W9-ABE-149

A GUIDE TO
READING
THE
ENTIRE
BIBLE
IN
ONE YEAR

A GUIDE TO
READING
THE
ENTIRE
BIBLE
IN
ONE
YEAR

Webb Garrison

Rutledge Hill Press®
Nashville, Tennessee

This is a revised edition of an earlier book published in 1963 by the Bobbs-Merrill Company, Inc.

All scripture quotations, unless otherwise indicated, are taken from the HOLY BIBLE, NEW INTERNATIONAL VERSION®. NIV®. Copyright © 1973, 1978, 1984 by International Bible Society. Used by permission of Zondervan Publishing House. All rights reserved.

Published in Nashville, Tennessee, by Rutledge Hill Press®, Inc., 211 Seventh Avenue North, Nashville, Tennessee 37219.

Distributed in Australia by The Five Mile Press Pty., Ltd., 22 Summit Road, Noble Park, Victoria 3174.

Distributed in Canada by H. B. Fenn & Company, Ltd., 34 Nixon Road, Bolton, Ontario L7E 1W2.

Distributed in New Zealand by Southern Publishers Group, 22 Burleigh Street, Grafton, Auckland, New Zealand.

Distributed in the United Kingdom by Verulam Publishing, Ltd., 152a Park Street Lane, Park Street, St. Albans, Hertfordshire AL2 2AU.

Typography by Roger A. DeLiso, Rutledge Hill Press
Design by Harriette Bateman, Bateman Design

Library of Congress Cataloging-in-Publication Data
Garrison, Webb B.
     A guide to reading the entire Bible in one year / Webb Garrison.
        p. cm.
     Includes index.
     ISBN: 1-55853-782-1 hardcover
     ISBN: 1-55853-783-X paperback
     1. Bible—reading. 2. Bible—Devotional use. Devotional calendars. I. Title.
    BS617.G35   1999
    220'.07—dc21   99-32877
                                                        CIP

Printed in the United States of America
1 2 3 4 5 6 — 03 02 01 00 99

Contents

Preface

This guide had a rather unusual beginning.

A small group of committed persons in Roberts Park Methodist Church, Indianapolis, set out to read the entire Bible. They quickly found that such a discipline requires planning and guidance. So, in response to this need, I agreed to prepare a reading guide.

Before the first monthly installment was finished, comparatively large numbers of persons in the congregation were showing interest. And a brief mention of the reading program in a column that I wrote for the *Indianapolis News* brought queries from all over the state.

Within thirty days, therefore, it became evident that a purely local program for one congregation had more than local appeal. I soon found that the biblical illiteracy of our times afflicts not only Methodists, but also Baptists, Disciples, Presbyterians, Lutherans, and others. And I was delighted to discover that surprisingly many persons of various denominational backgrounds are actually eager to know the Bible better.

—Webb Garrison

Introduction

Eager and excited, now that months of anticipation had given way to the reality of a trip, a group of New Jersey tourists pulled off the highway. It hardly seemed possible that, at last, they were in the Great Smoky Mountains National Park. As they had done four times in the last five miles, they jumped out of the car and started taking pictures of everything in sight.

Two mountaineers, rattling down the incline in their old car, looked at one another and laughed, seeming to say: "Ha! Another first-time crowd! They're hardly out of sight of Gatlinburg, but they're using up their film mighty fast. It'll all be gone before they get halfway to the top, and you can't buy more in the park!"

On any journey through a land of wonders, it is a major problem to choose stopping places. Especially on his first half dozen trips through the Bible, a traveler may be so overwhelmed by the wealth of vistas that he devotes too much time to the foothills and is weary before he reaches the first peak.

This guide is unlike any other in existence. It proposes to lead you at a pace that is appropriate to the stretch of highway being traveled. In some instances, you will be encouraged to skim through many pages in half an hour. At other times, you will be asked to read slowly and to meditate at length upon the message of a few paragraphs.

In order that individuals, classes, and congregations may begin reading at any time during the year, the guide is divided into twelve months of thirty days each. In months that include thirty-one days, use the extra day to make a rapid review. In February, plan your reading to "catch up" with the outline during the last week of the month.

Whether covering little material or much in your daily reading, the goal is always your personal enlightenment.

This is not an academic or scholarly enterprise. Such questions as authorship and date of composition will not concern us. Throughout, we shall treat the Bible as a unique source of sacred light. Directed toward the path your feet are following, that light will transform your pilgrimage. Without exception, effects of such illumination are personal and practical.

As described in Revelation (chapters 6–8), a supernatural force breaks the seals on a book, and John's eyes are flooded with visions of things never before seen. The imagery is especially valid today. Of the many books whose contents are "sealed" to the majority of folk, the Bible now heads the list. We revere it; we study it, after a fashion, in Sunday school; we quote a few verses from it; we do everything but read the *whole* Bible with eager attention to highway information it offers throughout.

When seals are removed from Scripture, new understanding comes. Men become capable of seeing things they never before glimpsed. Some of these things are in the Book itself, some are in life. Always, there must be a two-way flow between life and the Book. Each can shed light upon the other, so that there is a continuous increase in brilliance of the illumination.

It would be dishonest for me to pretend that you can claim the benefits of this light-bestowing process without paying the price. In order to win the prize, you must run the race. Without expenditure of time and attention and interest, you cannot hope to claim the benefits of systematic Bible reading.

Just as is the case with food for the body, food for the soul must be eaten by the person who expects to gain the calories involved. That sounds simple, but the simplicity is deceptive. For the gospel message that runs through the Bible from cover to cover is always proclaimed in the fashion of both/and. It is for everyone who will read it, yet it is also strictly personal. Its message is both universal and individual.

To make the Bible come alive, try to regard it as just off the press, with the ink still wet, having been prepared especially for your personal enlightenment. Do NOT read it for duty's sake. Do NOT read it as a discipline. Try to see it as inseparably linked with everyday events of your life. Try to regard it (though this is hard, hard, hard) as an on-the-spot news report of world-shaking events.

In the rare hours that you succeed in entering the mood and spirit of this Book, you will find it so full of action, so absorbing, so vitally informing, so urgent for your life today that if you are called away from your reading to view a telecast of the launching of a space shuttle, you will tend to be nettled at the intrusion of the trivial upon the cosmic.

Scripture's fundamental note is that of divine rescue. From the first page to the last, the Bible offers the incredible story of God's great acts designed to enable folks like us to burst the shackles of humanity. God opens for us a door that no person or event can close (Rev. 3:7–8); victory is the keynote of the whole incredible story. That basic biblical note is sounded in as many fashions as air is expelled from the pipes of an organ—with its many different sizes and shapes of tubes. But there is unity in diversity. Each tube is like every other in emitting air in such a way that a musical note falls upon the human ear. Just so, every part of the Bible emits evidences pointing to rescue—suggested in a multiplicity of ways.

In your reading, be continually alert for signals that will deepen or clarify or redirect your understanding of the grand themes of life—such issues as the meaning of the human race, the why of our existence on a planet prepared especially for us, how to win in the ceaseless rat race of existence, and ways of running the race with joy and victory.

Read also with specific interest in the problems, triumphs, burdens, and joys of your everyday life. Do not read as an exercise in piety—but read as a bewildered (or elated or weary or lost or triumphant) traveler who must study his guidebook to get the most from today's journey.

If possible, secure a copy of the Bible (or individual books from it) that you will feel free to mark and underscore. Even slight notations, such as exclamation points and question marks in the margins, will help you to conserve your discoveries and turn to them again and again.

Because the Bible comes out of life and is directed to life, it will speak most directly and clearly when used during normal activities of your daily life. Do some of your reading at intervals between periods of work (regardless of whether you work at home, in a factory, shop, or office.) Keep your Bible or Testament or individual Scripture portion conveniently at hand, so that you can turn to it as naturally as you would pick up the newspaper, turn on the television or go online.

Probably you will find it fruitful to jot down some of your major insights. If so, follow whatever fashion is appropriate to your interest and experience. You may wish to keep a notebook, in which you will record the flood of new understanding that is certain to come during these months. Perhaps you will wish to write comments about questions that trouble you as well as discoveries that excite you.

If you become a part of a weekly or monthly discussion group, you will find that insights of others will both supplement your own and raise the level of your private reading. If you read alone, you will have the special joy of knowing that a substantial number of others are reading with you, day by day, and entering with you into a spiritual comradeship that overcomes all barriers.

During the exciting year that is ahead of us as we read and listen and rejoice together, I shall try to point out major landmarks. But the glory of the journey is such that you can see many a mountain peak from your own perspective, and with these as points of reference, you will make every day—every hour—an exciting, joyful, victorious time of discovery.

A special reward grows out of the fact that hosts of other persons in many places are reading along with you. Every day, you can rejoice that you are not alone. You are part of a wide fellowship of kindred spirits—persons whom you will never know, but who are your companions along the daily journey.

At any earlier period, I would have used the beloved King James Version for my quotations. No other English translation is likely ever to challenge this classic one in terms of world influence or literary excellence. However, the inevitable evolution of the language, discoveries of more ancient texts, and increased biblical scholarship have resulted in many other translations better suited for study. For this guide I cite the New International Version (NIV) copyrighted 1973, 1978, and 1984.

A GUIDE TO
READING
THE
ENTIRE
BIBLE
IN
ONE YEAR

Genesis and Exodus

Genesis

Genesis is "the book of beginnings." Contrary to popular thought, though, it is not the beginning of the universe that is the most important part of its story. Rather, it is the beginning of God's dealings with mankind in general, and with the chosen people in particular, that makes this book so vital.

The story that unfolds is strictly and entirely the story of salvation—or the history of the manifold ways in which the Creator has offered rescue to men and women. From the beginning, the account is elaborate and tortuous, for the creature who is offered divine aid is the strangest mixture in creation. He is made in the divine image, that is, he has inside him the potential to achieve God-likeness, but because he is also of earth and from earth, he is confined and cribbed about by requirements of his body.

One-half of this paradoxical creature desperately wants to seize hold of divine gifts he can dimly see. But his other half—his earthly self—is lured by other goals. So he is in a state of ceaseless struggle. His responses to the overtures of God are never unmixed. He is sometimes eager, but he often balks and resists. Consequently, *salvation history* is a continuous series of ups and downs. At the very beginning, the climax—God's self-giving for the sake of man—is foreshadowed and hinted, though darkly, as "a light shining in a dark place" (2 Pet. 1:19).

As you read the dramatic story of the beginning of God's striving to help us achieve our true goal, never forget that the world was

15

created for this specific purpose. God's universe is a "university of life" designed to prod, persuade, awaken, and drive you and me to accept divine rescue. Therefore, the face of the whole world trembles in the balance as you prepare to accept or reject the good things offered you by God. What you do has a bearing upon a cosmic victory so vast that stars and planets and suns and moons are mere agents and instruments.

First Day *Read Genesis 1–2*

Nothing that exists came into being by chance. God created the laboratory in which man is the inquiring experimenter. Because God's creative acts were deliberate and purposeful, it follows that the world and life are "good." Notice how many times this vital factor is clearly specified in the account of creation.

What does this have to say about your own burdens and opportunities today? What pressing problems that confront you will look entirely different if you can succeed in seeing them as cooperating in God's stupendous work of establishing a creative context for your life?

If you are confronted by difficult decisions, take heart! Notice that, from the first, the creature who names and controls all other creatures is incapable of living in a state of ease. For Adam and Eve are torn between desire to obey God and hunger for the forbidden fruit of "the knowledge of good and evil."

Do you think it is possible to escape tension and turmoil by any process short of erasing the divine image that is traced upon you?

Second Day *Read Genesis 3–5*

Remember that we are dealing with *salvation history*. The Bible is not a textbook of political history, nor an encyclopedia of biology or astronomy or agriculture. From start to finish, the story told is that of the dealings of God with human beings. Always the emphasis is upon divine truths communicated through human words. Because the experiences and viewpoints and goals of the reader color every word he reads, the message of a given passage is not fixed and automatic. Instead, it varies from one person to another and from one time to another in the life of one reader. You may take it as absolutely certain that during this year's reading you will discover fresh meaning in passages long familiar to you.

In the story of Adam's fall, we find it to be a principle of life that no one can continue blameless in the sight of God. From generation to generation, every son and daughter of every father and mother is *human*—that is, frail and limited and prone to stumble. The fact that this has always been and always will be is the burden of the story in which the serpent plays the role of the Evil One.

Third Day *Read Genesis 6–8*

As with you and me, so it is with families and tribes and nations— how often God must have wearied of mankind!

But the darkness is never total. There is always a Noah standing for righteousness in the midst of a crooked and perverse generation. Always the world's Noahs obey the voice of God, even when the message they hear seems to make no sense. Such obedience—in which you and I can participate in this our time of new deluges—is vital in *salvation history.*

Always, inevitably, without exception, the divine-human crisis ends in rescue and victory and joy. Anything resembling ultimate defeat simply is not conceivable. Though men in their freedom rebel and defy their Creator, he has so shaped his total creation that right and truth must triumph. Because that is the case, there is no hopeless situation under the sun. Whatever the nature of the floodwaters that now roll over your soul, divine rescue and a new beginning await you if you will listen and obey.

Fourth Day *Read Genesis 9–11*

Here we find the first clear witness to a central riddle of *salvation history.* For reasons never quite clear from our human perspective but entirely adequate for God's own purposes, the Creator has actually entered into a covenant with mankind. Man did not earn or win or deserve the right to become a partner with God. This contract was entered into as a result of divine initiative and conferred upon man as a gift.

The entire Bible offers a running account of *salvation history*, so it may be described as "the story of the covenant." Not even the shameless conduct of a just-rescued Noah can cancel out the divine promise. Even the rebellious banding together of men, pooling human resources in an effort to build a tower to heaven in order to become more-than-human, does not void the contract.

The coming of Jesus Christ, at the time appointed by the Father, is the fulfillment of the covenant from the divine side. At Calvary, the Creator makes good his word. Precisely because that is the case, no view of the Cross is adequate that does not see it as the culmination of age-long processes initiated by God "in the beginning" so that saved men and women may accept a glory no mere mortal can achieve.

Fifth Day *Read Genesis 12–14*

In his acceptance of divine rescue and his entering into a covenant with God, Noah represents all mankind. But the Creator's dealings with creatures made in his image are to become more specific. Even God could not bring his Son into the world in a vacuum. For the Messiah to enter history, it was necessary that a particular people be set aside—chosen first by act of God and then by their response to the divine overture.

We do not know why the Hebrews were chosen as God's people, but we do know that they *were* selected for a unique relationship with God. The covenant was entered through their founder, Abraham. God's special promises to him and to his seed forever gain new and dynamic meaning in Christian thought, as we shall see before this year is over. For the present, we can only acknowledge that the bond of the covenant produces a people utterly unlike any other.

Sixth Day *Read Genesis 15–18*

From the beginning of the covenant relationship, difficulties, delays, and barriers are apparent. There is no quick, smooth working out of the divine purpose, even when it relates to the life of a single person. Over and over, there are reasons to think God's promises are empty words. But the very obstacles to the fulfillment of these promises serve to dramatize divine power.

In several of his letters, Paul wrestles with the matter of the covenant between Jehovah and Abraham. The promise, he concludes, was made to the spiritual rather than to the biological descendants of Abraham. Does this interpretation add to your appreciation of the Old Testament?

Seventh Day *Read Genesis 19–22*

Scripture comes out of life and is directed to life. These vivid chapters support the conclusion that the real issues of life change very little over time. People of the third millennium after Christ face the same temptations, testings, and opportunities that confronted Abraham in the second millennium before Christ.

What ideas in today's reading are particularly pertinent to issues you face? Do you think Jewish interpreters of Scripture were right in regarding Abraham's sacrifice of Isaac as the spiritual mountaintop of the Old Testament? What parallels, if any, do you see with God's offering of his Son upon the mount of Calvary?

Eighth Day *Read Genesis 23–24*

While the Bible is immortal literature, it is much more than that. It is a faithful representation of human dreams, frustrations, defeats, and victories. Instead of being a pretty story in which everyone is good, it depicts human nature exactly as it is. Some readers object to the sexual explicitness in Scripture, but that is part of its glory: we are dealing with real people, not characters out of fairy tales.

Notice that the haggling over the purchase price of a burial ground is a delightful description of Near Eastern bargaining. It helps to make Abraham a real person rather than an idealized figure. Much the same thing can be said about Isaac's courtship, if it may be called that!

Ninth Day *Read Genesis 25–26*

The birth of twins could present insoluble problems about which boy would inherit the benefits and obligations of the covenant. The faith of Israel, however, leaped blithely over such difficulties and asserted that God's word is always gloriously victorious; nothing can thwart the working out of the compact. Thus in the triumph of the younger brother over the older, we see a demonstration of the way in which the promise made to the chosen people overcame even the obstacles of biology.

Over and over, the divine promises are repeated. Not only does every generation require a fresh assurance, but all individuals who transmit the blood and the promise need assurance during crucial periods; they are fortified by hearing Jehovah repeat the fact that the covenant still holds.

Tenth Day *Read Genesis 27–29*

Part of the meaning of the strange story of Jacob and Esau rests upon reverence for the spoken word. It was through words, not through tangible agents or even angels, that God created the world. God spoke to Noah and Abraham, and his word triumphed over every obstacle. Psalm 29 gives a poetic description of the way Providence operates through God's voice. In John 1 and other New Testament passages, the Son of God is described as the Word of God. Even words spoken by humans are potent and enduring; once the decree of King Ahasuerus had been published, it could not be recalled (Esther 8:8). Having uttered a vow, Jephthah could not take it back even to save his daughter (Judg. 11:29–40). The word is the midwife presiding at the New Birth (I Pet. 1:23–25). Coming from the mouth of the Savior, it is a sword that makes holy war (Rev. 2:16).

Viewed from one perspective, it literally is true that no word ever uttered can be taken back. So regarded, words actually are among the most dynamic factors in human life, and tiny though it be, the tongue is the organ that most clearly separates men from beasts.

Even though Jacob engaged in trickery, the promise of God, transmitted through the spoken blessing of Abraham's descendant, held good. Nothing, absolutely nothing, is powerful enough to cancel out the promises of the covenant. Neither human frailty, nor family feuds, nor torturous marriage customs of a primitive clan can prevail against the divine word.

Eleventh Day *Read Genesis 30–31*

The patriarchs took marriage and the family very seriously. Although their views about sex do not coincide with those of the typical American, we cannot fail to see that they regarded sex as part of the mystery and grandeur of religious faith.

Nor can we fail to see that they were sensitive to religious faith as a factor in every situation. They were not above engaging in what we consider shady tactics, but they were perpetually erecting altars, making sacrifices, and renewing their vows of fidelity to Jehovah. Do you consider them to have been hypocritical or sincere? Why? What do you think of attempts to prepare an edited version of the Bible, leaving out passages that shock the modern reader or aren't "fit" for children to read?

Twelfth Day *Read Genesis 32–33*

All through the story of man's response to God's invitation there is a back-and-forth movement. This is geographical as well as spiritual and intellectual. Especially in the time of the patriarchs, the called one is forever having to leave the comfort and security of home in order to go into some far country.

But there is equal stress upon the importance of returning home. Over and over, individuals and groups "go back." Jacob's exciting and dangerous return is repeated generations later by the return of exiles from Babylonian captivity.

Some readers of the Bible are sure that this pattern of going out and returning home is a way of communicating a universal truth: In the providence of God, somehow and some day, all men will "return home" to enter into a saving relationship with the Father. So viewed, the going out and coming in of Old Testament individuals and groups serve to prefigure the message of salvation that is communicated through the parable of the prodigal son. Perhaps you will wish to debate this conclusion. Whatever you may think about it, do you consider the biblical message to be essentially pessimistic or overwhelmingly optimistic? What are the implications for your life this week?

Thirteenth Day *Read Genesis 34–36*

Formally and informally, sometimes in solitude and sometimes in a public ceremony, the changing of one's name was a frequent biblical event. For instance, Abram became Abraham, Jacob became Israel, and Saul became Paul.

Whatever else it indicates, the taking of a new name by an adult is a public declaration that a new person has come into existence. Thus the dictum "You must be born again" was firmly established long before the Savior spoke those words to Nicodemus.

Jacob's change of name made public the inner transformation, long in process and often interrupted, by which a clever young rogue matured as one worthy to be an ancestor of the Christ. Mark well, however, that Jacob did not lift himself by his own bootstraps. His transformation was not merely one of growth. Rather, he experienced a divine rescue whose effects were to make of him a person he could not become by any amount of striving.

Here is the eternal secret of the gospel, which is proclaimed over and over in Scripture but is perpetually hidden from those who have no eyes to see: GOD HAS CHOSEN TO DO THE IMPOSSIBLE FOR THOSE WHO ENTER THE COVENANT. HE WILL LITERALLY AND ACTUALLY REMAKE EVERY PERSON WHO WILL LET HIM. THIS COSMIC ACT OF SALVATION PRODUCES A TRANSFORMED INDIVIDUAL,

SO DIFFERENT FROM THE OLD PERSON THAT IT IS AWKWARD OR IMPOSSIBLE FOR HIM TO ANSWER TO HIS OLD NAME (cf. Rev. 2:17).

Fourteenth Day *Read Genesis 37–40*

Are you tempted to heave a sigh of relief?

"At last! We're on comfortable ground. Here is a story we can tell our children without blushing and without their demanding too many explanations! The story of Joseph is vivid, dramatic, and not too hard to understand …"

Not so fast. Remember that the one true function of Scripture is to communicate God's truth to children. If some of the crude and bizarre stories we have read in recent days puzzle or disturb us, so that we have to search very hard to find any spiritual truths in them, we face an opposite danger here. We can regard the story of Joseph as being merely a historical record of colorful men and events. To treat it in that fashion is to destroy it as a pointer toward truths that transcend history.

What warnings or promises do you think God is making through the vehicle of an account of Joseph's adventures? How do events in the life of this ancient man yield clues for your own journey today? To what degree is some type of "going down into Egypt" a necessary prelude to acceptance of divine rescue and participation in an exodus from one's personal "land of corn and plenty…and fleshpots"?

Fifteenth Day *Read Genesis 41–43*

Throughout Scripture, Egypt is a symbol of captivity to material things—worldliness in its absolute form. It was the domination of the world and the flesh, not simply the tyranny of Pharaoh, from which the chosen people were rescued by the mighty acts of God. Notice, too, that Joseph's success in politics and economics was the essential prelude to the captivity of Abraham's descendants. Grain and oil served as bait to lure Jehovah's chosen into a trap from which they could not escape by their own power.

Sixteenth Day *Read Genesis 44–46*

In recognizing the fearful threats posed by all the world's Egypts, never fall into the error of concluding that even a pharaoh can reign apart from the Creator who sustains all. The Egyptian captivity of the children of Israel was to the development of the chosen people what tragedy can be in the enlargement of an individual seeker for God.

Short of entering into a state of utter hopelessness, neither a clan nor an individual is likely to cease trusting in human resources. It takes desolation and helplessness to cause surrender, so that rescue by the divine is attractive and acceptable. Thus it can be affirmed with joy that God himself led his own people into the land of Goshen, because even God cannot rescue his people until they enter a captivity so absolute that they recognize themselves as captives.

Seventeenth Day *Read Genesis 47–50*

Enslavement in Egypt was gradual. At first the settlers considered themselves lucky to be in a land where the ruler was worshipped as divine. They did not lose their liberty all at once but a bit at a time over a period of generations.

Here is an example of the way people who are given freedom by their Creator drift into slavery, to false gods, and to dictatorship because of their habits and lusts. Yield a trifle here, retreat a bit there—nothing vital, mind you, just a reasonable concession to appetite or social pressure—and one day you will become aware of shackles that bind you hand and foot, fastened upon you so gradually that you failed to realize what was happening.

Exodus

The Book of Exodus is an account of historic events that transformed an enslaved tribe into a free nation. But because the tribesmen were people of the promise, the story is much more than mere history. It represents a specific instance—the instance in Hebrew history—through which a fundamental truth is expressed: God the Creator perpetually rescues his own from captivity to material forces and establishes them in a new land of promise so they may be free to keep their part of the divine-human covenant.

Because Exodus uses events of history as means to convey truths of the faith, the book reveals its radiant message only when read with believing eyes. Among the rescued clansmen whose sandals were hardly dry after crossing the wet sands of the Red Sea, only Moses listened intently enough to hear God reveal himself more fully than he had to Abraham. Among those reading Exodus during the next two weeks, only the ones who plod their way through the wilderness with eager certainty that God is leading them will fall on their faces before the glory of the Creator revealed at some personal Sinai.

Eighteenth Day *Read Exodus 1–3*

Marvels and wonders are essential ingredients in this story, which is an account of the Creator's dealings with creatures made in his image. Where there is no mystery or awe or transcendent glory, there is no sense of the divine presence. So long as one regards the events of everyday life as wholly explainable—not too large or complex for men to know them in their entirety—there is no sensitivity to the more-than-human.

Of all the incredible events in the career of Moses, perhaps the least emphasized is the paradox by which God used a prince from Pharaoh's household as his agent. By all logical standards, we would be tempted to think such a man would be the least likely instrument for the work of Providence. From the beginning of a career he did not choose but to which he was called, Moses was conscious that his highest task was obedience. It was divine power, not human, that was to set Abraham's descendants on the route back to the land of promise.

Nineteenth Day *Read Exodus 4–6*

Whether societal or individual, divine rescue is expensive. Its costs are great in terms of suffering and struggle, both divine and human. Instead of coming easily and quickly, rescue may be deferred through a series of delays.

Indeed, the lot of one seeking rescue may become worse as he responds to God's overtures. No Egypt is left without struggle. No pharaoh releases his slaves at the first sign of restlessness. One reason so many persons elect to remain in their personal Egypts, rather than be led out by God, is that freedom comes at a high price, and it is not won without a long struggle, the plagues of which may be more agonizing than slavery.

Twentieth Day *Read Exodus 7–9*

Reading about stupendous acts of God, worked in a strange and ancient land, the modern reader is likely to be baffled. Why did Pharaoh prove so obstinate? How could he have been so blind? Is it possible that a man with intelligence to rule a great civilization refused to recognize God's sovereignty except in cataclysmic, death-dealing disaster?

Remember, this is not merely the history of the Hebrews, but also *salvation history*. One of the qualities of divine truth is that it remains hidden from unbelievers. Two men look at the same plot of land; one takes off his shoes before the presence of his Creator, and the other calculates the cost of laying out a subdivision. Perhaps the most insistent message of these chapters is the warning: Are you playing the role of Pharaoh, obstinately refusing to seek the work of the one true God in events of your daily life? Will you stubbornly close your eyes until tragedy strikes inside the walls of your own house?

Twenty-first Day *Read Exodus 10–12*

Have you been struck by the insistence that God repeatedly hardened the heart of Pharaoh? The story seems to imply that divine forces were at work to prevent the Egyptian from seeing God's hand in national troubles. According to this line of thought, Pharaoh did not reject his opportunities by free choice but was forced by Providence to act as he did.

Such an interpretation bypasses the heart of the message. Faith asserts that NOTHING is outside the realm of the Creator, and NOTHING is strong enough to defeat his purposes expressed in the covenant. (Paul gives a detailed interpretation of this matter in Romans 9.)

No matter how powerful or clever or stubborn he may be, no human rebel against the government of God can succeed in overthrowing the divine rule. Regardless of how cruel or evil or warped a man may be, whatever he does is done within the context of Providence and not outside it. Because God's purposes cannot be thwarted, God succeeds in using any and all events for his glory and for the fulfillment of his covenant.

References to God's hardening his heart do not relieve any pharaoh from responsibility for free choice. Rather, these are yet more triumphant assertions of faith, declaring that GOD IS NOT ALOOF EVEN FROM SUFFERING, TRAGEDY, AND DEFEAT. Regardless of what may take place within the stream of history, eyes of faith sparkle with joyous certainty that, somehow, this too is operating to effect a rescue, an exodus into a land of milk and honey, and ultimately victory.

Twenty-second Day *Read Exodus 13–15*

Throughout the history of Israel, up to and including the twentieth century A.D., many ceremonies and symbols have been linked with the Exodus. The Passover feast is a solemn ritual that reenacts God's "passing over" of the Hebrew houses on the night Egypt's firstborn were slain by the angel of death. Therefore, the seven days in which unleavened bread is eaten are days in which the celebrants are reminded that Jehovah is a God of rescue.

Any attempt to penetrate to the depth of New Testament thought without some understanding of covenant events described in the Old Testament is futile. The bonds are clear between Calvary and the Exodus. Notice the foreshadowing of the gospel's central promise in the triumph song of Moses and his followers, which clearly emphasizes that the rescue from Egypt rested upon divine purchase (redemption) of the liberated ones (15:13, 16).

Holy Communion is an adapted and modified form of the Passover feast, pointing to, and actually offering, divine rescue through spiritual participation in the death and resurrection of God's supreme agent—his Son. The communion bread points back to the unleavened bread of the Jews and through it to manna eaten in the wilderness, as well as to Jesus Christ's broken body. The communion cup offers not only the rescue made available through the Savior's shed blood but also the leading out from Egypt of the chosen people whose doorposts were smeared with blood. In the same fashion, to eyes of faith, the waters through which Noah passed point to the saving water of baptism (see 1 Peter 3:21).

Twenty-third Day *Read Exodus 16–18*

Once the problems of captivity were solved by divine intervention, Abraham's descendants found themselves facing a host of new ones. Though liberated—made into a new people—by acts of God, they were not thereby freed from the limitations of humanity. Instead, they quickly discovered that their entrance into the land of promise would come only after a long struggle.

Once more we find that group rescue has many similarities to individual salvation. While struggling with enslavement to forces in whatever Egypt happens to hold us captive, we pant for liberty. But when freedom comes, those who become new persons in Christ Jesus find themselves confronted by a host of new problems. Individually and collectively, therefore, to cross the Jordan and enter Canaan requires not simply a single parting of the Red Sea by the hand of God, but also a faithful forty-year struggle to walk in the pathway designated by God.

Twenty-fourth Day *Read Exodus 19–20*

No doubt you will wish to read these chapters more than once because each time the revelation to Moses is pondered, new truths emerge. A lifetime devoted to considering the Ten Commandments is not sufficient to uncover all the spiritual treasure offered here.

Twenty-fifth Day *Read Exodus 21–23*

To a modern city dweller, these regulations seem more confusing than helpful. They do not apply to the world today. One of the problems linked with codes of law is that we must have laws to function as an organized society, but social changes make laws obsolete. Here is eloquent testimony about our incapacity to save ourselves. We cannot be governed by abstract principles alone. Regardless of how exalted these principles may be, specific laws based upon them must apply to specific conditions. Once those conditions change, the laws become empty.

It was the fatal mistake of institutional Judaism to become immersed in a sea of legalism. But it is far easier to recognize this error than it is to escape the necessity of placing rules upon religious groups, cultures, and nations.

As you consider this human dilemma today, think of some specific laws of Christian conduct that are accepted by other persons but that seem to you no longer applicable to actual conditions. Even if Moses, face to face with God, is limited in his ability to shape laws to govern human conduct, what does this say about a city council or a state legislature? Can you propose any human way out of the difficulty? Any divine solution?

Twenty-sixth Day *Read Exodus 24–27*

Both the glory and the mystery of the covenant is that we can accept God's gifts and know God through faith-powered experience, but we cannot describe, depict, or represent God so that he can be known by those who have not experienced him. This is the root of the prohibition of graven images. However deep his own religious experience, however great his skill with mallet and chisel, no sculptor can communicate truth about God without also suggesting falsehood.

Today we accept this principle when applied to visual representations or idols. But we do not always recognize that precisely the same difficulties are attached to the use of words. It is because any description or name may become an "idol" that God gives so mysterious a reply to Moses' question at his first divine call (Exod. 3:13–15). Likewise, the name of the King of Kings is known only to himself (Rev. 19:12). To say that God is the beginning, or that he is the end, is a distortion. At the same time, he is both beginning and end. He is Alpha and Omega simultaneously (Rev. 1:8).

In order to speak to one another about God, in order to engage in anything equivalent to what we now call "Christian education," we must have visual and verbal pointers toward truths that are not fully contained. This is the function of the religious symbol. It serves as a handle by which we can begin to grasp low-level truths that come into fullness only through a personal encounter with God.

For the Hebrew people, the ark of the covenant was a potent symbol. Made in costly and elaborate form, awe-inspiring and mysterious in its physical makeup, it was intended to point beyond itself to the divine-human covenant that is basic to the experience of the chosen people.

Twenty-seventh Day *Read Exodus 28–31*

Ceremonies, clothing, furniture, and food associated with religion always carry with them suggestions of the mysterious. That is also the case—particularly the case—with the vocabulary of religion. In worship we habitually use words to suggest meanings not ordinarily associated with those words in everyday speech.

This matter once more points to both the glory and the limitedness of man. Through the symbols, ceremonies, and vocabulary of religion, we can cultivate our own spiritual sensitivity and initiate beginners into the mysteries of the faith. That is glorious. But the greater the degree of success, the wider the gap becomes between insiders and outsiders. A stranger not familiar with the language of faith is bewildered by words, ceremonies, and symbols of worship; these serve as roadblocks rather than as highways.

Visualize the physical surroundings at your church and try to decide which things mean most to you and what effect they would have on a person without experience in Protestant worship. Should there be fewer candles, crosses, and flags, or more? Do you think verbalizations that might distract the novice should be discarded (for example, "washed in the blood")? Or should we hold fast to inherited symbols and try to help others discover their deepest meanings?

Twenty-eighth Day *Read Exodus 32–34*

Aaron's sin was not only a violation of the law against making an image of deity, it was also a concession to the popular desire for good things associated with Egypt. Never lose sight of the fact that *salvation history,* or the account of the divine-human covenant, deals as fully with man as with God. Divine readiness to rescue is always matched by human reluctance to make a full surrender.

If you and I were less "stiff-necked" than we actually are, if the gap between God and man was not absolute, there would be no necessity for a plan of salvation. It is part of the fallacy (or rather, heresy) of much modern churchmanship to minimize the radical nature of salvation and to proclaim a religion of achievement. Guard with your life against falling into this perversion of the gospel. Today, this very hour, try to see more clearly what variety of golden calf you are tempted to worship in order to gain the bounty of the particular Egypt that beckons you most invitingly.

Twenty-ninth Day *Read Exodus 35–37*

Repetition of monotonous details must not blind us to deep truths in today's reading. Limited and prone to fail though we are, we can yet have a part in the glorifying of God. We can make our offerings to

God with such free will and glad surrender that we add not only to the tangible apparatus of worship, but also to the glory of the Creator! Even though our feet become entangled in details of cutting acacia wood or meeting quotas assigned by the denomination, faithful self-giving through such media is part of the fulfillment of the covenant. It was for this that the world was established.

Thirtieth Day *Read Exodus 38–40*

Provided we open our eyes to God's presence in all that he has made, almost any event or object can serve to heighten our sense of wonder and mystery and holiness. From anointing oil to bronze fire pans, from fine-twined linen to gem-studded breastplates, any natural or manufactured thing can point to the all-powerful God through whom it exists and by whom it is sustained.

The capacity to see God not only in holy articles associated with worship and inherited from previous generations, but also in the most commonplace and ordinary things of daily experience, is among the most sublime of faith-powered gifts (Rev. 5:13). Thanks be to God, here is a gift that can be cultivated! If you do not "see" God in fresh fashion today, in some strange or some very familiar experience, it is because you are not eagerly straining to find evidence of the Creator in every aspect of his creation.

Leviticus, Numbers, Deuteronomy, Joshua, Judges

Leviticus

For most practical purposes, this book might as well not be included in the Bible. It has few points of contact with modern Christian thought or life and is seldom opened. In our pilgrimage through the Bible, Leviticus can claim only the briefest pause.

It is startling to recognize the bond between Levitical laws and the everyday life of the Savior's people, as evidenced by the relationship between Leviticus 12 and Luke 2:22–24. Nevertheless, we cannot ponder the message of this book but must skim through many chapters in half an hour, looking for major landmarks that project above the surface.

First Day *Skim Leviticus 1–14*

Quick glances at the ceremonies of Israel reveal the role of blood in the worship of the chosen people. The word blood appears many times in these chapters, and few rites proceed without the ceremonial use of blood.

Central in the entire Old Testament, not merely to the legal codes preserved here, is the symbolism of blood as the vehicle of life. Mysterious and elusive, this carrier of life is forbidden as an item of diet; it is taboo. Even otherwise clean animals, those that die a natural death or are killed by beasts, are unclean because the blood has not been drained from their bodies. There is no atonement for murder, and the land on which human blood has been shed is polluted (Num. 35:29–34).

Because blood is the carrier of life and thus is the most precious part of an organism, it constitutes the best offering God can be given. Abraham was tested by being asked to sacrifice the blood of his only son. So we begin to perceive why blood symbolism is so deeply embedded in the unfolding of *salvation history.*

Our Father's self-giving for the sake of humanity took the form of pouring out his most priceless gift, the blood of his Son. Jesus' blood, voluntarily shed as a sin offering to cleanse us of guilt, becomes, in effect, the modus operandi of rescue. Just as blood coursing through our veins conveys life, so the shed blood of Jesus Christ transmits spiritual life. In effect, that blood *is* grace (1 John 1:7; Rev. 1:5), for it constitutes the purchase price of salvation (Rev. 5:9–10).

Blood symbolism is rooted in antiquity, and understanding it is necessary to understanding the New Testament as well as the Old. So in this "desert of dry bones" that is Leviticus we can rise on wings of faith-founded metaphor to new understanding of Calvary and the Lord's Supper. From this perspective we gain fresh meaning from Christendom's colossal repertoire of blood-centered meditations, prayers, and hymns, typical of which is William Cowper's glory song that begins:

> There is a fountain filled with blood
> Drawn from Immanuel's veins;
> And sinners, plunged beneath that flood,
> Lose all their guilty stains.

Second Day *Skim Leviticus 15–27*

These chapters reveal a people acutely conscious of being set apart from the rest of mankind and obsessed with zeal for observance of religious law. Instead of setting aside special places and occasions for obedience, Israel uses the law as social cement, holding society together. There is no hint of the modern distinction between sacred and secular; the law addresses everyone and deals with all aspects of life. The Sabbath is the pulse beat of the culture, as organic as the rhythm of the human heart.

Obsessed with religion, these folk, in conscious covenant with their Creator, must always give him their best. Only unblemished male animals (prized by stock breeders then as now) may be offered. It is not just any handful of cereal, but fine flour that is used at the altar. Because the Lord accepts only the choicest, he requires that unblemished human males be set aside for the holy priesthood (21:16–24).

In a land perennially unable to feed all its hungry, the fear of God is brought into the kitchen by laws prohibiting many sources of food. No family can ever sit down to a meal without consciousness of religious overtones. This factor goes far to create a state of intoxication with the Lord. At the same time, there is an incredible degree of social solidarity. Descendants of Abraham are so conscious that they differ from other people that assimilation of the outsider is slow and difficult. A culture so permeated with religious rites actually constitutes a people *set apart* (18:1–5; 20:23). But more is involved than conscious separation; Israel is *set apart to God*. This is symbolized by the tithe, through which one-tenth of the national production is set aside. It is not actually an offering, for it never does belong to the people and is not to be put to ordinary use, even in dire emergencies.

This absolute domination of religious law formed a people through whom God would pour himself into history in the person of his Son.

Numbers

As in the case of Leviticus, we must skim this little-read book. Its English title comes from Moses' census, or numbering of the tribes. It is designated in the Hebrew Bible by a word taken from its opening sentence, "In the wilderness," for the book deals with Israel's life during her forty years of wandering. While a meditative reading is not profitable, an overall look reveals powerful and fascinating qualities in the life of the covenant people, destined to be the social womb through which the Son would be delivered to effect salvation.

Third Day *Skim Numbers 1–10*

Israel's whole life was permeated by God-consciousness. Still some areas of experience and conduct were especially holy, hence potent (3:38; 4:15, 19–20). Potency of the holy is the base on which the ceremony of lie detection rests (chapter 5). Power so permeates the holy that it is explosive. Dealing with it, a novice may bring disaster upon himself and all his people.

Partly for this reason and partly because conducting complex ceremonies required discipline and training for the leader, there developed special classes of men "set apart." Descendants of Aaron, became priestly specialists in worship and descendants of Levi were designated as their assistants. As guardian and manipulator of the holy, the priest could, to a degree, direct the flow of divine power. He was not a servant of the people, not a paid official of the tribe, but an earthly representative of the Most High.

The Christian Church has tried to preserve something of this quality through the practice of ordination. Within the life of the congregation, the modern ordained minister administers the sacraments, of which Holy Communion and baptism are especially important among Protestant Christians. Do you think of your minister chiefly as a priest or as a friend? Is your minister an employee of the congregation or an appointee of God? What are the implications for the life of the church? How important do you consider the sacraments in the process of salvation?

Fourth Day *Skim Numbers 11–21*

Interspersed with sections of religious law and descriptions of ceremonies, there is a thrilling and frightening account of the rescued people as they react to their new freedom and responsibility. Not once, but over and over, the people who so recently thought they wanted liberty more than life, complain at their new lot. Not satisfied with grumbling, they repeatedly engage in active rebellion.

These incidents take place against a backdrop of Providence, for their miraculous feeding in the wilderness is calculated to make them sensitive to God's concern and aware that they are totally dependent upon him.

No matter how earthshaking a miracle may be, it is likely to be taken for granted when it becomes a daily experience. At first, Abraham's descendants marveled as they gathered manna, but soon they wearied of it and cried for red meat. Though this was only one of many sources of complaint and rebellion, it is symbolic of them all.

Over and over, God punished them through sickness, natural disasters, and military defeat, but they never learned. Over and over, the cycle was repeated. Divine bounty and forgiveness soon were taken for granted; men complained and rebelled; God punished them sorely and then forgave the repentant ones; for a while, they rejoiced and offered noble sacrifices—but they soon slipped back into sin to launch another cycle.

Fifth Day *Read Numbers 22–24*

In a way, it is a shame we ever began telling the story of Balaam and his ass to Sunday school tots. Many of them have grown up to think of it as nothing more than a fairy tale. So regarded, it is interesting and amusing but has little significance for the lives of educated adults in the scientific age.

Actually, the story of the prophet and his beast is a vivid case history in divine revelation.

A fundamental tenet of Scripture is illustrated here, in that God actually communicates with men. While he uses inspired prophets and seers, God also uses everything in existence. EVERYTHING IN CREATION HAS CAPACITY TO WITNESS ABOUT THE CREATOR (Ps. 19:1–4).

There are many biblical instances in which a sensitive soul hears God "speak" to him without being exposed to sounds of human speech. To Noah, the rainbow "says" that God has entered into a compact with men. The attuned ears of Jeremiah, exposed only to the squeaking of a potter's wheel, "hear" divine warnings and promises. And that passionate listener, John, reports in Revelation how in quick succession he heard God's voice poured out through a trumpet's blast, thunder, and the cry of an eagle.

Do you think Balaam's ass spoke an early Hebrew dialect—or did his actions simply point the prophet to God so that Balaam had to resort to human words to report the message he received? Have you ever been "spoken to" through an event or thing that did not employ language? Is God less eager and able to speak to us today than during the time of the patriarchs? How literally shall we take the idea of a sword's serving to convey a message (Judg. 3:20)?

Whatever you may conclude about the mystery of Balaam's beast, this I should like to declare as a personal conviction: If you will deliberately tune your ears to God's wavelength, there will be many days when you will hear life-changing messages from heaven, and rarely will your Creator fail to whisper in your ear during a day.

Sixth Day *Read Numbers 25–36*

Internal solidarity, evidenced by the adoption of more elaborate laws, continued to mature during the desert wanderings. This transformed Israel from a motley band of refugees into a stalwart group of clans.

But there was no advocate of world peace among the people of the covenant! The fierceness of their warriors was matched only by the cruelty with which they treated their conquered foes. There was almost fiendish exclusiveness: come what may, the blood of the chosen people must not be contaminated. There could be no compromise with worshipers of false gods; those who could not be assimilated (i.e., brought into the life-stream of Israel) must be exterminated.

The whole idea of a divine-human covenant with a chosen people requires that they be set apart, fiercely exclusive, totally unwilling to enter into compromise with the world. In order to give his Son to all mankind, God had to take for himself an earthly bride in the person of an Israel who would remain true to him, rejecting all the amorous advances of those who bowed at the altar of Baal and other pagan gods.

Deuteronomy

This set of codes, whose title means "second law," is the last of the five books of Moses. In clear contrast with much earlier religious law directed to desert nomads, it deals largely with the life of an agricultural people settled in villages and towns. Influence upon New Testament writers has been immense, with Matthew and Paul being especially vocal in their tribute to Deuteronomy's spiritual power and witness to the Savior dimly glimpsed.

Seventh Day *Read Deuteronomy 1–4*

A formal address by Moses, these chapters give a capsule interpretation of divine law. It rests entirely upon God's promises, which he made voluntarily; but, in order to gain the rewards that are offered, the covenant people must act boldly and faithfully.

God's word stands forever; the covenant cannot be destroyed. Ultimate fulfillment is more certain than the coming of morning after night, when the Hebrew day begins. Both individuals and the chosen people as a whole (functioning as a sort of corporate individual or "social person") are prone to turn aside from God and thus bring down his wrath. Such fire from heaven, poured out over and over, serves to convict and convert erring ones. Here is the womb from which the transformed soul must be born: the covenant state, with all its paradoxes and alternating currents and its inevitable human failures, has assurance of absolute victory through divine rescue.

Eighth Day *Read Deuteronomy 5–7*

Moses' second public address, as transmitted by generations of the pious, is essentially a commentary upon the Ten Commandments. Notice particularly the winged words of 6:1–15 and the repeated emphasis upon Israel's unique role as a chosen people set apart.

Ninth Day *Read Deuteronomy 8–11*

Promise and warning…warning and promise! How the two aspects of the covenant relationship do continually alternate!

Viewed from a perspective other than that of a brief human life, promises and warnings actually coexist and thereby establish a field of tension whose intensity may vary, but whose fierce tuggings never cease. Establishment of this environment for the development of souls is basic to God's creative work. Only in such a context can creatures made in the divine image so respond to the Creator that they shake off the limitations of the dust from which they came and enter into endless glory in the company of the Father.

Tenth Day *Read Deuteronomy 12–15*

Even in the time of joy and victory that is symbolized by entrance into Canaan, the rescued one is never wholly free of the tendency to bow down before false gods. The lure of Satan and the world is ceaseless. In this life, spiritual power never reaches a point where the covenanter, with Egypt still fresh in his memory and the glory of rescue still vivid, can rest.

Relax for a new moon or two, cease to be aggressive against the forces of evil, drift into contentment…and defeat is near. That is the reason why scrupulous attention to the Law is vital when security threatens; awakening and convicting statutes cause fresh winds to blow over the soul.

Eleventh Day *Read Deuteronomy 16–19*

Part of the eternal human dilemma lies in the relationship between the individual and the group. Truly human individuals cannot develop in isolation; a social as well as a biological womb is necessary. But the impact of the group upon the individual is such that we are continually trying to "improve" society for the sake of the persons whom it includes and shapes.

To have a king or not to have a king? In one form or another, that is a perennial riddle (see 17:14–20). We cannot function as an organized society without a power structure, but poor leaders are worse than none. Once more, we recognize that we are incapable of saving ourselves; if we are to enter an ideal state, it must be by God's grace and not by our own cleverness.

Twelfth Day *Read Deuteronomy 20–23*

No activity, no event, no circumstance is outside the area of the covenant and its concerns. Conduct of battle, siege of a city, discipline of a son, recovery of a stray farm animal, and robbery of a bird's nest are activities within the law and not apart from it.

Thirteenth Day *Read Deuteronomy 24–27*

Never under any circumstances must Israel forget that she has been redeemed, not by her own power but by the favor of the Lord. At every harvest time, rejoicing over the bounty of the earth can be a special occasion for remembering the divine rescue (26:1–11). Every occasion for remembrance can be the stimulus for erecting altars and memorial stones, which, in turn, serve to evoke new rememberings.

It is such remembering and dedicating, over and over, through all the activities of a God-intoxicated culture, that gives Israel her unique nature and constitutes her as the bride of Jehovah (26:1–19).

Fourteenth Day *Read Deuteronomy 28–29*

Blessings or curses…bliss beyond imagination, or afflictions severe and lasting…in the covenant relationship there is no middle ground of neutrality.

Fifteenth Day *Read Deuteronomy 30–31*

Man's freedom comes at the point of moral and spiritual choice. We are not free, in the sense that we can do anything we please. We are of earth and are chained to earth with bonds far stronger than iron. Even as we soar into space, we take our earthliness with us.

But it is our glory that we can shake off the shackles of earth in the realm of the spirit. Each of us has set before him "life and prosperity, death and destruction" (30:15). Each of us not only may make this cosmic choice; each of us must make it.

Sixteenth Day *Read Deuteronomy 32–34*

Few passages in literature exceed the power and sweep of the songs of Moses. As you revel in their magnificent promises, remember that Christians, followers of Jesus Christ, are the recipients of all the bounty promised by the Father. Israel's whole history, God's entire covenant of grace, comes to focus in you. Hence you may read these glory songs with your own name inserted; it was that you might accept the Father's good gifts that heaven and earth were created!

Joshua

The historical books of the Old Testament depict the growth of a family (Abraham's descendants) into a group of tribes and then into a nation. Throughout, emphasis is placed upon the importance of the group. It is the collective Israel, "the bride of Jehovah," with whom the story is concerned.

At the same time, the story centers upon a few individuals. Joshua, successor of Moses, is one such stalwart leader. Just as we associate Moses with the divine deliverance that produced the Exodus, so we associate Joshua with the fulfillment of God's promise to establish his chosen people in a land of abundance. Over and over

God raises up a leader like Joshua to play a vital role in leading groups of people into some land of Canaan.

God is never an absentee landlord. He not only created and sustains the physical environment essential to human existence, he also has an organic role in human history. God's absolute entrance into that history is through the person of his Son. In the Old Testament God worked through Abraham, Moses, Joshua, and others. In the New Testament, God entered history in the person of his Son who came in the fullness of time.

Seventeenth Day *Read Joshua 1–4*

An ironic commentary upon what we call "progress" is to compare the role of national leaders then and now. Joshua's rise to leadership was in response to a divine call. His first duty was obedience to God. His most pressing daily task was meditating day and night upon the Book of the Law.

In our epoch of "enlightenment," leaders derive their power from voters rather than from God, and the first duty of elected officers is to please the persons who can keep them in office. Their most pressing daily task is to ascertain what the majority of voters want, then try to act accordingly. They are not governed by morals but by consensus.

In these thousands of years, how far have we really come? Is there any reasonable hope for an ideal society—a utopia—on this planet? Do you accept or reject the notion that social dilemmas, like individual ones, remind us of our limitedness and can serve to persuade us to seek divine rescue rather than human achievement?

Eighteenth Day *Read Joshua 5–7*

Every advance is achieved at a price. Even in the process of accepting and acting upon divine help, we remain finite. We are prone to forget our limitations when we are relatively comfortable. This is the perennial error that we make, individually and socially. Over and over, God leads his own out of their personal Egypts and, by the thunder of his trumpets, causes the walls of fortified cities to fall. Over and over, rescued ones cease to obey the Lord, break faith, and in their self-sufficiency rebel against their deliverer. Over and over, proud ones are denied entrance into the promised land for which they had set out in enthusiasm.

Hence, perpetually and perennially, children and grandchildren actually settle in lands of promise never entered by those who "grow up" and cease to think of themselves as little children in the sight of a Father who demands absolute obedience as the price of rescue.

Nineteenth Day *Read Joshua 8–10*

We are inclined to remember Joshua largely for his role in that strange battle when the sun stood still. This memorable event, like the rain of stones from heaven, was a dramatic message conveyed through deeds rather than words (see comment on fifth day, Num. 22–24.) In spoken language, these marvelous signs of God's special concern for Israel simply say that the Lord is fighting on the side of the chosen people.

Today's middle-class churchgoers tend to use the marvelous events of Joshua's military campaigns simply as interesting and vivid stories—and frequently fail to show Sunday school pupils how they are the outward fruits of individual and national faithfulness to God. The real message of Joshua's story centers in his ceaseless search for greater obedience (1:8). His building of an altar, offering of sacrifices, and reading of all that "is written in the Book of the Law" (8:30–35) are the central public events of his colorful career. Supernatural aid in battle was simply a visible effect of his far more important campaigns in the realm of the spirit.

Twentieth Day *Read Joshua 11–13*

Bloody and cruel as the account is, the record of the wars of Joshua is not to be struck from the Book that deals with *salvation history.* In our present-day recoil from the horrors of war and our enthusiasm for world peace, we tend to adopt a point of view in which wars are fought in a vacuum, as it were. That is, we are prone to regard war as taking place outside the ongoing creative work of God.

Here is a wholesome corrective.

Let us never fall into the error of believing that anything whatever can exist "in its own strength." God is the maker of all that has been; God sustains all that is. Even when men, in their freedom, fall upon one another and slaughter the innocent with the guilty, God has not turned his back upon his creation. Providence is ever present and exalted, operating on so vast a scale that human eyes perceive the details only with difficulty.

Were we sufficiently sensitive, we could see the Creator in every aspect of creation. That is essentially the witness of these chapters. Blithely indifferent to contrary arguments, rising on wings of belief above all the objections of logic and doctrine, they declare that God is *the* active agent in human history. God is working out his purpose even in our darkest hours. For those who accept his offer of redeeming grace, every circumstance whatever is an agent operating to strengthen the bonds of the covenant.

Twenty-first Day *Read Joshua 14–20*

The assignment of territory by lot is further evidence of the Israelites' dependence upon divine guidance. Such a notion sounds strange today. We are prone to rely upon the wisdom of a human expert or to call upon some impartial jury of average men and women to arrive at a verdict, i.e., "the truth."

Only in a God-centered culture is it possible to seek the will of the Creator through what we are likely to consider pure chance. Israel found it logical to make important decisions upon the basis of the fall of Urim and Thummin—small stones that functioned somewhat like dice.

Casting of lots was a standard religious ceremony (see Exod. 28:29; Lev. 8:8; Num. 27:21; Deut. 33:8). It was employed by Jesus' apostles to select a successor to Judas (Acts 1:26). Gideon's fleece was simply another device for "testing God," or seeking to know his will (Judg. 8:36–40). Some device for casting lots was probably used in such crises as that described in Judges 20:23. The apron-like ephod of the priest was used to determine God's will in cases of doubt. For example, David employed it to decide whether or not to attack in battle (1 Sam. 30:7–9). It was frightful to be unable to get any answer through the use of such devices, and this crisis of silence sent Saul in disguise to consult the medium of Endor (1 Sam. 28).

I think what this means is this: NOTHING TAKES PLACE APART FROM GOD. THEREFORE, GOD AFFECTS THE OUTCOME OF CASTING LOTS AND THROUGH THIS PRACTICE "SPEAKS" TO THOSE WHO HAVE ENOUGH FAITH AND SKILL TO UNDERSTAND WHAT HE SAYS.

However you may react to so primitive a view of Providence, it nevertheless remains provocative. For if you and I can become convinced that a given outcome represents the will of God, and if we order our conduct in the light of this conviction, then it follows that, for us, whatever comes is bound to bring us closer to God rather than cause us to turn aside from seeking him. Such a point of view is radically different from fatalism—passive acceptance of whatever comes, resignation that what will be, will be.

A vital trust in the providential ordering of life's events, even to the assignment of a place to live (about which we moderns fret so much), produces individual and cultural peace of mind of a variety far deeper than that of shallow contentment.

Twenty-second Day *Read Joshua 21–22*

Even the assignment of territory is conditional; even the blessing of a Joshua rests upon acceptance of terms. Those terms, in the present case, are no less than a scrupulous daily concern for God's will as expressed through religious law (22:5).

Twenty-third Day *Read Joshua 23–24*

Once more, the people of the promise hear a warning that their special relationship with God is like a two-edged sword. Obedience to God alone will bring blessings, but loyalty to any other god will arouse God's anger and cause his wrath to be poured upon the heads of his people. There is no middle ground; it is either/or (24:15).

As a small boy learning the catechism, I was bothered by the idea that God is "jealous." But the sense of that adjective is positive rather than negative. God so yearns to give us all his good things that he frets every time we turn aside from him to seek a foreign god. Let us not fall into that delusion of Satan that tells us that idols and false gods have vanished from this age of enlightenment. To put any other goal ahead of the desire to know and please God is to bow down at the shrine of some modern Baal and thereby to invite the wrath of Jehovah.

Judges

Having settled in the Promised Land, the people of the promise developed a town culture that contrasted sharply with that of wandering shepherds. Heads of clans could no longer govern the people satisfactorily—but it would be many generations before a true nation could take shape. In this interim period of several centuries, tribal chieftains and heroes, or "judges," were important and colorful leaders. Hence their title attaches to the book that preserves many records from the period.

Twenty-fourth Day *Read Judges 1–3*

It was the role of the judge not only to lead in battle and govern in time of peace but also to serve as agent or spokesman for God (see 8:23). During the period of the judges, the distinction between religious and political leadership did not exist. Part of the power of the judge came from the conviction that a judge was first a messenger of God and second a leader and governor of the people.

Twenty-fifth Day *Read Judges 4–5*

Sisera, the most powerful Canaanite chieftain of the period, possessed the most advanced weaponry of the day; he commanded nine hundred chariots of iron. Military force alone could never defeat him.

To bring the mighty warrior low, ironically, God raised up, not a stronger fighting man, but a woman, the judge Deborah. Her weapons were words and moral certainty. After his defeat in battle, the great Sisera hid in Jael's tent, and with more irony, this great fighter died at the hand of this women (see also Abimelech's end, Judg. 9:50–54).

You recognize, of course, that such accounts represent history interpreted from the viewpoint of a belief in all-inclusive Providence. Only one of many ways in which history can be viewed and reported, it is quite alien to the method of most present historians. But the important thing for us to underscore here is that all historical reports are shaped by the beliefs of the historian. There is no such thing as absolutely impartial and objective reporting of what happens.

We are dealing with spiritual history, in which events are interpreted from the viewpoint that God is the decisive agent in all that takes place. That certainly is the message of the Song of Deborah.

Twenty-sixth Day *Read Judges 6–8*

Have you noticed how many chapters begin with the same theme? Just as military victory is credited to the work of Providence, so defeat is regarded as a call to self-appraisal and repentance.

In a culture where disasters are regarded as divine punishments, complacency is impossible. Over and over, the tribes are driven to their knees. From that perspective, they look up and out to be overwhelmed with consciousness of having wandered from the path that leads to life. Confessing guilt and begging forgiveness, they rise to serve God with fresh ardor.

This cyclical pattern is one of the chief characteristics of the record of the people of the covenant.

Twenty-seventh Day *Read Judges 9–11*

"God sent an evil spirit between Abimelech and the citizens of Shechem" (9:23); "God repaid the wickedness [of] Abimelech" (9:56); when Israel served false gods, "He sold them into the hands of the Philistines" (10:7).

How do such statements help us understand Israel's inner life? What significance for our life today is in the point of view expressed here?

Twenty-eighth Day *Read Judges 12–15*

Divine participation in human procreation is a recurrent motif in Scripture. You will instantly see parallels between the birth stories of Isaac, Samson, and John the Baptist.

What really matters here is the conviction of the covenant people that the birth of a son or daughter is neither accidental nor casual. Rather, God the Father is both interested and involved. No baby comes into the world apart from the work of Providence. Human mothers and fathers are merely agents—essential ones, to be sure, but only agents—for the working out of the divine will as it moves through the stream of human heredity.

No interpretation of the Virgin Birth of our Savior is really coherent unless it takes into account the biblical attitude about God's role in human procreation.

Twenty-ninth Day *Read Judges 16–18*

For the typical moviegoing, Bible-neglecting church member, Hollywood has succeeded in distorting Old Testament biographies of Noah, Moses, Samson, and more. The goings-on of the judge Samson with Delilah, LIKE EVERYTHING ELSE IN THE OLD TESTAMENT, finds a place in the sacred record only because the account has power to communicate truths about God in his relationship with mankind.

Do you find it difficult to focus your reading so that you rise above the sordid in Samson's brief biography? If you succeed in using the story as a lens for high-level seeing, what vivid new truths emerge here?

Thirtieth Day *Read Judges 19–21*

Flagrant sexual perversion...bloody civil war...near extermination of blood descendants of Jacob's youngest son....

All this within a score of generations after God reached down into Egypt to rescue Abraham's seed. All this from the people set apart—holy, dedicated to the Lord. All this within the framework of the continuing covenant between God and the people whom he called to be his own.

Ending as it does on a note of near-despair, the record of the days of the judges offers hope in every time of national and international darkness. The end is not here. More is yet to come. God has not turned his back upon the world. In the fullness of time, the Savior will come. Victory, not defeat, is the ultimate assurance.

Ruth, Samuel, Kings, Chronicles, Ezra, Nehemiah

Ruth

A hasty glance at this little book suggests that while it has a certain sentimental appeal as a romantic short story, there is little religious content.

But underneath, the currents run deep, for Ruth tells of events central to the family history of David, greatest of Hebrew kings and ancestor of the Savior. Through the marriage of a foreign woman with a man who stands in the line of succession from Abraham, the covenant is given new breadth. Potentially, it now beckons everyone, not just those who inherited the bloodlines of Israel. That is to say, Ruth becomes "an inheritor of the promise" by her own act of choice. That she thereby becomes an ancestress of the Savior adds mightily to the power of the drama that involves heaven as well as earth, God as well as man.

First Day *Read Ruth 1–4*

Because Israel is the bride of Jehovah, Ruth deals with divine-human marriage as truly as with that between a Hebrew man and a Moabite woman. Ruth's entrance into the covenant relationship is a harbinger of the "New Israel" of which Paul makes so much in his letter to the Romans. Inheritors of the divine promise are not simply those who have Abraham's blood in their veins. Rather, all who will may enter the covenant state as freely as Ruth accepted God's lordship along with Hebrew law and culture.

Samuel

When the sounds of Hebrew speech are transcribed into written words, only consonants are used. This primitive form of shorthand is a considerable spacesaver; a document is twice as long when written in Greek as when written in Hebrew. A group of scholars centered in Alexandria prepared a famous Greek version of the Old Testament, the Septuagint, during the third century B.C. Because the Hebrew Book of Samuel doubled in size during translation, for convenience it was divided into our present two volumes.

In some respects it is strange that the prophet Samuel, and not the great king David, should be named in the title of this history of the early kings of Israel. Seen through eyes of faith, however, history is as truly a record of the mighty acts of God as of the doings of kings. Hence, unless a political leader is also a religious prophet (often the case with the great names of Israel), a prophet takes precedence over a king. It was David, and not Samuel, who was destined to advance the bloodline leading to the Savior; but it was Samuel, and not David, who came to symbolize religious fervor not adulterated by secular ambition.

Second Day *Skim 1 Samuel 1–9*

Instead of concentrating upon the familiar and often sentimentally interpreted story of Samuel's birth and boyhood, notice why he had to be raised up to judge the land. It is an old, old story—human depravity here revealed through the vehicle of the religious institution. Given power, the religious leader always tends to fall away from God. Self-interest of the official (2:12–29) takes many forms but is never permanently curable. Corruption in the religious institution leads to a break in the dialogue between God and his people (3:1, 21); social rottenness develops and then spreads through the whole culture like a cancer.

But this is not the only convicting and humbling note sounded here. Let us beware of thinking that our institutions can manipulate divine power. Whether symbolized by the ark of the covenant or by some other "dwelling place of God," the ongoing work of the Creator is bigger than men. It is lethal, and may seem erratic. No one can control and direct God's power; all must bow down before it and confess their limitations.

Third Day *Skim 1 Samuel 10-15*

Man's rebellion against God, even within the covenant relationship, is as inevitable and continuous as is divine rescue. In these vivid chapters, the new little kingdom totters under the effects of disobedience to God. No one is guiltless. By acting as a priest to make offerings (13:8–14), Saul foolishly claims powers that do not belong to him; later he permits his men to keep booty he was told to destroy (15:3, 10–31) and victorious Israelite warriors commit the great sin of eating blood (14:32).

Over and over, repentant ones offer sacrifices and set up stone memorials. But no degree of contrition can wipe out the offense. Obedience, not sacrifice, is demanded by God, so it is mercy that the people must ask of God, not justice.

Fourth Day *Skim 1 Samuel 16–22*

As with many biblical stories such as those of Joseph, Samson, and Ruth, there are subtle dangers here. Color, vividness, and power of description give these chapters the qualities of good fiction. Precisely because it is easy to become absorbed in David's adventures and to interpret them upon the human level, there is danger that we overlook the spiritual overtones.

Notice that the most powerful motivating factor here is the divine will. God is at work in the unfolding of Israel, and it is he who elevates and deposes kings. Battles, friendships, and intrigues are simply instruments that further the purposes of the Creator.

Again, let us not become so absorbed with delight in David's exploits that we fail to see their symbolism. In offering himself as champion of his people, to give his life for them if need be, David is a forerunner of the Savior. As a military substitute against Goliath, he takes upon himself the risks that belong to the nation, collectively. So he points, though dimly, to Calvary—where Jesus serves as a spiritual substitute. In and through the Cross, our divine-human Champion steps forward to do battle with Satan, taking upon himself the sins of the whole world.

Fifth Day *Skim 1 Samuel 23–31*

While human heroes and villains are the most conspicuous characters walking the stage of history, their freedom to make history is limited. God acts in every situation and through every event. It is he, for example, who sends Abigail to feed and placate David (25:32). Though the pride and stupidity of Saul are agents working to put him at the mercy of David, it is the Lord who actually gives him into the young rebel's hand (26:23).

Since God is the decisive agent in the outcome of any event, cosmic or trivial, it follows that those who fear him will try to discover the divine will in every situation. David's perpetual inquiring of God (23:2–3; 30:7–8; 2 Sam. 2:1; 5:19; 5:23) seems to us to have been on a crude level; we would not today cast lots or consult oracles. In your opinion, is the difference between such inquiring and the use of prayer a difference of degree or of kind? Why?

Whatever you may think about methods of asking for divine guidance, notice that the outcome is very different when you fail to seek it and let yourself be guided purely by your own wishes. Literature includes no more suggestive contrast than that between David's marriage with Abigail and Bathsheba. Both had been wives of other men, but in the case of Abigail, there is encounter between man and woman based upon mutual surrender to God (see 25:23–35). In the case of Bathsheba, the encounter is the fruit of concession to lust. That Bathsheba rather than Abigail should enter the bloodline of the Savior does not excuse the sin of David. Rather, it witnesses with dramatic eloquence to the fact that God's power to rescue men and his willingness to use their failures as well as successes is without limit.

Sixth Day *Skim 2 Samuel 1–6*

We have noticed the vital power of words—through which humans gain powers not granted any other creatures. We have seen the significance of those special words we call names and have noted ways in which metaphors can point to truths they are too small to contain.

These chapters are rich with the power of symbolism. For it is David, the shepherd king, who prefigures and points to the coming of the Shepherd of Men and the King of Kings. It is the Canaanite stronghold of Zion, or Jerusalem, that David captures and makes his capital. Ever afterward, the City of David, however designated, will be a central symbol of the Hebrew-Christian faith. To those who have ears attuned for messages from God, "the sound of marching in the tops of the balsam trees" speaks more forcefully than any words (5:24); to those who use their literal meanings as bases from which to leap forward in faith, radiant truths are seized through such symbols as: the Good Shepherd, the New Zion, and the City of David.

When religious symbolism is concentrated in persons or things rather than in words, we have tangible "vessels that contain the holy." A king who has been anointed by God's priest is such a vessel. Therefore to slay him—even in righteous wrath—is to rebel against God, to take the work of Providence into one's own hand (1:13–16; 4:10). As the supreme tangible example of the holy, the ark of the covenant is actually dangerous. Regardless of how good his intentions are, Uzzah's stumbling against it constitutes an act of suicide (6:6–7).

Do such notions appear utterly strange to you? Or has our journey through this portion of the Old Testament increased your capacity to wonder at the work of God? As we try to travel the Information Highway, do we still become lost in the woods of life, requiring rescue to reach a goal we can never attain by our own strength?

Seventh Day *Skim 2 Samuel 7–13*

Success is the road to failure.

But conscious failure and repentance offer a new start; no failure is final unless we choose to make it so. Having gone down into the

Egyptian captivity of adultery, and having had the angel of death enter the royal household, David accepts the forgiveness that even he cannot win with his sword.

It is then, and only then, that the new man, who can pour out his penitence in Psalm 51 and who is to be used by God to bring Solomon into the world, enters into the New Covenant. Instead of speaking directly to David, as he did to Abraham, God uses an agent: Nathan the prophet. Modified and expanded, the new promise to the new human partner—the nation of Israel rather than the family of Abraham—preserves the original qualities of boundlessness and limitedness, coupled with assurance of absolute victory (see chap. 7).

Lust, greed, vanity, perversion, and hate pervade these chapters. God is not working through plaster saints, but through flesh-and-blood humans whose wars are as savage and whose murders are as brutal as any that history records. Yet the promise cannot be defeated. The covenant is so strongly maintained by God that nothing man can do is sufficient to shatter it. Israel, the bride of Christ, will in due time bring forth the divine-human Son, whose role will be that of overcoming Satan and canceling the effects of sin so that men, made in the image of God, may accept the prize they can never win.

Eighth Day *Skim 2 Samuel 14–19*

These chapters also depict colorful men in a brawny era. In the fast-moving story of intrigue that sets father against son, there are few references, direct or indirect, that we can consider "religious." God is in all that occurs, to be sure (17:14), but the emphasis here is upon the character of David, who is destined to become idealized as "the perfect ruler."

Ninth Day *Skim 2 Samuel 20–24*

No matter how hard it may be to see his movements, God is the source of all that is. Nothing exists apart from the ongoing work of creation and the sustaining hand of the Creator. All victories and all deliverances are actually the work of God, not of man who enjoys his moment of triumph. Hence an occasion of "success" is a time that demands one's gladdest and most fervent praise—even if few can match the winged words of David as reported in his song of praise (see chap. 22).

God is also involved in all tragedy and trouble (21:1; 24:10–15). Days of tribulation are heavenly traffic lights, calling on men and nations to stop their mad rush for gain. A time of distress can drive even a king to his knees and send him out to erect an altar and make a special offering to God (24:18–25). For the faith of Israel, this is the meaning of tragedy: sons of the covenant suffer in return for sin, and their suffering is redemptive because it can turn them back to God, if they are humble enough to accept his rescue.

Kings

These two books made up a single volume in the Hebrew original, and the actual division was not made until the sixteenth century. Most Greek Bibles prefer the title "Kingdoms," which in them is applied to these books and to the books of Samuel.

Like the books of Samuel, these are filled with—sometimes vivid—details that are often all but meaningless to us today. Here are accounts of the most glorious decades of Israel as a political community and also the so-human story of civil war, military defeat, and foreign captivity.

While these books have even less evidence of conveying deep spiritual truth than the books of Samuel, they are vital to the unfolding story of the covenant. They tell us (often in what seems like tiresome detail) how Israel's material success led to her spiritual decay. To be reawakened, the chosen people had to be led into a new Egypt, as it were, and from bondage in Babylon, a new rescue could revitalize their sense of destiny.

Tenth Day *Skim 1 Kings 1–7*

These chapters symbolize both the individual and the national paradox: eagerness to serve God and him alone, countered by a tug from sin that is too strong to resist.

Solomon receives a powerful challenge from his dying father (2:14). He accepts as the chief principle of his reign that God "has established me, and placed me on the throne of David my father" (2:24). Nevertheless, after vowing loyalty to God, he sends his agents to slay his ambitious brother and hurries to contract an alliance with Egypt (2:25; 3:1).

To his eternal glory, Solomon becomes the builder of the temple. But that great king, made wise because of his earnest prayer for wisdom and not long life or riches (3:11), makes sacrifices and burns incense at shrines in the high places, and in his old age, he will degenerate into open idolatry (11:1–8).

Eleventh Day *Skim 1 Kings 8–14*

Solomon's great public work, the temple, is built to house the ark, the holiest of Israel's inheritances that is merely a receptacle for the stones on which the Ten Commandments are written. These stones, in turn, are merely pointers to the God of whom they speak, who is too glorious to be contained in anything visible (8:27).

It is the covenant, no word of which has failed (8:56), to which all these tangibles witness. By the glory of the temple and all its contents, the chosen people are impelled to bow down at the greatness of Jehovah and to wonder why he should have chosen Israel for his bride. Always, there is clear recognition that the principle of the covenant makes it a conditional instrument (8:25; see also 2:4; 6:12; 9:4–9).

But in practice, leaders of the nation set apart to follow God repeatedly fail. In Judah, loyal to David's line, and following after Rehoboam, the covenant is repeatedly broken from the human side. This is seen in Jeroboam's rebellious act of erecting golden calves and calling upon all Israel to worship them (12:25-33). It is the repeated and flagrant breaking of the covenant that will send the chosen people into new captivity where they will once more long for divine rescue rather than boast about their human achievements.

Twelfth Day *Skim 1 Kings 15–22*

How very brief is any human hour of glory! Kings were a dime a dozen in these years; Zimri conspired, murdered, and made war in order to reign for seven days (16:15). As with individuals, so with nations. David's kingdom began to break up even before his death, and the once-powerful nation degenerated into mutually hostile states.

With God's power no longer evident in political leaders, prophets such as the "troubler of Israel" (18:17) had to speak against the idolatry of the times. Even smashing victory over the prophets of Baal, with fire called down from heaven by an Elijah, could not bring lasting reform; "the people still sacrificed and burned incense on the high places" (22:43).

What parallels do you see between this Hebrew period and the United States? What major differences do you see? Do we place too much trust in the White House, Congress, NATO, or the United Nations?

Thirteenth Day *Skim 2 Kings 1–7*

Accounts of miracles of the New Testament have attracted great interest and have been the subject of much debate. Probably because the accounts are seldom read; the mighty works of Old Testament prophets are not widely discussed. Notice, however, that under Elijah and his successor, Elisha, all the great miracles are reported: healing of illness, marvels in the natural world (iron floating, water mastered), and the dead raised to life. The calling down of heavenly fire to strike opponents dead has no counterpart in the New Testament. To center upon minute details of such accounts is fatal to the discovery of their inner meaning. For believers these startling events shout about the majesty and wonder and infinite power of God. As you ponder these strange stories, are you bewildered and repelled by them, or do you hear in a new way the central motif of the biblical symphony?

Fourteenth Day *Skim 2 Kings 8–12*

Having sunk into the pit of infamy, the descendants of Abraham wallow in their own filth. If history is interpreted in terms of individuals, we have to confess that there are many periods of utter hopelessness.

But viewed from the perspective of God's total dealings with mankind, darkness is never absolute. God is active, even in defeat and tragedy (10:32). God will continue to raise up reformers who will abolish whatever pagan altars dominate their cultures. Such reform, however, is itself always limited and never absolute.

These bloody pages therefore speak an oddly paradoxical verdict: man can never sink so low that he slips through the fingers of Providence, nor can he ever climb high enough to achieve a God-centered culture from which all the pagan shrines have been banished.

Fifteenth Day *Skim 2 Kings 13–18*

To read *spiritual history*, as revealed through the pages that record the deeds of Hebrew kings, is to become wholly pessimistic about human nature and at the same time to become utterly optimistic about divine love. For the long, sorry story tells us (over, and over, and over, and over, as though repetition is necessary to drive home the truth) that we always fall short. No reform is absolute or enduring, no progress is unqualified. In our own strength we cannot achieve anything approaching an ideal godly society.

Yet God does not cancel his promises. He reaffirms the covenant, punishes in wrath only to forgive again in redemptive love, and refuses to write off the human race as an experiment that has failed. Over, and over, and over, and over, as though no number of repetitions can cause him to waver, he holds out forgiveness and offers rescue that can lead to absolute spiritual victory.

Sixteenth Day *Skim 2 Kings 19–25*

These tumultuous generations were marked by two sets of events that were to affect the whole course of covenant history.

First, the Book of the Law was discovered in the Temple. Lost or hidden during long periods when kings sank so low that they even practiced human sacrifice, the written code became the basis of Josiah's sweeping reforms. Note, however, that the sun of fidelity to God peeped out from clouds of idolatry only briefly; the nation returned to its pagan practices upon the death of Josiah.

The second crucial set of events centered around international affairs. After being threatened by Assyria and becoming a tributary to Egypt, the people of God were overwhelmed by soldiers of Babylon. With the temple sacked and their cities burned, Abraham's descendants were taken away into captivity.

Note, however, that every page of the record affirms the conviction that God is the decisive agent in all that takes place. When national victory comes, it is because he has given it. But disaster is equally his work! FOR EYES OF FAITH, WHATEVER COMES WILL SERVE TO CONVEY A GOD-CENTERED MESSAGE. EVERY EVENT, WHETHER IT LEADS TO REJOICING OR MOURNING, SERVES AS AN AGENT OF REVELATION AND SPEAKS ABOUT GOD TO THOSE WHO LISTEN WITH EARS ATTUNED TO THE STILL, SMALL VOICE.

Chronicles

These volumes roughly parallel the books of Samuel and Kings. Like all historians, the chronicler selects his evidence to defend a particular point of view. He presents an overwhelming case for the conclusion that kings (and their people) incurred divine wrath by failure to worship God without compromise. Tangible sins, like making alliances with foreigners, were results of inner decay—a breach of the covenant by which the children of the promise owed ABSOLUTE trust and loyalty to God.

Seventeenth Day *Skim 1 Chronicles 1–10*

Although to us these chapters constitute a valley of very dry bones, to devout Hebrews and early Christians the genealogies included here were of absorbing interest. It was considered vital to trace the transmission of the covenant and its promises through unbroken lines of descent. The normal pattern of the bloodline was from father to eldest son, but there were numerous exceptions. Reuben's adultery (Gen. 35:22) cost him his place in the line of succession and the birthright went to his youngest brother, Joseph (1 Chron. 5:1). Though the story of David's many marriages is scrambled, it is clear that he had a number of sons before Solomon (1 Chron. 3:1–9). To seek a logical explanation for Solomon's place in *salvation history* is to become entangled in fruitless speculation. Divine choice, not man's doings, is at work here (1 Chron. 28:5–7).

However devious the pattern of descent, faith has an explanation that covers every situation in principle. Sin on the part of the human recipient of divine grace—breach of the covenant by the partner of God—deflects *salvation history* from its normal course.

In many instances, such as that of Reuben, the sin is specified; in others it is only implied. Saul's disobedience and his dabbling in the occult cost him the throne and his life (1 Chron. 10:13–14). David's scorn for God's unqualified demands cost him the life of his first son by Bathsheba (2 Sam. 12:13–20). Solomon, without parallel among kings, succumbs to the lure of foreign women (Neh. 13:26). Judah's faithlessness sends the whole nation into Babylonian captivity (1 Chron. 9:1).

Unlike any other collection of sacred literature, the Bible underscores the limitedness of its heroes, prophets, and holy men. Instead of elevating its chief figures into divinities, the Bible perpetually reminds us that there is no one faithful—no, not one (2 Chron. 6:36). It is this perpetual and inevitable human factor that accounts for the erratic and sometimes inscrutable path of *salvation history.*

Eighteenth Day *Skim 1 Chronicles 11–19*

Woven into this account of David's personal and national triumphs, there is a strand that runs through the entire biblical record. Precisely because of the covenant relationship, and not in spite of it, the chosen people (individually and collectively) live in a state of paradox and tension. They must be in perpetual fear of God; if they happen to become callous, they are warned by some mighty event to return to a saving state of dread (1 Chron. 13:12). At the same time, they must continually be in a state of joy, powerful enough to evoke such praise as David's song of thanksgiving (1 Chron. 16; see also Ps. 100).

This double orientation of life carries over into the realm of signs, portents, revelations, and words. We have already noticed Old Testament emphasis upon the power and mystery of these devices for communication between God and man as well as between man and man. In our reading of the psalms and especially of the New Testament, we shall be reminded over and over that words are frequently employed to convey meanings at two or more levels. It is not strange, therefore, but natural and logical that Nathan's vision of glorious kingship on the part of David's offspring (1 Chron. 17:11–14) should (to faith-directed eyes) be a harbinger of the coming Savior who will occupy the throne of David and establish the new Zion.

Nineteenth Day *Skim 1 Chronicles 20–29*

No one, asserts the scriptural record, ever gets all he wants. Our capacity to yearn always exceeds our ability to perform. Even David cannot build the temple of his dreams; he must go to his grave denied this central satisfaction of his life.

How do you account for the emphasis upon his sin in making a census? Did Satan tempt him to rebellious pride, so that he numbered his subjects in order to magnify his own importance and thereby to reduce his fear of God? What is the divine message here, for the statistic-minded modern church?

Twentieth Day *Skim 2 Chronicles 1–9*

Solomon's encounter with the Queen of Sheba is colorful and easy to read, but details of his economic and military exploits and the long lists of materials and furnishings for the temple are meaningless to us today. We tend, therefore, to skip over the account of years in which the house of the Lord was translated from a dream into reality.

Woven into that tedious story, however, are warnings that temple-builders and God-seekers perpetually need to have repeated. Glorious as the covenant is, wonderful as its promises are, the divine-human contract is conditional. Punishments for faithlessness are on the same grand scale as rewards for fidelity (2 Chron. 7:11–22).

Even a Solomon cannot win or achieve the right to build a house for the Creator of all houses (2 Chron. 2:6–16). Divine glory (2 Chron. 5:14; 7:2), conferred by the presence of God himself, is what sets his house apart from all others. The visible temple, no matter how costly and beautiful and magnificent, means nothing unless God is in it. And no matter how close the bonds between God and the priests of his chosen people, God is always withdrawn, hidden "in thick darkness" (6:1), forever beyond such intimacy that he can be manipulated. Let Solomon's people, therefore, guard with their very lives against the danger of thinking that, because they have erected the temple, they control the Lord and may relax in their passionate striving to know and serve him better.

Twenty-first Day *Skim 2 Chronicles 10–19*

Clearly there is nothing new in these chapters; they simply repeat the basic notes sounded in many chapters of the books of Samuel and of the Kings.

Why do you suppose there is so much biblical repetition? Would it not be equally convincing and more readable to present just two or three vivid case histories that communicate a given message? Is it really necessary to overwhelm the reader with dozens of instances that tell the story of divine constancy, human failure, mutual pledges between Creator and creatures, faithlessness that leads to religious reform (always incomplete), and reaffirmation of loyalty? Even with all these repetitions of a few fundamental notes, do you think they are heard and heeded by most church folk today? If there is a cure for the basic human dilemma, what is it?

Twenty-second Day *Skim 2 Chronicles 20–28*

Whatever else it communicates, this record of the rise and fall of kings and the coming and going of national attitudes shouts loudly about the limitedness of man's influence. Nothing human is permanent. Whether a change be in the direction of evil or of good, it is fluid and transient.

Yesterday's spiritual victories do not carry over into today's life. Baal must be overthrown again in every generation (2 Chron. 23:17). Social salvation is a myth; mankind can never hope to arrive at an ideal society by means of human progress and reform. We cannot save ourselves. Society, like the individuals who constitute it, is limited and fallible. Divine rescue is a social as well as a personal necessity; no reform is absolute or eternal, no progress is great enough or enduring enough to eliminate the need for divine intervention in the affairs of men and nations.

Twenty-third Day *Skim 2 Chronicles 29–36*

Repeating, for the most part, details already reported in portions of 2 Kings, these chapters simply document the verdict which we arrived at yesterday. Hezekiah's cleanup is followed by Manasseh's orgy of idolatry; we are impelled to join our own voices to the plaintive cry that "men never learn."

Oddly, however, this is the one true source of hope. Because we cannot put any trust in ourselves, we are forced to trust in God. When we have failed on a sufficiently conspicuous scale to recognize our own failure, only then are we ready to join Manasseh in the humble entreaty for divine rescue that leads to overpowering recognition that the Lord really is the one true God (2 Chron. 33:10–13).

3

Ezra

Ezra, the valiant priest, probable author of the Chronicles as well as the little book that bears his name, here records a new exodus by the chosen people. Instead of Egypt, the captor has been Babylon. Instead of a great horde of liberated ones, there are just 1496 men and their families. Instead of a whole people (all the seed of Abraham), the rescued ones are merely the righteous remnant of a once-great nation.

Besides these factors, there is the important difference that going back cannot be identical to going out to a new land. This time, the people led by God are returning to their old home in hopes of restoring some of their past glory. So their whole orientation is different from that of Moses' people, eager to claim a God-promised land and in it to grow from a group of families into a nation.

Twenty-fourth Day *Read Ezra 1–4*

Here we find tears mingled with shouts of joy (3:12–13), for the new temple is hardly under construction before human adversaries, moved by jealousy (4:1–5), succeed in stopping the work. But the combination of weeping with rejoicing, symbolic of man's incapacity to achieve a tension-free state, cannot silence the praise of these people. Their glad song (3:10–11) comes from the lips of those just back from exile. Even overwhelming national disaster cannot shake their faith in divine love or their confidence in divine favor.

Part of their delight stems from the fact that a new note has been sounded in the old symphony of the covenant. Cyrus of Persia—a man outside the ranks of God's people—plays a major role in the building of the new temple. Even though Abraham's descendants are employed as his agents to perform the work, we here begin to get a hint that the whole concept of the chosen people is in process of radical revision.

Twenty-fifth Day *Read Ezra 5–7*

First-person comments are rare in the Old Testament, so the almost casual personal remarks of Ezra (7:27–28) are a bit startling. Devout and courageous as this priest certainly was, we cannot avoid recognizing that at its highest and noblest, rebuilding is not the same as building.

So the whole movement of Ezra and his people witnesses to pre-occupation with the past (return of part of the gold and silver vessels that long adorned the temple, for example). Such looking backward always involves some degree of hardening, intellectually and spiritually. It involves some degree of inhibition of the novel—even when originating from God.

In the end, this looking back is to prove the undoing of the covenant people. They will become so zealous to interpret the inherited law that they refuse to participate in the new revelation offered through the incarnation of the Creator in the person of Jesus of Nazareth.

Twenty-sixth Day *Read Ezra 8–10*

Here we are confronted by the concept of social guilt. According to it, all in Hebrew society (even Ezra himself) are stained by the sins of their fellows (9:1–7). The great sin involved is that of contamination—failure to remain deliberately set apart from all other peoples.

As a result of recognized guilt on the part of all the chosen people, there arises a new understanding of the divine-human contract. Since God has chosen to destroy the nation that developed in the land of promise, human understanding of the covenant must have been in error. It is not the entire Hebrew people who will inherit the promise, but only a righteous minority, a remnant.

Subsequent generations will see the visible remnant dwindle in number until at last it includes, strictly speaking, only one member: Jesus of Nazareth. But his victory over Satan and his death lead to a revision of the covenant idea, so that after Calvary the chosen people (made up of all who accept the salvation offered by the risen Lord) will rapidly expand in number and will include all races and nations—the new family of God raised up to take the place of the Israel who played her essential role by giving birth to the long-promised Son of God.

Nehemiah

This earliest of Hebrew autobiographies, coming from the pen of a layman rather than a priest or Levite, is essentially a story of action on behalf of God as contrasted with meditation about the nature of God.

Twenty-seventh Day *Read Nehemiah 1–4*

The vivid and often emotional words of Nehemiah witness that action can never be divorced from the principles that motivate it. To build for God is to evoke jealousy, ridicule, and opposition. Such building is therefore costly and dangerous.

This case history therefore poses some basic problems. Is persecution by foes of God an inevitable mark of one's genuine devotion to God alone? Are there any situations in which public opinion is so overwhelmingly on God's side that one can build a temple without opposition?

Twenty-eighth Day *Read Nehemiah 5–7*

Few portions of Scripture approach these chapters in preserving spontaneous conversation with God, woven into reports of daily events (5:19; 6:9, 14; see also 13:22, 29, 31). Nehemiah speaks to the Lord as naturally as he would to any human companion. His relationship with the Lord is accurately conveyed in the hymn that says, "he walks with me, and he talks with me; he tells me I am his own."

Occasionally men and women have entered into a personal relationship with God so that the gulf between the divine and the human has been bridged.

Twenty-ninth Day *Read Nehemiah 8–10*

Periodic rediscovery of the written law is basic to Israel's cycles of regeneration. From floundering without any sure guide, the people a few generations away from fervent dedication to God find a source of certainty in the law. Such discoverings and enterings into new covenants always involve both warning and promise—"a curse and an oath" (10:29).

Here we find light shed upon a dilemma of Protestant Christianity in our time. There are but three great streams from which spiritual vitality may flow: holy ceremonies and the institution that transmits them, a body of holy writings, and religious experience. Large segments of Protestantism have practically abandoned the authority of the church and her holy ceremonies. Religious experience still suffers from the excesses of a kind of evangelism that elevated emotional factors at the expense of intellectual ones. And insistence upon verbal literalism, followed by a wave of purely literary and historical study, has cut the foundation from the Scriptures in many communions.

For new hope in the church, we today need precisely what the returning exiles found: a holy Book to which we can turn with the delight of new discovery, from which we can draw authority and through which we can come into personal encounter with the God to whom it points. That is the real purpose of this discipline in which we are now engaged.

Thirtieth Day *Read Nehemiah 11–13*

Discovery of a long-lost holy code is not in itself any guarantee of lasting gains. It is vital that those who ponder the sacred writings shall find in them new meanings that apply to the current situation (13:1–3), and as a result of those insights order their lives differently.

When study of the law degenerates into making commentaries upon what scholars of earlier generations have found, the spirit is dead and the letter reigns. Our year's reading has reached a significant milepost: one-fourth of our time is gone, and we have surveyed considerably more than one-third of our total material.

It is the future, not the past, that calls us! We dare not be like the returning exiles who seek to recapture the past, romantically interpreted. We must be divinely led immigrants, consciously called to enter a new Canaan whose wonders we shall never exhaust. That land of promise lies ahead of us, across the intellectual-spiritual Jordan that separates the New Testament from the Old. Though we are led by a more-than-earthly light, we have yet some time of preparation and of hardening before we shall be ready to cross that river.

Esther, Job, Psalms 1–89

Esther

This little book is among the most colorful in the Bible. It reads like good fiction, with a fast-moving plot. Though there are many impressive lessons in the realms of ethics and morals, the spiritual content is far below that of most Scripture. For religious purposes, its chief role was that of giving support to the observance of the feast of Purim. It is neither quoted nor mentioned anywhere in the New Testament.

First Day *Read Esther 1–5*

Persecution of the Jews began early, frequently became intense, and has continued across the centuries. Whatever else may be said of them, the Jews are absolutely without counterpart. Not a true racial group, but a community held together by religious ties, their survival is one of the marvels of human history.

So this exciting account of ancient plots and counterplots is a sort of summary (better, a symbol) of Jewish survival during the centuries that these people have existed. Haman's role is also symbolic, for economic and political factors have often motivated the Jew-baiter.

The writer of the Book of Esther is absolutely sure that the Lord of hosts, Creator of the heavens and the earth, has a personal interest in these chosen people. What do you think of that idea?

Second Day *Read Esther 6–10*

Through the years in every culture, change occurs in the meaning of words, symbols, ceremonies, and customs. Change also takes place in economics, politics, science, literature, music, and religion. Hence it is not unusual for people to wake up to the fact that they are reciting liturgy or going through rituals without fully understanding why.

Such a situation creates an intellectual vacuum. We are so made that we are dissatisfied without explanations. Consequently, history is written backward through the development of stories to account for the origins of things passed down from previous generations.

Lost in antiquity is the origin of Purim, which is celebrated by Jews on the fourteenth and fifteenth days of the twelfth month, Adar. In the Book of Esther, this unintelligible name is explained by its connection with the Persian word *pur*, the device for casting lots (Esther 9:26). It was pur, the divining tool, that Haman used to determine the date set for the slaughter of the Jews, and hence for the two days of celebration when the king changed his mind.

Job

If this ancient drama had to be summarized in one sentence, perhaps the most nearly suitable one would be the question found in chapter 4 verse 17: "Can mortals be righteous before God?" (cf. 15:14; 25:4). The entire action, like the argument of Paul's letter to the Romans, revolves around the question of how a creature can enter into the righteousness demanded by his Creator.

There are but two basic answers to that question. Many religious systems teach that righteousness is a goal to be won by great striving. Dozens of passages in the Old Testament, considered without regard for the larger context, support such a view. Many critics of Jewish thought assert that Judaism is essentially a legal system that interprets a religion of achievement.

Opposite to the view that a creature can by striving succeed in escaping the limits of creaturehood is that righteousness is an unearned gift of God. Righteousness then is a fruit of mercy or grace, and it operates through the process of salvation or rescue. Religion, therefore, is a goad that continually pricks us, urging us to accept the gift from God: "acquittal by mercy" that can never be won through justice.

Because the entire Bible deals with this fundamental issue, and because the Book of Job presents most of the basic arguments, all neat summaries of its message are suspect. Here, the questions are more basic than the answers. This is a book to make one examine one's surest convictions; instead of becoming simpler, it becomes more profound each time it is read.

Third Day *Read Job 1–5*

Suddenly plunged from prosperity into tragedy, the upright Job reacts by entering black despair. Though he speaks more fluently than most, I wonder if his vivid imagery (chap. 3) leaves any mature person untouched? Have we not all felt utter defeat that makes us wish we had never been born?

Out of his despair, Job raises the fundamental questions of human existence: Why am I here? Is there any purpose to my life?

His "comforter," Eliphaz, presents one of the stock arguments central to many religious systems and prominent in much Old Testament thought. Trouble and suffering, he says, are direct results of sin, which may be either deliberate or unconscious. The chastened one, who uses tragedy as a lens to magnify his view of Providence, gains marvelous new power by which he wins prosperity and peace.

Fourth Day *Read Job 6–10*

Eliphaz's promise of prosperity in return for righteousness is empty, Job asserts. A person's meaning is centered in a life span that is bound to end in futility. To die is to go to "the land of gloom and deep darkness" (10:21–22). To die is to cancel out having lived. Therefore, all striving is useless.

Furthermore, Job says, if a man does his absolute best so that he is spotless by comparison with other men, he is no less guilty in God's sight than is the most wanton sinner. That being the case, what is the use of trying? (9:29)

Although this lament, like that in the song "Sixteen Tons," is troubling, Job realizes that God actually does concern himself with man. Why this absorption of the Creator with so futile a creature? Why? Why? Why?

Blithely leaping over Job's main argument, Bildad reiterates Eliphaz's assurance of future material blessings in this life as a reward for righteousness. Job retorts with a fresh statement of a major motif of the whole drama: "How can a creature attain acquittal, when the Creator is judge?"

Fifth Day *Read Job 11–15*

Zophar shakes his head to silence Job and repeats the assurance that if he will just cease sinning, God will bless and prosper him.

Your answer is too simple, Job retorts. With one eye shut, I can see flagrant sinners (robbers and idolaters) who are enjoying peace and prosperity. God, the omnipotent and ever-present, obviously has a hand in such victories by evil men.

Despairing of help from human wisdom, Job yearns to take his case before God. If permitted to do so, he will argue that man's days are numbered (14:1–2, 10–12). Man is actually impotent, a helpless bit of flotsam moved hither and thither by tides that the Creator directs. Therefore, it is an absurdity—a travesty upon the idea of justice—that God should require righteousness of man.

Sixth Day *Read Job 16–20*

Job's reasoning continues along these lines: God has attacked me; there is no doubt of it. My superhuman adversary has overwhelmed me. There is no use for me to yearn for death since I cannot take hope into the grave with me. If God is going to give me justice, it will have to be soon—for life ebbs away daily, hourly. To tell me that I am suffering for my sins is a waste of words and simply puts my friends on the side of the persecuting God. How I do wish my claims could be written to last forever! I know that, someday, God will assess the evidence and declare me guiltless.

Zophar bypasses the main issue and suggests that apparent prosperity of the wicked should not trouble a good man, for it is sure to pass and be followed by woes sent from God.

Seventh Day *Read Job 21–25*

Still angry at divine injustice, by which all the enterprises of the wicked seem to thrive, Job protests once more that it is useless to struggle for righteousness. Death treats everyone alike and wipes out all differences between the good and the bad.

Eliphaz repeats the basic argument of all the "comforters." It is sin, he insists, that causes Job's woes. If he is not guilty of deliberate acts of rebellion, he is certainly guilty of sins of omission. To gain peace and prosperity, he must make peace with God.

Job cries that the accusation is false. He is innocent and would give his life to confront God and defend himself. But the hope is futile; one can look at the way evil flourishes and the wicked prosper and know that God is an absentee landlord who cannot be found in order to be called to account.

Bildad's answer, in chapter 25, once more repeats the fundamental question of the drama—whether or not righteousness is possible to man (see 4:17; 15:14).

Eighth Day *Read Job 26–28*

Windy words of Bildad and his comrades, according to Job's reply, have added nothing to the God whom they would defend. God is Lord of all and needs no human champion.

Job insists that this great God is his persecutor, who has attacked an innocent and righteous man.

Returning to the persistent question of life's meaning in the face of inescapable death, Job concedes that death actually does make null and void all triumphs of the wicked. This fact underscores the deeper riddle. Man, the magnificent master of all things, has seized every treasure but one—understanding of himself and his meaning. Hidden from the eyes of every creature, "the place of understanding" is known only to God. The closest man can come to wisdom is to fear the God who alone possesses it.

Ninth Day *Read Job 29–31*

In these closing chapters of Job's great argument in his own defense we find some of the most stirring lines of the entire drama. For here (as, indeed, in all his protests) Job speaks for all mankind and not simply for himself. Looking back upon his life, he repeats his plea of innocence and his demand for a meeting with his divine adversary. Summarized, his plea runs: Though I were a knight in the shining armor of righteousness, revered among the leaders of men, I have become a joke to the rabble—and this by the hand of God. It is God's purpose to bring me (along with all living things) into the house of death. Yet I cannot keep silent. I must cry out, though I know I will not be heard. I cannot refrain from protesting my innocence and challenging God to meet me so that I may answer all his charges and be pronounced guiltless.

Tenth Day *Read Job 32–35*

So far, the great themes of the drama have simply been repeated over and over. Though expressed quite differently each time, the arguments of Job and of his "comforters" have not changed substantially since first advanced. With the entrance of Elihu, the son of Barachel, the tempo changes and new motifs begin to appear. Brushing the older men aside, Elihu addresses Job in a symphony of words whose burden runs: The fault lies with you, Job, rather than with God. You say God does not answer you. That is absurd. The silence stems

from your dull ear. God speaks in more ways than one—through ter-
rifying dreams, for example, and especially through suffering that
leads to despair. Not once, but over and over, God speaks through
acts of rescue.

You, Job, have concluded that there is no justice under the sun.
In doing so, you dull-eared one, you have simply added rebellion to
your other sins. Take a look at the glories of creation, and recognize
your folly. For neither your sin nor your righteousness can touch
the Creator of all. You say God does not hear you? It is because you
do not call in the right way. In rebellious pride you dare to challenge your God—and then to wonder that he does not bend his will
to yours!

Eleventh Day *Read Job 36–38*

Continuing his powerful argument in three chapters that form one of
the most moving of all tributes to life-shaping belief in Providence,
Elihu asserts: Instead of being withdrawn, as charged by Job, God is
actually central to every event. Providence permeates all situations,
without exception. God conceived and sustains all natural processes
that give and take life, that bless and curse. He is so wholly
unsearchable that it is impious folly to challenge him; "he does great
things which we cannot comprehend" (37:5). "God is clothed with
terrible majesty" (37:22); he is to be worshipped ("feared"), not
challenged by proud and rebellious men whose sole claim to wisdom is conceit.

Twelfth Day *Read Job 39–42*

Human argument having ended, the Lord himself at last confronts Job.
Instead of commending him for his righteousness or chiding him for his
guilt, God underscores the gulf between creature and Creator. Chapters
38–39, showing Job how very little he knows about the world's origin
and operation, are among the most sublime of all tributes to the God
who shaped and sustains all that we call "the natural world."

Momentarily stunned, Job is further challenged in chapters 40 and 41 to demonstrate power like that of God, if he is to dare challenge or question God.

Prostrate, literally overwhelmed by his face-to-face encounter with God, Job blurts out a moving confession of his own impotence and repents of having played the rebel by questioning the will of his Maker (42:5–6). Here the drama proper comes to a stunning and climactic end.

There are two schools of thought concerning the epilogue (42:7–17). Some interpreters take it literally, holding that Job was showered with material blessings as a reward for his faithfulness. Others hold that the passage is symbolic, promising God's richest rewards (not necessarily material ones conferred in this life) to those who learn life's most paradoxical lesson: the one road to righteousness is that of contrition for inability to achieve righteousness.

Psalms

More than any other book of the Bible, Psalms has its modern counterparts. Christian hymnals relate to public worship much as the psalms related to temple rites in Israel. To recognize the psalms as religious poetry adapted for public worship and set to music is to see that this book is radically different from, say, 2 Chronicles. So readers who seek the deepest meanings from individual psalms must bring their own inspired imagination to the reading.

It is a delightful paradox (true of all Scripture, but especially vivid here) that one gets from the reading what one seeks. Truth and meaning are products of the meeting of the message with the seeking mind. This has the startling effect of making the meaning a variable, so that two readers (or one reader at two periods of his life) will get quite different sets of meaning from a single psalm or other Scripture passage. Recognized everywhere in the Bible and stressed throughout the New Testament, this fundamental aspect of communication was expressed for all time by Elihu when he told Job that "the ear tests words as the tongue tastes food" (Job 34:3).

If you have not already recognized this factor, which demolishes the view that the literal meaning of Scripture is fixed and final for all persons and all time, this fresh reading of Psalms may help you seize upon dynamics of meaning and interpretation as forces offering you breathtaking new truths from old and familiar words.

Thirteenth Day *Read Psalms 1–7*

All through your reading of Psalms, look for vivid examples of poetic imagery. Through metaphor and other poetic devices, it is possible to express profound truths that cannot otherwise be conveyed by words. Yet, taken literally, the statements are not "true." Deliberate stretching of words is one of several factors that make Psalms so breathtaking. Try, for example, to communicate the meaning of Psalm 7:14 in literal, nonpoetic fashion, and then compare your effort with the lines of this verse as it stands.

Notice how many of these seven psalms are evoked by trouble, tension, and danger. Notice also how frequently the words of a psalm speak for you and me by expressing our private thoughts more vividly than we can.

Now turn back to Psalm 1 and put in writing your idea of the two distinct ways in which its promises and warnings may be understood. Do you think Israel's devout ever stopped with taking this psalm literally at the level of material blessings? Can you think of a way to express hope for spiritual blessings, so phrased that no one could interpret the promise on lower levels?

Fourteenth Day *Read Psalms 8–14*

How strife and wickedness do flourish! Is there any social order, any system of government, under which evildoers will be subdued while those who seek the Lord bask in peace?

Whatever answer one may give, the meaning of life and of civilization is at stake. This is precisely the focus of many psalms. Such powerful ones as Psalm 8 deserve to be memorized. Committed to memory or read frequently over a period of years, a passage like this demonstrates the fluid nature of meaning—for its riches will never be exhausted. Just when you conclude that, finally, you fully understand what Psalm 8 says about God and man, you are likely to be flooded with fresh insights persuading you that as yet you have hardly made a beginning!

Fifteenth Day *Read Psalms 15–19*

Many devout persons have been troubled by the emphasis on blood and battle in Psalms. According to this point of view, many passages portray God as cruel and vindictive—ready to hear prayers for rescue and vengeance that are essentially pagan in tone.

To what degree do you think these matters reflect the limitedness of the men who wrote and sang the psalms? Do failures and imperfections on the part of even zealous worshipers reflect upon the character of God? Mentally stepping outside our own culture and viewing it from a distance, what do you see about our public worship that you would like to change? Can you discover any prejudices and blind spots that affect your own prayers?

Ponder the verdict of Psalm 18:25–26. What bearing do you think it has upon the deep questions suggested here?

Sixteenth Day *Read Psalms 20–23*

Today's reading provides an especially vivid example of a feature that marks the entire Psalter. Throughout, there is the dramatic alternation between exultation and despair that puts Psalm 21 in sharp contrast with Psalm 22. Both triumph and tragedy are prominent in these ancient songs, for both have places in every normal life. It is part of the timeless message of Psalms that tragedy and triumph alike may be creatively related to God.

No situation, no event, no circumstance can cut off dialogue with God, so long as we fervently want it! We can take both our woes and our ecstasies to God, and in both moods we can hear the still, small voice. The sharp contrast between Psalms 21 and 22, forming a prelude to Psalm 23, can hardly be accidental. Rather, this arrangement is an example of the highest literary artistry, demonstrating the fact that only one who has cried to God from both the pit of despair and the pinnacle of success, and has been answered in both situations, could possibly witness through such a set of lines as those that form the Shepherd Psalm (23).

Seventeenth Day *Read Psalms 24–29*

There are times when the devout find praise to be their chief employment; instead of asking God for things, the loosened tongue can only pay tribute to divine glory as in Psalms 24 and 29.

At other times and in other moods prayer becomes a process of telling God about the affairs of everyday life. Such conversation with God is dominant in Psalms 25, 26, 27, and 28. Notice how these inspired verses show us the way of prayer. Nothing is too big or too little to find a place in our prayers; we can talk with God about anything and everything: our longings, our youthful sins, guilt, loneliness, plots of our enemies, our dark hours, and our radiantly joyful days. Prayer, as demonstrated in the psalms, is as broad as the human spirit and as deep as life itself.

Eighteenth Day *Read Psalms 30–34*

Notice today how the language of devotion reflects the circumstances around which prayers and praises are framed. From these psalms alone, we can get a coherent idea of the land and culture from which the psalmists speak. Some of the allusions in today's reading are: strong mountain, sackcloth, rock of refuge, pit, fortress, a broad place, a broken vessel, a besieged city, the heat of summer, the rush of great waters, lyre, harp of ten strings, war horse, famine, young lions. Such a list could be compiled from any half-dozen psalms and from many passages in the historical and prophetic books of the Old Testament.

Once more, we are made vividly aware that God speaks to particular people in particular places. He never broadcasts a verbal message to everyone everywhere, but he relies upon sensitive individuals to hear his nonverbal messages and translate them into the words, images, and thought forms that prevail in the time and place. This aspect of divine revelation presents both major difficulties and monumental opportunities in Bible study. It is always the reader's task to find in his own vocabulary some equivalents for words and concepts that flourished in the climate of thought from which Scripture sprang.

Nineteenth Day *Read Psalms 35–37*

Evil, wrongdoers, and enemies always beset those who try to follow the path of righteousness—whether in a shepherd culture or in an industrial age.

Is it chance or deliberate arrangement by ancient singers that accounts for the fact that these three psalms are grouped together?

In Psalm 35, the singer (whose pleas readily become my own) begs God to join the battle of life—on his side. Reflection tells me, in Psalm 36, that God actually does rule the world and me, no matter what circumstances may prevail for the moment. In Psalm 37, I conclude that I must be more patient. I must cease my groaning and let God act in his own good time. Measured against the time scale of the Creator, everything human is like a puff of smoke or like flowering weeds that adorn the pastures for a few hours in the spring. Let my own effort, therefore, be directed toward holding fast in my place of refuge. God will take care of the wicked without my help.

Twentieth Day *Read Psalms 38–41*

All four of these psalms are in the first person. All four are both individual and universal, for through each of them there runs a note of victory in dire distress.

Let me never forget that it is not success, but stress, that turns me to God confessing my failures and weaknesses as a prelude to pleading for divine forgiveness and rescue. In this sense, trouble (as a basic ingredient in human life) is one of God's richest gifts.

The next time you are in distress, even despair, you will find it helpful to remember this quartet of songs. Read them with your own name substituted for the "I" of the ancient singer; make David's lamentations, pleas, and cries of victory your own.

Twenty-first Day *Read Psalms 42–48*

Every seeker for God goes through periods of doubt. It is normal to experience a "dark night of the soul" in which all spiritual striving seems useless. Psalms 42, 43, and 44 come from a mood of near-despair. But the rest of the psalms in today's reading reflect a different mood.

God is an active agent in whatever happens, these psalms declare. Whether you experience victory or defeat, you are not outside the realm of providential purpose and care. So the real secret of happy and victorious living is not to get what one wants but to use every situation as a lens through which to see God. Calamity, earthquake, and defeat can be used as avenues through which to approach God more closely. Treat every situation from joy to anguish as an opportunity to know God better, and you will find joyful victory no matter what life may bring.

Twenty-second Day *Read Psalms 49–53*

Throughout Psalms, there is recognition of the grand issues and dark riddles of human existence. Today's reading centers here. Since all (good and bad alike) must die, the inspired singer ponders life's meaning and finds that it resides in God above.

Before an all-powerful God, good men and evil men are alike. God in his heaven looks down and laughs at man's struttings, pretensions, and mighty strivings directed toward ephemeral goals. Only God endures. Hence it follows that the only human effort of more than fleeting significance is that aimed at permitting the Creator to impart his own qualities to his creatures in greater measure.

Twenty-third Day *Read Psalms 54–59*

Today's psalms reflect the constant turmoil that marks human life. Though the nature of one's enemies may vary widely, conflict is as basic to existence as air and water. So these psalms are universal— above and beyond time and circumstance. They speak for troubled men and women everywhere. How could a man so plagued and tormented have produced these great hymns of praise and confession? In a sense, the answer to that question is the "hidden secret" of the Psalter. Though reason can never quite build a convincing case, faith asserts that only those who are desperate will accept God's best gifts because all their own resources have failed. Consequently, only tension, trouble, and disappointment can serve as soil to yield a crop of timeless songs, prayers, and praise.

Twenty-fourth Day *Read Psalms 60–66*

To be human is to suffer stress and tension, but they need not be endured as purposeless, nor suffered in solitude. God is in every situation of tragedy, exile, and turmoil. He tries his own as the silversmith tries his precious metal; he takes us through fire and water because he loves us.

There is no condition that does not permit prayer. When we enter into dialogue with the Creator, we "feast on marrow and fat" even though we are fainting in a waterless desert. So all the earth can join in joyful praise to our great God—praise that echoes through terrible affliction and provides automatic reward, because crying out in trouble strengthens bonds of fellowship with God.

Twenty-fifth Day *Read Psalms 67–69*

Is God the ruler of nations as well as of individuals? Does he literally affect the course of world history—wars, conquests, treaties and alliances—or has he delegated control in these areas to man?

The whole history of Israel, and the whole Bible as a record of the covenant between God and a particular people, are at stake here. Whatever else these psalms may do, they insist (sometimes to the perplexity of peace-minded moderns) that God is not far off in some abstract heaven. Rather, God is involved in the "blood, sweat, and tears" of both individuals and nations. The nation or the person having a life-directing relationship with God gains some human friends and makes some enemies thereby. All life is affected in the here and now, not simply in some nonphysical hereafter.

If this outlook is accepted, it would seem natural that those who are God-fearing should pray for heaven's vengeance upon their enemies, as a prelude to rescue. Do you consider such bloody petitions as included in these psalms to be pagan or Christian? Why?

Twenty-sixth Day *Read Psalms 70–72*

Whether or not David himself wrote all the psalms to which his name has become attached is beside the point. What matters for us is the vivid fashion in which they portray the problems and challenges of life.

On the surface, it seems that for a mighty ruler who has been "a portent to many" (71:7), David is strangely obsessed with his need for divine aid. This powerful warrior before whom strong men quail is perpetually calling for help!

Not only in today's readings, but in many of David's other prayers and Solomon's Psalm 72, there are suggestive undercurrents. Perhaps these inspired men glimpsed more clearly than ordinary folk the paradox by which human need for divine protection increases rather than decreases as one gains prestige, power, and wealth. Of all men, the king is the most needy! Material success, whatever its form, constitutes a source of danger that has no equal. Measured by whatever human standard, your achievement is a rise to a height at which you can easily become dizzy and may fall to your injury or death. Instead of relaxing in your quest for divine guidance and protection during periods of success, follow David's lead and search, ask, and pray with new fervor every time you score a triumph.

Twenty-seventh Day *Read Psalms 73–77*

Why are the godly so restless and troubled while the godless are so often complacent if not actually triumphant?

All religious systems must face that question, and none offers a universally acceptable answer. Perhaps there is a clue for us in the frequency and fervor with which this question is raised throughout the Scriptures, and especially in psalms such as these. Can it be that discontent with things as they are is a mark of the God-seeker? Is it possible that a sensitive soul, attuned to the voice of God, simply cannot be completely at ease in the world of flesh and of things?

Whatever your conclusion, notice that the very process of wondering why God does not act to bring about justice and right can yield an answer. Over and over here, the psalmists who cry out in their impatience over injustice and wrong answer themselves by taking a look at history. It is the verdict of the ages, they conclude, that God actually is in control. Through faith, we must hang on to that belief, even when events of the present moment (viewed from our limited human perspective) seem to challenge the notion that God, truth, and right really do rule.

Twenty-eighth Day *Read Psalms 78–80*

Delete from these psalms a few references to long-vanished ways, and they become contemporary. So far as their basic theme is concerned, they might have come from twentieth-century U.S. life as appropriately as from that of ancient Israel.

A basic characteristic of the divine-human covenant is especially prominent here. We have noticed earlier that the characteristic relationship of individuals and nations with their Creator is one of change rather than constancy. *Salvation history* is marked by ebb and flow, by advances and retreats, by new surrender to God and fresh rebellion against him.

So vivid is this quality that in today's reading we find hints that the covenant is almost an organic state, whose pulse-beat is essential to its existence. The periodic cry, "Restore us, O God of hosts," is as fundamental to seeking and serving God as the heart's pounding is to the human body. Those who succeed in maintaining a placid and undisturbed state are likely to be spiritually dead; no matter how vigorous the outside appearance, their blood is no longer circulating.

Twenty-ninth Day *Read Psalms 81–86*

Not simply in today's reading, but throughout the Book of Psalms, there is much testimony to the reality of divine-human dialogue. Many of these passages point to heights and depths that we dull and timid ones today hardly dare seek in our prayers. Burning, life-directing hunger for an answer from God (85:8; 86:1) creates conditions in which prayer ceases to be monologue and becomes dialogue.

Oh, the grandeur and sublimity of direct quotations from God! Passages such as Psalm 81:6–18 gain in power each time they are read. It is a major role of the Psalter to persuade you and me that in rare and exalted moments we can hear God speak directly to us, too.

Thirtieth Day *Read Psalms 87–89*

A modern poet has suggested that God is closer than a man's breath, nearer to him than his own hands and feet. That is a way of acknowledging that Providence is so fundamental to existence that every situation and circumstance is pervaded by divine purpose and care. We cannot get away from God, no matter how hard we try. He is involved in everything.

God gives singers and dancers their bounce (87:7). God is in the personal "dark night of the soul," using one's despair as a context in which to create hunger for light. God is in the tragic eras of his own chosen people; in periods that seem to challenge the notion of a divine-human covenant, the Creator is at work stirring men to logic-defying faith in order to cry triumphantly, "Praise be to the Lord forever! Amen and Amen" (89:52).

Psalms 90–150, Proverbs, Ecclesiastes, Song of Songs

First Day *Read Psalms 90–94*

Even in the book whose function is to stir the mind and heart, these psalms represent a mountaintop. All of them, but especially Psalms 90, 91, and 95, include so many sublime ideas so magnificently expressed that every doubting and troubled soul can find new life here. If you have not already done so, you will surely want to memorize one or more of these psalms.

You have noticed, have you not, how they permit you to breathe the crisp, clear air of the mountains? When you are so troubled that life seems useless, these psalms help you find strength to keep inching upward until you actually enter the place of refuge and find yourself sheltered behind the rock of salvation.

Men and their doings pass away. Friends and foes alike have a life span like that of autumn weeds. All human institutions, including powerful nations that strike terror into the hearts of the whole world, will vanish like puffs of smoke. God alone is enduring. God alone is powerful.

God, give me vision to see that my only refuge is in you, and give me courage to accept that refuge. In the place that is at one and the same time hidden from sight and visible to all who will consent to see it, I can sing glad praises. Here, nothing can touch me. Weak and puny creature that I am, during every hour that I linger here, the qualities of the Creator himself attach to me.

Second Day *Read Psalms 95–100*

There are many other joyful passages in Scripture, some in verse and some in prose. Nowhere, though, does any group of half a dozen chapters rise higher than these triumphant ones. Maybe you will want to make a note inside the cover of your Bible, reminding yourself to turn to them when you have had a special blessing and cannot find words to express your joy and gratitude.

Joy so great that it can be poured out only through song is the dominant note from the first line of Psalm 95 to the last line of Psalm 100. That the Lord reigns, absolutely, is the fundamental fact of existence. During the rare hours that I really know this, I cannot keep from singing! Life's circumstances, no matter what they may be, simply serve to magnify the utterly unbelievable wonder that I, a creature, may know the Creator! Glory be to him; in knowing my God I bring to life those divine qualities that lie dormant inside me!

Third Day *Read Psalms 101–104*

Notice how intensely personal these (and many other) psalms are. In today's reading, no poem of praise omits the small words that point to one of the axles on which my world turns—words like I, me, and my. Although the ancient seekers, sometimes puzzled and sometimes overjoyed, are speaking for themselves, they are also speaking for me. To the degree that I succeed in making their lines not words in a book but outpourings of my own heart, I shall enter into their experiences and victories.

Throughout these psalms, humanity and divinity are contrasted. A particularly vivid description of man's utter futility occurs in Psalm 102:3–11, and a spine-tingling tribute to the unspeakable glory of God is found in Psalm 104:1–30.

Instead of leading to despair, as would be the case with an agnostic, for the believer the recognition of the gulf between God and man is a source of triumph. The victory of faith is trumpeted full blast in

Psalm 103, and the net result is overpowering. By crossing the gap between the divine and the human, we can gain significance in the midst of our chaotic world. Glory! A human being—I myself—can become a tiny bit like the God whom I both revere from a distance and meet face to face!

Fourth Day *Read Psalms 105–106*

We have here, in a sense, a poetic summary of *salvation history*. In relation to secular history, the time span is from the days of Abraham to the establishment of the chosen people in the land of promise; but, as an expression of the covenant relationship between God and his people, this summary is timeless.

God initiated the covenant (105:8–11); God is faithful in every situation; Providence is involved in all possible circumstances, from famine (105:16) to plague (106:29). Whether through negligence or outright rebelliousness, people can neither escape nor flee from the hand of God.

Though we are beneficiaries of this covenant relationship, we are by nature incapable of keeping our part of the bargain. We cannot help being rebellious. Overpowered for a time by consciousness of deliverance, we soon forget. We test the God who has saved us, fashion idols, and pollute the land with monstrous deeds performed in the name of piety.

Is there, then, any solution? Yes! The heart of the covenant relationship, the secret shouted so loudly that few of us succeed in really hearing it, is the fact that God does for his own what we cannot do for ourselves. God is perennially busy in the cosmic process of rescue. Here is reason enough to praise him and rejoice "from everlasting to everlasting" (106:48).

Fifth Day *Read Psalms 107–109*

Turn where you will in Scripture; if you stay with a passage long enough and really open your mind and heart, you will find a personal message that applies directly to your life.

At first look, the diversity of these psalms is discouraging. They are alike in only one respect: each voices a note of praise to God. You and I cannot avoid noticing that the praise of Psalm 107, with its theme of divine deliverance in response to human pleas (vv. 6, 13, 19, 28), and the praise of Psalm 108 sound from a higher plane than that of Psalm 109. It almost seems that the violent language of Psalm 109, with its pleas for vengeance upon the heads of enemies, is out of place in Scripture.

Perhaps its inclusion has a purpose. Maybe the sharp contrast between these psalms is a way of calling upon you and me to examine our own ways of praising God. How ready we are to feel that our praise is pure, while that of someone else is tainted! How easy it is to see the fly in the ointment—provided it is someone else's ointment!

Just how pure is your everyday run-of-the-mill praise of God? Compared with the lowest and most selfish notes sounded in Psalm 109, are your prayers lofty and selfless? How do they sound by comparison with the praises voiced in Psalm 108:1–4?

Sixth Day *Read Psalms 110–115*

Winds of eternity blow through these psalms. Different as they are in other respects, each of these psalms speaks—directly or indirectly—to the contrast between God's enduringness and the instability of men and nations.

Recognizing the fact that God's great covenant with mankind is established forever is to discover an escape hatch in the roof of the dungeon of life. To change the figure of speech to a more contemporary one, setting out upon the adventure of praising God's name "from this time forth and for evermore" is like entering a shelter that no missile can destroy.

Given such a source of security, you do not need to worry about stockpiling supplies and holing up in the mountains. Really to know the everlasting God and fully to praise him is so absorbing a task that anyone joyfully engaged in it has no time or energy left to worry about terrorist attacks or random shootings.

Seventh Day *Read Psalms 116–118*

One of the rewards of systematically reading the entire Bible is the frequent discovery of familiar lines. An example of this is Psalm 118:24, words often used in public worship but which take on new power when we recognize them as linked to divine rescue in time of distress.

Other much-quoted verses in today's reading are Psalm 116:15 and Psalm 118:22, the latter often being applied to the Savior. Here, in an Old Testament setting that seems far removed from proclamation of the Good News of Christianity, we find that the central idea of divine rescue is already well developed. *Salvation history* is the story of the development of that idea into a rounded system of thought that comes to focus on the divine-human Savior.

Any point of view that says the Old Testament and the New Testament are poles apart with no common core must be rejected. Instead, we must recognize that there is a subsurface unity embracing the entire Bible. From cover to cover, it proclaims that God does for men and women what they can never do for themselves.

Eighth Day *Read Psalm 119*

Comprising the longest chapter in the Bible, this psalm contains some of the most highly stylized poetry in Holy Writ. There are twenty-two stanzas—one for each letter of the Hebrew alphabet—and each stanza has eight lines, all of which begin with the appropriate Hebrew letter.

These features disappear with translation into English, so we are once more confronted with the riddle of language. God has so ordered human behavior that ideas may be expressed through patterns of conventional sounds (spoken words) and through shapes (written words). Within a given language group, meanings can be expressed fairly accurately, but translation from one language to another always involves losses as well as gains. Those well-meaning but misguided persons who are ready to fight to defend one of several meanings of a word or verse in the English Bible have failed to reckon with the intricacies of translation. It is beyond the limits of human skill to produce a modern-language version of Holy Writ that is identical with ancient Hebrew versions.

Yet the riddle and marvel of translation has its positive as well as its negative side. Through our God-given capacity to work with words, we can transmit sublime truths and poetic images—"sweeter than honey" (Ps. 119:103)—from one generation to another through the centuries. Civilizations, different in almost every other respect, can unite in seeking God and in praising him with words that do not look or sound alike but which express the same longings of the creature made in God's image.

Ninth Day *Read Psalms 120–129*

All these psalms, as well as the next five, bear a special title. Regardless of how that title may be rendered in translation, it seems to have been applied to special pilgrim songs of the Hebrews. Travelers who climbed the hill to the temple, about twenty-five hundred feet above sea level, "ascended by degrees" as they approached the great shrine of Israel.

That pilgrim who ceases to climb upward is not actually headed toward the holy place of the Lord God of Hosts, no matter what he may think of himself and regardless of how other men judge him. Climbing is integral to the religious quest. No matter what level one may reach, to cease ascending is to die inside.

But this aspect of the human response to the divine overture is no cause for melancholy and weeping. Rather, it is a basis for great joy! Though born of struggle, these songs of the upward-climbing pilgrim are triumphant. They suggest that to join a band of like-minded seekers and with them to ascend the holy hill is to enter a state of victory. It is not arrival at a given goal that constitutes religious success, but the joyful process of struggling to get a little higher every day.

Tenth Day *Read Psalms 130–135*

These psalms, mostly very brief ones, give a first impression of diversity almost to the point of confusion. Just about anything, it seems, can form a subject for a holy hymn of praise!

Here we have agonized personal longing (Ps. 130), followed by a short stanza of humble praise (Ps. 131). The national destiny of the chosen people (Ps. 132) seems so grand a theme that praise of community harmony follows a bit lamely (Ps. 133). It almost seems that a brief exhortation to take part in public worship (Ps. 134) has nothing in common with poetic praise of God the Creator contrasted with impotent pagan idols (Ps. 135).

A second reading reveals that there is unity even in diversity, for the constant factors here are God and man. However much they differ in length, style, and subject matter, these psalms are alike in treating the divine-human relationship as the most important aspect of existence. Regardless of how stirring or sublime it may be, no piece of literature or work of art or system of thought can deserve the label "biblical" unless it deals not with God in the abstract or with man in the concrete, but with God and man in a state of conscious relationship.

Eleventh Day *Read Psalms 136–139*

It is impossible for man, formed by God to become like God, to enter any situation from which the steadfast love of the Creator is absent. Divine love permeates the total environment, affecting both societies and individuals every moment of their existence. In this respect, the history of civilization, with all its varieties of Babylonian captivity, is cut from the same cloth as that woven by one individual.

From the cradle to the grave, people are swathed in protective layers of providential care. From the beginnings of civilization to the days of galaxy exploration, the covenant relationship shapes the destiny of all created in the image of their Creator.

Twelfth Day *Read Psalms 140–144*

No matter how hard we try, you and I cannot fully comprehend the situations from which our psalms came. Distance gives the Old Testament world a halo all its own; we are inclined to think it natural that immortal songs of praise should have taken form in those glorious days when it was easy to obey God. For simple people of simple times, we say, it was as though heaven and earth were closer together than they are now.

Let us be done with such inane musings!

Samuel and David had to wrestle with the world, the devil, and the flesh just as strongly as you and I. Regardless of the times or circumstances, everyone who tries to know and serve God is sure to be dogged by evil people. Every drama has its villains who "spread out the cords of their net" (140:5), offer banquets featuring forbidden "delicacies" (141:4), set a hidden snare in the pathway (142:3), overwhelm the innocent and make them "dwell in darkness like those long dead" (143:3), speak lies and offer "right hands [that] are deceitful" (144:8).

Away with excuses for our failures to rise to the level of God's heroes of other days! They had their trials and troubles, too. Certainly, the road that leads to the city built without hands is rough and dangerous now, but it was no smoother in the days of Abraham and Isaac and Jacob. We must view the spiritual achievements of ancient Israel with wonder from afar, because they did not have things easier then. In contemporary America, as truly as in ancient Israel, God will raise up men, if they will surrender to him and accept from him the rescue they cannot win through striving.

Thirteenth Day *Read Psalms 145–150*

I sometimes fear that too much of the time and energy of the typical modern Christian is devoted to trying to understand God and not enough time is spent in praising God who is beyond understanding. The Psalter begins with a promise of bliss to the person who learns to enjoy seeking the hidden things of God, and it ends on a full-throated chorus of praise.

All that God has created reflects the greatness of the Creator (see Ps. 19). Among created things, humans are unique in their capacity for formal praise of the Creator through words and melodies. Until one engages in such creative praise, he has not accepted the full legacy that is due him. So viewed, the Book of Psalms contains the key to life. Everyone who accepts and uses the God-given key enters into a life of creative delight that constitutes humanity at its best. Praise the Lord that this is so!

Proverbs

Every culture develops its own collection of terse sayings, or proverbs, that offer folk wisdom in capsule form. A look at the Proverbs of Israel might lead readers to conclude that they are very much like those of other peoples and other periods and thus hardly deserve to be in sacred Scripture.

While there is some reason for such a conclusion, slow, meditative reading of Proverbs challenges the assumption. Most of the individual sayings can be interpreted on two or three levels. As is the case with folk wisdom in general, there is much wordplay and employment of figures of speech. Such material is not intended to be quaffed in huge gulps but should be sipped. Then Proverbs yields much spiritual nourishment. While it is true that few of the sayings are on the exalted level of, say, the Sermon on the Mount, it is equally true that such passages as the Sermon on the Mount must rest upon solid foundations long a-building. The Book of Proverbs is such a foundation for Christian thought.

Fourteenth Day *Read Proverbs 1–3*

As sought by generations of the chosen people, wisdom is not identical with knowledge or skill. It is possible for one who is ignorant, as the world measures learning, to be wise in the sense of the biblical quest.

God is masculine, but Wisdom is feminine. "She" is a coworker with the Creator and plays a vital part in bringing the world into existence (3:19). That work, you will recall, is accomplished by the power of words; as creation is described in Genesis 1, God *speaks* the world into being.

Wisdom is an agent of God, an intermediary who communicates the knowledge of God to the children of God. In this respect, she is a sort of dim prototype of the Holy Spirit.

Because Wisdom has fabulous gifts to confer, she must be eagerly sought over long periods. Any man who devotes his life to courting Wisdom can become so infatuated with her that he is not tempted by the shiny baubles that constitute bait in the traps set by the adversary (personified as an adventuress in Proverbs 2:16–19). To yearn for Wisdom is to enter the bliss of Psalm 1. By yearning for the divine gift of Wisdom, one can rise above the limitations of creaturehood.

Fifteenth Day *Read Proverbs 4–7*

On a literal level, these chapters are an indictment of lust and immorality. On a higher level of theological interpretation, they offer an analysis of the cosmic drama in which the forces of good and evil fight for the prize of the human soul.

Wisdom is on the side of God and of right and does everything in her power to hold any man who is attracted to her. She is opposed by the evil woman, "the adventuress...the wayward wife with her seductive words" (7:5), who represents the attractive tug of tangible goals. The struggle between these two women is somewhat like that between Christ and Satan, for, in both instances, the fate of a man made in the image of God is at stake. Far from being a helpless pawn, man actually decides the issue. He can succumb to the seductive speech of the woman of the world and follow her like an ox going to the slaughter (7:21–22), or he can seize hold of Wisdom, hanging on grimly and sleeplessly so that he actually saves himself "like a gazelle from the hand of the hunter" (6:5).

The fight is on, and it is a fight to the finish! Withdraw from it, no man can. Win it by the grace of God and the power of his agents, any man may!

Sixteenth Day *Read Proverbs 8–10*

God's first great act was creating Wisdom (8:22–31). As a go-between, offering the Creator's good things to creatures made in his image, Wisdom is perpetually beguiling. Wisdom does not wait for men to become enamored of her, but she takes the initiative and stations herself where the pilgrim cannot fail to hear her pleading voice (8:2–3).

Wisdom never gets an uncontested hearing, though. Her opponent, the foolish and noisy "wanton" who personifies Worldliness, actually imitates her manners and repeats her invitation verbatim. (cf. 9:4; 9:16).

Therefore, the pilgrim is never safe, and his journey toward the holy city is never finished. Life is a perpetual battle in which spiritual victory is beyond achievement. The most that a man can do is to busy himself in ceaseless seeking, occupying himself so fully with the courtship of Wisdom that he "shows the way to life" (10:17).

Seventeenth Day *Read Proverbs 11–13*

No compartment of life is sealed to the influence of one's faith. What one deeply believes and what one seeks for a lifetime goal, will affect everything one does: use of money, tongue, and time—even the manner of dress and walk.

Consequently, a dividing line runs through society, separating men into two distinct categories: the righteous and the wicked. Life attaches to the former and death to the latter. Challenge this as too neat and simple if you like, but by whatever standards you use to arrive at your own classifications, make today a time when your personal scales are tipped toward righteousness and life.

Eighteenth Day *Read Proverbs 14–16*

Much twentieth-century religious thought emphasizes difficulties and dangers in arriving at clear-cut definitions. According to this view, right and wrong are not absolute but relative. Gray, in a wide variety of shades, is far more common than either black or white.

No such doubts plagued the culture out of which the Book of Proverbs came. The characteristic structure of a wise saying is that of antithesis between two alternatives: "A fool spurns his father's discipline, but whoever heeds correction shows prudence" (15:5). Here there are no shades of gray, no in-between stages; all is either/or. However persuasive the arguments that challenge such an outlook upon life as being oversimplified and dogmatic, the fact remains that the mindset that produced Proverbs makes people realize that life is a constant succession of choices. The decision to walk toward the light rather than toward darkness does affect the goal that a pilgrim reaches.

Nineteenth Day *Read Proverbs 17–20*

This collection of sayings touches most areas of life, and it is not so formless as it seems at first look. Through the whole there runs the unifying thread of emphasis upon the human capacity for speech. This great gift, rightly employed, can make life sublime; misdirected, it makes life futile.

The one whose whole life is a courtship of Wisdom will find delight in brief maxims that represent the distilled thought of the past. Unlike the outpourings of a fool's mouth, each such proverb is a spiritual-intellectual mine, whose richest treasures come only after much digging (see Prov. 17:3, 16; 18:18; 19:16; 20:24, 30). Brief as they are, such sayings challenge one to examine his or her own system of values and conduct.

Twentieth Day *Read Proverbs 21–23*

To a degree that is both fascinating and astonishing, twentieth-century Americans accept the idea that change brings progress. As a culture, we are thoroughly committed to the notion that the passage of time brings improvement—"every day, in every way, we are getting better and better."

Proverbs challenges this outlook. Speaking across four thousand years and from a wholly alien culture, the voice I hear is that of my own heart. Only externals change. Men and women are the same in all generations. The lure of alcohol as a way of escape (23:29–5) is the same among camel-riding desert tent dwellers and SUV-riding suburban homeowners. Regardless of techniques that may be used, no modern philosophy of education rises one inch above that of Proverb 22:3. Though we now focus upon atomic weapons instead of war horses, the verdict of Proverb 21:31 is for all ages and conditions—past, present, and future.

Twenty-first Day *Read Proverbs 24–26*

To court Wisdom instead of living with that contentious woman Worldliness is to enter into dialogue. Wisdom is not limited to human speech as a means of communication; she can whisper in her lover's ear through any experience. Everything that God has made has capacity to convey divine messages to the seeker who looks and listens for rapport with God.

Tasting honey, the awakened one makes a great leap of understanding and "sees" that Wisdom is like this sweet stuff (24:13–14). A costly piece of jewelry allows Wisdom to whisper that stinging reproof from a friend is like this thing of beauty (25:12). Aghast at hearing of a practical joker who throws firebrands at the innocent, Wisdom's courtier knows she is using this experience to warn him against tossing fiery words (26:18–19).

Twenty-second Day *Read Proverbs 27–29*

We are not alone. We are social as well as solitary. We are strange creatures, made in the divine image but also bound to earth by feet of clay. Our full development requires us to be at one and the same time an unduplicated individual and a unit of organized society.

Though specific patterns change, man's social structures pose about the same problems and opportunities in every age. How to get along with one's friends, relatives, neighbors, king (or boss) is as basic a problem when communication is by email as it was when by messenger (27:17). Then and now, our relationship with God is the basic factor that governs the way we get along with our fellow man.

Twenty-third Day *Read Proverbs 30–31*

The beginning of wisdom is to realize how little one knows. It takes only a casual glance, just an instant of direct attention, to be entranced by the awesomeness of nature. The wind, the waters, a soaring eagle, a sunning lizard…any one of these is enough to convict the wisest among us of gross ignorance. We know so little, and God knows so much.

To recognize our littleness, to bow down before the awe-full greatness of God who made and sustains the total universe and us within it, is to begin to escape from the clutches of that wanton woman, Contentment.

Ecclesiastes

Ecclesiastes, meaning "the book of the preacher," is as puzzling as it is intriguing. Highly distilled theology and philosophy are presented here, sometimes in verse and sometimes in prose that has many qualities of poetry. Modern readers are tempted to bypass this little collection of Wisdom's formulas because of its obscurities, or they hastily conclude that it is too cynical to be included in a Christian's spiritual diet. However, if you approach the book as an instrument through which God will speak directly to you about the affairs of your life, you may find such thrills that cold shivers run up your spine as you stand with bowed head in the presence of the Most High.

Twenty-fourth Day *Read Ecclesiastes 1–2*

There are two ways to view life: you can look at it as containing only visible things, or you can look at life as containing intangible elements also. Anyone who limits their view of life to those things that can be touched and tasted, seen and sold is driven to an inevitable conclusion which the "Preacher" summarizes (1:2) and then repeats (2:24).

If truth and meaning and joy are inseparably linked with life in the physical body, then all striving really is busywork (1:13). If the intangible and invisible do not have eternal significance, if human logic rules supreme and beliefs deal only with chimeras, then the epitome of success really is to eat, drink, and be merry.

Twenty-fifth Day *Read Ecclesiastes 3–5*

God has put a sense of past and future into the minds of men (3:11), yet the human heart is so fashioned that it cannot understand what God is doing. This is where the trouble arises. Work might be satisfying—planting and plucking up, casting away stones and gathering them together—were it not for that elusive glimpse of eternity. As it is, those who win only tangible successes (whether in ancient vineyards or in modern corporations) reach the end of their days realizing that they have toiled only "for the wind" (5:16).

This utterly frustrating situation, says the Preacher, is the work of God, who has deliberately arranged things so that his creatures will sooner or later come to see that their furious strivings are futile: "God tests them so that they may see that they are but animals" (3:18).

Twenty-sixth Day *Read Ecclesiastes 6–8*

Emotionally and intellectually twisting and writing, doubling and redoubling upon the trail of his own thought, the Preacher repeats his earlier arguments in different form. Neither material success nor length of days actually contributes one iota to life's meaning. Neat answers simply are not to be found; even the pursuit of wisdom is futile, for it perpetually eludes the seeker (7:23). Everything seems to be topsy-turvy; the wicked are rewarded, and the righteous are punished (8:14).

Troubled, perplexed, and burdened, this mixed-up seeker gets his answer in a flash of insight. The truth is, he concludes, that ultimate answers are hidden from earthbound creatures. They toil to discover how the Creator orders his universe and are doomed to disappointment. "Despite all his efforts to search it out, man cannot discover its meaning. Even if a wise man claims he knows, he cannot really comprehend it" (8:17).

Twenty-seventh Day *Read Ecclesiastes 9–12*

No categorical solution to the human condition comes in these final pages. I believe, however, that the last two verses answer the riddle. Coming after the Preacher's breathtaking vision of the end of things, they form a sort of denouement in which the central theme of the drama is condensed.

Convinced of the futility of every human activity, the overwhelmed one is in a mood to turn to God for divine gifts that must be accepted in lieu of personal achievements.

Only out of the pit of despair is one impelled to look up and out. Until a struggling seeker descends to rock-bottom defeat, where all human activity spells "vanity of vanities," he simply will not cast himself utterly upon God. So long as we retain the least glimmer of hope in our own strength, efforts, and the progress of society, we do not make divine rescue our one goal. To put the fate of our souls into the hands of a malefactor dying upon a cross, we must have despaired of every other source of help.

So viewed, this dark and difficult little book suddenly glows with more than earthly light. Though he never spells out his message in a few easy sentences, the Preacher insists throughout that a more-than-logical act of rescue by the Creator is the one thing that can give significance to the creature made in the divine image.

Song of Songs

Chances are, here is a little book that you have never studied in Sunday school! There are two widely divergent positions concerning it.

Many modern Christians (probably the majority of Protestants) take the "literary" view. According to it, this is a pagan love song— no more and no less—which won a place in the Bible only because Solomon's name is attached to it. So regarded, it is poetry of a fairly high grade whose subject matter makes it quite unfit for any religious use.

But this point of view has been prominent for only two or three centuries. During more than fifteen hundred years the song was generally regarded as the love song between Jehovah and the chosen people (or between Christ and the church). So viewed, the lines are not sensuous, but exalted enough to occupy a central place in the devotional life of such a great leader of Christendom as Bernard of Clairvaux.

Twenty-eighth Day *Read Song of Songs 1–3*

For my part, I shall take the position that those who long ago helped shape the contents of the Bible were not schoolboys, but great and godly men. Consequently, I shall insist upon reading the song as the love plaint of Israel, daughter of Zion (Isa. 16:1) for her divine Lover. Here is the nuptial music of the covenant!

So viewed, the placement just before the Book of Isaiah is deliberate and tremendously significant.

Israel and her divine Lover engage in the fervent and secret language of love. Their rapid exchanges defy logical outline. Each sometimes whispers sweet nothings, sometimes bursts into lyric praise. It is not possible in some instances even to say which of the two is speaking.

This much, however, can hardly be overlooked: the vocabulary of lovemaking conveys high-level ideas about the exotic and delightful state produced by the union of God with those he created. In more direct language (and more exalted poetry), we have here an ancient forerunner of Christian love songs such as "In the Garden" and "The Lily of the Valley."

Twenty-ninth Day *Read Song of Songs 4–5*

In every age and among all circumstances, sensitive men and women have had a sense of being sought after by God. This is the basic idea of the "call" to religious service. In it, God is seen as taking the initiative. He does not wait for men and women to seek him, but he continually beguiles them to come to him.

Artists have expressed this compelling concept through paintings depicting Christ knocking at the door of the heart. In his poem "The Hound of Heaven," Francis Thompson suggests that God pursues the wayward soul as a hound follows its quarry. Today's reading employs softer and warmer imagery. The divine Lover (5:10–16) is not stern or fearful but is engaged in eager courtship! Now pleading, now chiding, now tenderly pursuing, he devotes all his ardor to the task of wooing the human soul.

Thirtieth Day *Read Song of Songs 6–8*

Fervent and ceaseless as it is, the wooing of the divine Lover will not lead to union until the soul responds in kind. For a really fruitful and transforming encounter with God, one must literally pant for the instant of embrace. The soul must focus upon the coming of the Lover in order to surrender to him. The soul must cry:

Come away, my lover,
    and be like a gazelle
or like a young stag
    on the spice-laden mountains (8:14).

When such a mood dominates the hungry soul, when yearning for God is so intense that it cannot be haltingly expressed except in the language of romantic love, then the soul is ready to enter into the transforming surrender that the Bible exalts as the apex of human achievement.

Isaiah and Jeremiah

Isaiah

In order to play the role of prophet, a person must have a sensitive ear and a nimble tongue. The function of a prophet is to hear and understand the divine messages that people in general fail to notice, then put those messages into such form that they have public influence.

Because of the nature of prophecy, it is inevitable that many more "proclaimers of divine secrets" are forgotten than are remembered. Many a self-styled prophet is more attuned to his own inner groanings than to the voice of God. Others, who really do succeed in hearing messages from on high, lack the capacity to communicate those messages so that listeners are impelled to take heed.

The messages that form the Book of Isaiah stand in the front rank of Jewish-Christian prophecy. It takes only a casual reading to discover that, though all the garments are cut from the same bolt of cloth, the hands of more than one tailor have been used by God. There are three natural divisions in the book: chapters 1–9, 40–55, and 56–66. They deal, respectively, with Judah in the eighth century B.C., the sixth-century Babylonian exile, and the fifth-century return to Jerusalem.

What matters, for our purposes, is the remarkable fashion in which a stream of prophecy that flowed across three pre-Christian centuries served as a herald of the coming Good News. Jesus Christ, the supreme agent of communication between God and man, so embodies the divine that we revere him as the Word of God. Everything that he does and says speaks to us about the Father. No previous channel conveyed so full, so overwhelming, and so definitive a stream of revelation.

But the essential truth that God and his people are in a covenant relationship, with God rescuing those who accept his unearned grace, resounds throughout Scripture. In this sense, the Old Testament is precisely like the New Testament. Indeed, without the centuries-long work of Providence by which a chosen people were prepared to hear the definitive message from God, it would have been futile for that message to have been sounded.

The Book of Isaiah stands in the front rank of the agents of preparation. Foreshadowing much that is clearly articulated in the Son of God, Isaiah is to the solemn movement of *salvation history* as John the Baptist is to Jesus Christ. Read as a preparer of the way, this noble book will bathe your whole understanding of the gospel with brilliant new light.

First Day *Read Isaiah 1-4*

Whatever else he may be, Isaiah is a man with a message! Sometimes he spews out challenges that sting; sometimes he pours out promises that soothe. But he always requires that we who read shall take a stand; neutrality is not an alternative.

God's own people have rebelled against him, the prophet charges; Zion's haughty daughters are "walking along with out-stretched necks" (3:16) while they deliberately explore the depths of iniquity. So great is their sin that Jerusalem has become a new Sodom.

Though it is seldom expressed explicitly, Isaiah everywhere implies that his prophetic warnings are voiced in a time of prosperity. Having grown strong and comfortable, the people of the covenant have ceased to rely upon divine help. They worship the fruits of their own labor. They do not need any gifts from God; they are getting along quite nicely on their own, thank you.

All this will change in "the day of the Lord," the prophet declares. Then things will be reversed, with the proud laid low and God alone exalted. Boys will play the role of princes (3:4) and the latest arrangements from the beauty parlor will yield to baldness (3:24). Poured out upon the heads of mankind, in a series of divine acts that are in some respects beyond history rather than within history, the day of the Lord will establish justice and give meaning to history. In that day, the mood will once more be that of divine rescue. Zion's daughters will be cleansed, not through their own efforts, but by the work of the Lord who will provide "a refuge and hiding place from the storm and rain" (4:6).

Second Day *Read Isaiah 5–9*

Once he has been overpowered by his vision of the Lord "high and exalted" (6:1), Isaiah is no longer his own master. He belongs to the Lord, for whom he is a spokesman—a mouthpiece, in the literal sense. In this role, the prophet runs the gamut of religious experience, from despair to exultation. Partly for this reason, and partly because all his messages fall upon the ears of a people too dull to hear God speaking directly to them, Isaiah's prophecies are not arranged in orderly sequence.

Yet, in spite of the fact that his messages spill out in almost chaotic fashion, all of them revolve around a few central ideas that are repeated in a variety of ways, somewhat like the theme of a symphony. Almost any segment of his book, selected as arbitrarily as today's five chapters, will yield many of the same emphases.

Faithlessness of the chosen people must be punished, Isaiah repeats. Israel must be led out of her new Egyptian captivity, which consists of bowing down to idols of materialism. In order that these rebellious people shall turn their hearts to repentance, they must be chastened.

So far, nothing radically new has been said, but now the prophet's message takes a strange turn—one that was frequently anticipated earlier but nowhere clearly spelled out. GOD WILL USE A NATIONAL FOE AS AN INSTRUMENT. MILITARY DEFEAT WILL REESTABLISH CONDITIONS IN WHICH THE PEOPLE OF THE COVENANT WILL CEASE TRUSTING IN THEIR OWN STRENGTH AND TURN TO THEIR CREATOR FOR RESCUE. This radical interpretation, that a national calamity will be a dramatic message from God, is so basic to Isaiah's prophecy that it is repeated several times in our reading for today (5:26; 7:18–20; 8:7–8; 9:8–11).

Because God's dramatic signs can be viewed from many perspectives, they are even harder to interpret than are verbal messages. What one sees in a divinely ordered event, such as the birth of a child (8:1–4) or invasion by Assyrian armies (8:7–8), depends upon where one stands and with what eyes one looks. It is the role of the prophet to ponder such signs, to soak himself in them until they are part of him, and then to translate the divine messages into words that challenge people who are too dull or too busy to notice the signs that abound everywhere.

One such sign that Isaiah emphasizes is the coming of a child through whom God will rescue his people (7:10–17, 9:6–7). Christians consider this a milestone in *salvation history*. Here is a finger pointing forward to the grandest of all acts of rescue; the climax of the drama: the birth of the child for whom the divine-human marriage was consummated, he who was at the same time Son of God and Son of Man, the pivotal figure in the drama of Creator and created.

Third Day *Read Isaiah 10–13*

Viewed from one perspective, any occasion on which God pours out his wrath constitutes "the day of the Lord." Punishment is a major ingredient of that day, and God can use any circumstance or event as his agent to effect such punishment.

But there is also an element of glory in the day of the Lord. Once Assyria has served God's purposes, functioning as the rod to chasten godless Israel (10:5–6), Assyria herself will be laid low (10: 12, 25). Next, when Babylon has executed God's anger (13:3), the Lord of Hosts will march against that great nation and turn its cities into waste places (13:19–22).

So far as *salvation history* is concerned, therefore, it may be concluded that all men and nations play their special roles in the implementation of God's purpose. What seems to be a national calamity, actually can be the stimulus to rededication of the chosen people.

Having grown lax in their performance of covenant vows, they will be stirred to fresh zeal by onslaughts of Assyrian and Babylonian armies.

The covenant is never canceled. God never withdraws his promise, no matter how flagrantly man abuses his confidence. Consequently, there is no possibility that the ultimate triumph of God shall be threatened. Out of what seems calamity, there always comes a fresh appetite for rescue. When the oak is cut level with the ground, "a shoot will come up from the stump of Jesse" (11:1). God's punishment is never total; he always preserves a remnant, and always that remnant will turn back to him, reaffirming the covenant to write another page in the book of *salvation history* (10:21).

Fourth Day *Read Isaiah 14–18*

There are two main impressions offered by these chapters.

First, many of the places and powers that Isaiah talks about are forgotten and their names mean nothing to us. Moab and Babylon may sound faintly familiar, but who has ever heard of Heshbon and Elealeh, of the road to Horonaim, or the waters of Nimrim?

We tend to focus our fears and yearnings upon the powerful of this earth, but the truth is that God so overshadows kings and generals that, by comparison, the most exalted rulers are like new growth on a vine, soon to be chopped off with a pruning hook (18:5). Whether they be our friends or our foes, the nations of earth are like chaff on the mountains (17:13). No man or nation has more than fleeting significance. God alone is powerful. God alone is everlasting. God alone commands our awe, our fear, our loyalty, and our worship.

Fifth Day *Read Isaiah 19–24*

"Tumult and trampling and terror" (22:5) pervade these pages. "In that day," nature herself is turned topsy-turvy, for the mighty Nile becomes "parched and dry" (19:5). From fishermen and weavers of Egypt to merchant princes of Tyre, affairs of the people are suddenly thrown into chaos. Archers of Kedar and horsemen of Babylon are alike dashed to the ground. Egypt's fabulous City of the Sun, stronghold of idolatry, becomes tributary to the Lord of Hosts (19:18).

Here is a definitive repudiation of the plea, "Peace, peace." Let the soul who enters into covenant with God recognize that there can never be an armistice. No culture, no society, no nation can long escape divine wrath. No institution, no stronghold, no monument will endure beyond the life of a puff of smoke; "the earth will be completely laid waste and totally plundered" (24:3). In this uncertain and insecure life, the only way anyone can find security is to become prostrate before the Lord of Hosts, whose glory outshines the moon and sun (24:23).

Sixth Day *Read Isaiah 25–29*

God's offer of rescue is made to mankind in general; indeed, it is potentially universal and unlimited. But for it to be accepted by individuals, rescue must be introduced into history. This, in turn, requires a specific and not a general place, and particular men, and not mankind. It is the function of Jerusalem, the holy mountain, to serve as the valve or spigot through which salvation flows.

In the same fashion, it is the role of the chosen people to serve as the channel through which God may move to encounter all the nations. But this chosen vessel is a vessel of clay. Jacob continually fails and must be scourged and reawakened. That is what happens in time of national and international turmoil. Never lose sight of the fact that God's hand is involved in calamities and disasters. God is the keeper of the vineyard, and he will not turn his back upon it even for an instant. By using their foes to chasten the chosen people, God revives the sense of covenant with them and guarantees the continuing movement of *salvation history*.

Seventh Day *Read Isaiah 30–34*

God is terrible! Oh, how terrible he is! (30:13–14, 27–33; 32:14–15; 34:1–17).

The wrath of God is poured out for the healing of the nations. He strikes fear into the hearts of men in order to cause us to bow down before him (30:18), to cease trusting in some Egyptian alliance, to turn away from our idols of silver and gold made with our own hands. The day of the Lord is a day of reckoning, the role of which is to awaken us out of our complacency (32:9–11).

Because of its awakening role, the day of the Lord is not only a day whose terrors no tongue can describe, it is also a time of joy and exaltation (30:19, 26). When the land mourns, then God is known in his glory (33:9). Then and only then do the eyes of men succeed in seeing that Zion alone is fixed and eternal (33:20)—the one source of stability in an unstable universe.

Eighth Day *Read Isaiah 35–39*

Much that is reported in these chapters is also confirmed in secular history. National and international events are dramatic and stirring. Sennacherib, the powerful and ambitious King of Assyria, brings armies and lays siege against Jerusalem, which has been reduced to such weakness that the city does not have enough warriors to mount the spare horses of their foes (36:8). Sudden death strikes the encamped Assyrians, who abandon the siege and flee in panic (37:36–37). King Hezekiah falls gravely ill, but recovers to reign over Judah for another fifteen years (38:16). Babylonian diplomats make their appearance, presaging the rise to power of that great eastern empire whose expansion will bring an end to the Hebrew monarchy (39:1–7).

It is against such a background that Isaiah the prophet gives his unique interpretation of history. God is in history, using men and events, he declares. Whatever comes must be interpreted in the light of a faith that cannot waver. Regardless of how absolute defeat may seem, God always preserves a remnant (37:31–32) through whom the covenant is maintained and to whom ultimate victory will come (35:10; 38:20).

Ninth Day *Read Isaiah 40–42*

The flail has threshed out the grain; the razor from beyond the river has shaved off every hair. Rebellious children of the covenant have come through the years of the Babylonian captivity predicted in chapters 1–39, and now they are chastened.

What is the outcome?

A new movement in the cyclical unrolling of *salvation history*! Now that his chosen ones are panting with thirst, the Lord is ready to open up fountains (41:17–18). Prostrate, Abraham's descendants no longer trust in their own strength but throw themselves upon God alone. Now Jerusalem sees with new clarity that even mighty Babylon is like grass that withers—while "the word of our God will stand forever" (40:8).

Here is good news, indeed!

Out of despair, there comes a new kind of joy. From the ashes of defeat, there springs a totally unexpected kind of victory. Out of captivity, there emerges freedom in God. Israel has been made new through suffering.

But that is not the end of the story. These reborn people, transformed through acceptance of rescue, have a role to play in history. The new servant of God (sometimes the nation, sometimes Jerusalem, sometimes an individual "suffering servant") is the divine instrument through which healing will come to the nations.

Rejoice! Rejoice! Rejoice! Through his servant, God will level mountains and make rough places smooth, turning darkness into light, so that instead of having forsaken people as hopeless, God has established his covenant anew!

Tenth Day *Read Isaiah 43–46*

"Don't be afraid," God soothes Israel through the lips of the prophet. "You are my son. You belong to me. You were born of my covenant with Abraham. Come what may, my blood flows through your veins. Nothing can change that fact. Nothing can sever our relationship."

Basic to the divine-human bond is "a new thing" (43:19). God the Creator continues his work and brings it to a cosmic climax in the covenant. Something utterly new is forever emerging! Divine forgiveness makes guilty sinners into new persons (43:25; 44:22). Divine mercy brings water out of dry ground (44:3). *God is all in all.* "I am the first and I am the last" (44:6)…"and there is none like me" (46:9). In the covenant relationship, God continues his work as Maker.

God is utterly unlike the impotent idols we humans make with our hands. God uses us and all things as his instruments. In his hand, mighty Cyrus and the hosts of Persia are but pawns (45:4). This powerful Maker, this Creator of all that is and of all that is to be pours out upon us a stream of "everlasting salvation" (45:17). His deliverance, always potent to transform the whole of existence, is perpetually near! (46:13).

Eleventh Day *Read Isaiah 47–50*

Babylon the great, daughter of the Chaldeans, rules the world. But she did not reach these heights by her own strength alone. She is an instrument of God, who deliberately gave Israel into her hands (47:6)—sold Israel into slavery for her sins (50:1).

Basking for a moment in the sun, Babylon has dared to think herself almighty and everlasting (47:10). It is therefore time for her to learn who really is in control. Both to punish rebellious Babylon and to restore the people of the covenant to their glory, Israel is about to be redeemed once more (48:20).

What glorious fruit God has caused to grow upon the tree of Babylonian captivity!

Made prostrate in order to be eager to accept the helping hand of God, Israel will rise up stronger than ever. She sat down by the waters of Babylon to weep (Ps. 137), but now rises up to rejoice that in such a situation she succeeded in hearing a new message from on high (48:6). Worship of Jehovah, so long tribal and national, has become international. God's suffering servant will not only bow before him in Jerusalem, but will also be "a light for the Gentiles" in order that salvation may bathe the whole earth (49:6).

Twelfth Day *Read Isaiah 51–55*

Songs of triumphant praise abound here. No passages in Scripture are more eloquent and moving. Commentary upon them is superfluous, if not presumptuous.

Here is the climax of the covenant. Here is Calvary foreshadowed. Out of the marriage between Israel and the Lord, there comes the Suffering Servant—the Redeemer. It is for this that the world was created.

Thirteenth Day *Read Isaiah 56–59*

Almost immediately there is a change in the mood and style of the writer. Even before a side remark reveals that the outcasts are now back home (56:8), we sense that the conditions of the Babylonian captivity no longer prevail. Instead of comforting promises about the redemptive work of the Suffering Servant, we encounter a volley of stinging rebukes.

Restored to their homeland, the people of God have fallen and failed once more. Immorality and idolatry flourish. God is forgotten, and his holy day is profaned. Injustice and wickedness prevail. Even the solemn religious ceremonies dedicated to God are futile, for they are empty and pretentious (58:4).

In this situation, the prophet takes yet another giant stride in the human pilgrimage whose goal is a glimpse of the height and the depth of God's redemptive love. God will restore the penitent, he exults. The sins of his people do not cause the covenant to be canceled. BUT INSTEAD OF REJOICING AT THE REDEMPTION OF ABRAHAM'S SEED OR THE SONS OF DAVID, THE PROPHET SINGS HIS PRAISE THAT "those in Jacob who turn from transgression" WILL BE VISITED BY THE REDEEMER (59:20–21).

No longer regarded as transmitted through biological processes or by a select nation into which one enters by birth, the covenant is now seen to be spiritual in nature. Once this startling leap of understanding has been made, we are not far below the pinnacle from which a few sensitive ones will grasp the fact that God offers salvation to THOSE WHO BELIEVE IN HIS SON.

Fourteenth Day *Read Isaiah 60–63*

God's free salvation, poured out for all persons, necessarily enters history at a particular place as well as through a special agent. That place is the city of God—Jerusalem. Because the light of the world shines in her streets, she will enlighten nations (60:3). Foreigners will rebuild her shattered walls (60:10), and those who are in captivity will be set free (61:1). Jerusalem's people will become recognized as God's earthly representatives (61:56), and divine righteousness will spread over the earth (61:11). This new instance of the divine-human marriage, in which the Holy City becomes the bride of the Lord (62:4–5), promises utter transformation.

But that transformation is temporary. The mighty promises of God have hardly been sounded before he begins once more to shout his anger that the chosen people have not responded (63:1–6). They perpetually rebel and arouse divine enmity. No matter how mightily saved or how wonderfully restored to some Jerusalem, God's own people always backslide and become like strangers who have never bowed before him as king (63:15–19).

Fifteenth Day *Read Isaiah 64–66*

Small wonder that anyone who really looks around yields to despair—until another look shows that the human race is the handiwork of God. Such recognition, leading to hope in hopelessness, evokes a mighty groan (64:9–12).

God replies, reciting a list of grievances (65:1–7) whose punishment will contribute to the formation of "new heavens and a new earth" (65:17). In the end, God's chosen people will find victory rather than defeat. Regardless of struggle and failure in the past and defeat in the present, God will establish a glorious and triumphant reign in the future. No matter what the conditions of earthly life, anyone who really believes in God has such radiant optimism that nothing can dispel the joy.

Jeremiah

It hardly seems possible that we have reached the twenty-fourth book of the Old Testament. With half our year of reading to be completed in just two weeks, we find the age of the patriarchs behind us and the coming of the Savior awaiting us.

That is precisely where Jeremiah found himself. From the past, he inherited a rich legacy of law, history, songs, and ceremonies. He recognized himself and his contemporaries to be on the receiving end of a stream of divine revelation and guidance that began with Abraham. And to a degree seldom matched in *salvation history*, Jeremiah found messages from God in the events of secular life.

Jeremiah lived through one of the most chaotic periods in Jewish history. Three world powers were struggling for supremacy, and little Judah lay in the path that their armies naturally took in meeting one another. Egypt, Assyria, and Babylonia alternately offered threats and protection, after a fashion. Judah's leaders turned first to one, then to another of these pagan nations. Jerusalem entered a series of futile treaties; she was first made a tributary, then captured outright, and finally destroyed about 587 B.C.

Throughout this tumultuous epoch, Jeremiah tried to persuade the people of the covenant to rely upon God instead of their own strength or the promises of foreign kings. He never succeeded more than briefly and partially. But no event or circumstance could silence this man!

To a degree unmatched in the Old Testament, he offers dramatic as well as verbal messages. It seems that he is perpetually doing something as well as saying something to attract attention and persuade the people of Judah to bow down before God. Failure never daunts him. Reverberating as they do with the voices of diplomats, the noises of battle, and the groans of prisoners, these pages are yet exuberant and triumphant. Nothing can defeat our great God!

Sixteenth Day *Read Jeremiah 1–3*

It is a basic affirmation of Scripture that God speaks to us without ceasing. He uses not only words, but every kind of experience and object—from an almond tree branch to a boiling pot. But there is no flow of communication (or revelation) unless some sensitive one sees or hears in order to understand and act. Hence the stream of divine-human dialogue is not continuous, but broken. It comes in spurts and is poured out in history through men like Jeremiah.

In these opening chapters, the prophet's message is as blunt as it is damning. Israel has fallen into idolatry, he asserts. Not only do the people engage in all kinds of pagan worship, but they try to preserve their nation through alliances with sinful nations rather than by dependence upon Jehovah. Judah has violated the marriage contract between God and man. She has turned her back upon the ark of the covenant. But the situation is not hopeless. God calls for repentance in order that he may show mercy. In a future era of divine victory that the prophet labels simply "in those days," rebellious Judah and wanton Israel will be joined together and all nations will flock to Jerusalem to bow before the Lord!

Seventeenth Day *Read Jeremiah 4–6*

In spiritual matters, there are no impossible situations. Everyone (even those favored by God) falls and fails, wallowing in sin and all the while enjoying it. But the possibility of a return to God—no, the certainty that a remnant will return—is never challenged.

To reawaken sleepers and to make restless the comfortable, a merciful God uses national disasters as tools. His judgment is within history as well as beyond history. When priest and prophet alike have become corrupt (5:30–31; 6:13–14), when both the great and the small have turned their backs upon God, he uses other nations to punish his chosen people.

No matter how far we may have wandered from the path to life, once we are brought to a state of despair we are ready to find strength in God. Therefore, a ray of hope always shines. It may become very dim, but it is never extinguished. Man's follies and failures cause the Lord to sow desolation, not once but over and over. But God "will not destroy [them] completely" (4:27; 5:18). However hard it may be to order our lives by a promise that is almost totally obscured in a given historical situation, nevertheless, the assurance of meaning and of victory gleams through the mists of our chaotic existence. Hope, and not despair, is the final word.

Eighteenth Day *Read Jeremiah 7–9*

Part of the paradox of the Hebrew-Christian faith is that, though hope in God is ultimate and decisive, the happy verdict does not necessarily apply to a particular person or epoch. We have almost a spiritual counterpart of the statistical principle that is the foundation of modern science. Given large numbers of cases over a long period, the scientist can predict a cumulative result, but confronted by a specific instance, the laws of probability give no answers.

God's ceaseless covenant with mankind is conditional in about the same sense. Individuals and epochs may depart from the covenant; indeed, many are certain to do so. The ultimate triumph of the divine purpose does not relieve anyone of freedom and responsibility. Indeed, part of the plight of Jerusalem in the time of Jeremiah is the tendency to rely upon the fact that God has chosen Israel as his bride. This gives a false sense of security, leads to a new low in social degradation and a new high in pagan practices, and hence causes God's heart to break. No lines in Scripture exceed the power and pathos of those which describe the grief of God at the waywardness of his people (8:18; 9:2). Lovingly though the punishment is administered, God's judgment upon Israel is so fearful that words can hardly describe it (9:11–16).

Nineteenth Day *Read Jeremiah 10–13*

I cannot today resist noting that these chapters confirm the judgment that tendencies toward idolatry are never eliminated. Man, simply because he is man, is prone to bow down before less than God. With half an eye, one can look about our own land today and see modern counterparts of the idols whom Jeremiah's people displayed in their solemn processions.

Man, being man but wanting to be a god, fails most utterly when his efforts are directed toward scaling the heights. No failure is like spiritual failure. Jerusalem, chosen from heaven to be the bride and beloved of her Maker (11:15; 12:7), has become more vile and filthy than her neighbors who have not yet made an effort to rise above their wallowings.

As you read these gripping chapters, are you beginning to feel a sense of revulsion? Do you abandon hope in man's capacity to live up to the best that he knows? Are you spiritually seasick at the waverings and failings of the chosen people who so badly muffed the most glorious of opportunities?

If so, you are again entering the mood that makes spiritual victory rest upon divine rescue rather than human achievement. Jeremiah's scintillating description of the way finite goals transform the best of men into the worst, begins by indirection to lift up the distant vision of a man upon a cross who will die in order to accomplish for mankind what our race cannot do for itself.

Twentieth Day *Read Jeremiah 14–17*

Throughout this vivid book, and especially in today's chapters, we are confronted by a paradox. In all its forms, organized religion is prone to fail and to fall—yet, when such instances of human depravity are most abundant, God raises up some amateur through whom the covenant is revived.

Jerusalem's respected religious leaders have sold out. Instead of offering yeasty and transforming messages from on high, they wink at the sins of their people and support the status quo (see 5:30–31; 8:13–14). Priest and prophet alike "ply their trade" (14:18) in utter blindness. That is, they act the part of the professional religionist instead of the spokesman for God. They are being well paid to speak soothing words of peace, when they ought to be shouting warnings that would shake the foundations of society.

It is in this apparently hopeless situation that God raises up men like Jeremiah. It is when the institution fails most completely that individuals respond to the divine call most grandly. It is when conduct of religious officials seems to question the validity of religion itself that some layman steps forward so thoroughly surrendered that God uses his lips to pour out authentic new warnings and promises.

Twenty-first Day *Read Jeremiah 18–21*

Anyone who thinks the lot of a genuinely God-inspired prophet to be soft and easy will revise his judgment after reading these chapters!

Jeremiah is so attuned to the still, small voice that he hears God speak in every situation of life. For example, he gains a vivid message from on high while watching a potter at work (18:1–11). Not only does he receive messages through a great variety of media, he also uses unconventional methods in making public what he hears from God. Unable to persuade men by use of words alone, he arranges a dramatic setting in which to smash a clay jar to symbolize divine punishment (19:1–2, 10–11).

Just how popular this makes the prophet, we learn in such passages as 20:1–2. Convinced that he is a voice crying in a wilderness of idolatry and degradation, Jeremiah runs the emotional gamut. At one moment, he sings with delight (20:13); the next moment, he is overcome by despair (20:14–18). He hears God in a time when nearly every ear is dull. He speaks with power and passion—and nobody responds.

Dare we draw a tentative and hesitant conclusion?

Is it possible for any prophet who presents an authentic message from God to be universally popular?

What does this suggest concerning the programs of middle-class churches today that seek to serve God by means of pleasing all and offending none?

Twenty-second Day *Read Jeremiah 22–24*

Jeremiah's denunciation of false prophets and priests continues, interspersed with warnings about fearful judgments certain to come upon the heads of those who follow such leaders.

In hopelessness, however, there is hope. Echoing Isaiah's verdict that "a remnant will return," Jeremiah catches a glimpse of light in the darkest hour of Israel's history. Both in the last climactic months before the nation falls (23:1–8) and in the aftermath of Babylon's victory (24:1–7), Jeremiah sees hope. God, who punishes sin wherever he finds it, will never give up. Always, he will woo and pursue. Although a new deluge comes in our day, tomorrow at least a few repentant ones will thrive in the sunshine of God's love.

Twenty-third Day *Read Jeremiah 25–29*

Were it not for the dramatic incidents that punctuate his message, Jeremiah's prophecy would seem repetitious to the point of monotony. During a period of more than twenty-three years (25:3), he has said about the same thing, over and over. Public reaction remains uniformly unfavorable, varying from indifference to indignation. Opposition of the religious establishment remains firm; "false prophets" continue to be satisfied with the status quo and to resist reform. Under such circumstances, why bother continuing to seek new ways to make public a message through drama (25:15–17; 27:2; 28:12–13) as well as speech?

The answer is that Jeremiah is not a free agent. The choice is not his to make. He is a tool in the hand of God. Although playing a very different role from that of the king of Babylon, the prophet is like the ruler because both are instruments of Providence (25:9). Jeremiah is voicing a system of crisis theology; in a time when it seems that God has deserted his chosen people, God is using Jeremiah to offer a reinterpretation of the covenant. Therefore the prophet has no choice. Even at the risk of life and limb (26:11), he must speak. He is a mouthpiece for a message larger than he.

Seldom achieved even by the most dedicated of God-seekers, this is the ideal state of the religious leader. This is the goal toward which every preacher and teacher and church officer should aim: surrender so complete that they become voices for God rather than for themselves.

Twenty-fourth Day *Read Jeremiah 30–31*

There are woes, calamities, and punishments. Precisely because we are human, we shall never escape these conditions of our humanity. But neither present nor future signs of doom represent God's final word.

Always, that word is positive. God is perpetually saving his people (30:10), binding up our wounds (30:17), and establishing conditions for rebuilding (31:4). This is true of history in general and of every period and epoch in particular. That is to say, the divine-human covenant is a basic factor in creation—as characteristic of it as are those forces that regulate the sun, moon, and stars (31:35). Consequently, the verdict of Jeremiah (like that of Scripture in general) is in the end one of unqualified optimism. The covenant itself is perpetually being made new (31:31), and the final outcome was assured before the world began: "…you will be my people, and I will be your God." (30:22)

Twenty-fifth Day *Read Jeremiah 32–35*

Regardless of the holy zeal that moves his lips and the social evils that stir him to speak, Jeremiah, it seems, enjoys his role! In such passages as 34:17–22, the wonder is not that the prophet spent time in the guardhouse (33:1), but that he survived his first frontal assault upon entrenched evil.

That the king and his officers tolerated Jeremiah is solid ground for hope. Things never get altogether bad. Man is perpetually involved in the cyclical movements that grow out of the covenant, of course. The succession of events is monotonously sure: in every generation, men will fail and fall as their fathers did; God will cleanse (33:8), restore (32:38), and accept his children into a New Covenant relationship (32:40). This pattern is as much a part of the life situation as the day-night cycle (33:20).

Yet something more is involved. There is an element of what we moderns tend to call "progress." Although the rolling of the wheel takes it in perpetual circles, it is also moving forward. Absolute and not just relative gains are promised through a "Branch" from the tree of David (33:15). Individuals and cultures really do continue to call upon God, even though sin and evil never vanish. Answering such calls, God does not always repeat his answers. He gives new ones from time to time: 'I will answer you, and will tell you great and hidden things which you have not known" (33:3).

Twenty-sixth Day *Read Jeremiah 36–39*

Anyone who thinks of God's prophets as men withdrawn from the world and shielded from ordinary problems in order to meditate and pray will gain a fresh outlook from the fast-moving chapter 36. Few passages in the entire Bible exceed this chapter in emotional impact.

Having survived his frontal assault upon the king of Judah and having prepared a revised edition of his scroll, the much-imprisoned Jeremiah sees, firsthand, many of the woes he has predicted. Egyptian control of Judah is followed by Babylonian. No matter what puppet ruler happens to be on the throne, Jeremiah gets about the same treatment. A climax is reached in the episode of the cistern (chap. 38), but the prophet lives to see his king blinded and led away in chains (39:7).

Fresh messages from God, in such a time as this!

Twenty-seventh Day *Read Jeremiah 40–45*

The writing style employed by a historian is quite different from that used by a prophet. That is the case even when both write prose or both write poetry. Here, the use of prose in the historical sections helps to emphasize the differences between reporting political events and "speaking for God."

Even in historical sections, however, the religious viewpoint is dominant. All the woes that come upon God's people stem from one cause: wanton idolatry (44:23). Egypt and Babylon are instruments of God in working out the divine purpose: chastening the chosen people so that they will turn away from idols and prostrate themselves before God.

Egypt has both historical and symbolic meaning, here and elsewhere in Scripture. Groaning under Babylonian rule, Judah's "remnant" turns hopefully to Egypt. They prefer the service of the queen of heaven (44:17) to remaining in Judah and wearing the yoke of captivity. It is part of the basic message of Jeremiah that every choice of an "Egypt" is futile and self-defeating. All who elect what seems an easy life in some Egypt enter a new idolatry that will launch a fresh cycle of war, famine, and pestilence (42:11–17).

Twenty-eighth Day *Read Jeremiah 46–48*

In our pride, we continually engage in a subtle form of idolatry paying homage to the state by bowing down before symbols of human power that range from ancient monarchies to totalitarian"isms" of many kinds.

God has spoken very plainly to Jeremiah, reminding him that such aggregations of power are finite. Seen against the backdrop of ongoing divine creation, no nation is of significant duration. Egypt and her sacred bull will pass away, along with Philistia and her great mercantile cities. Moab's wealth and fortresses are futile to protect her.

Just now, the prophet asserts, it pleases God to use Babylon as his sword. Every battle that helps reveal the futility of human pride serves as a day of the Lord (46:10). The more clearly we recognize that nations—all nations—come and go, the more likely we are to see that the only genuine source of strength is trust in "the King, whose name is the Lord Almighty" (48:15).

Twenty-ninth Day *Read Jeremiah 49–50*

Intoxicated by the glory of the Lord, Jeremiah continues to call the roll of great cities and mighty nations. One by one, they shall go to their doom. As his chastening rod, God is presently using Babylon. But when its invincible armies have served their purpose, Babylon will go down in such defeat that the very earth will shake.

Is there no security in this insecure life?

Yes! God overthrows the proud and topples the strong to show that man's one sure source of strength and comfort is trust in his Maker. He himself is our Redeemer and our advocate (50:34). No matter how dreadful the present moment may appear, the covenant stands. Always we have the assurance that a remnant will return (50:4–20; cf. 46:27–28).

Here is a major paradox of *salvation history*: the downfall of the proudest human institutions serves to awaken us and point us to the God who alone is eternal and omnipotent.

Thirtieth Day *Read Jeremiah 51–52*

War is the apex of human conflict. All the factors affecting lesser struggles are involved in war, so in a sense, it is the definitive example of our human dilemma. Because of the sinful conditions of humanity, we can never find tranquillity. Struggle is an ingredient in existence.

Although he does not set out his conclusions in one-two-three order, Jeremiah implies that God is the author of the factors that produce conflict. When men vie with one another and someone gets hurt, that does not mean that God has turned his back upon the world. Even in a time of utter desolation, such as the sack of Jerusalem described in chapter 52, the believer must hold fast to the conviction that God is intimately involved in what happens.

Here is a faith that cannot be shaken.

How strangely modern the book of Jeremiah sounds, now that we have reached its end! Although the great nations of today have different names, and their arsenals of weapons are unlike the war implements of Babylon and Judah, today's mood is the same as yesterday's. Use modern names instead of ancient ones and Jeremiah might almost be writing in the twentieth century.

Can we reach the citadel from which he looked down on the affairs of men and nations? Is it possible for us, too, so to fear the God of Jeremiah that neither man nor beast nor engine of war holds any terrors? Can we make the covenant so binding upon our own lives that it becomes increasingly sure under test? If so, with Jeremiah we become invincible—not through anything we are or do, but through the God in whom we trust absolutely.

From Lamentations through Malachi

Lamentations

If we could read these exquisite verses in their original Hebrew, we should more readily grasp the prophet's literary power. In the first two chapters all three lines of each verse begin successively with one of the twenty-two letters of the Hebrew alphabet. Chapter 3 has sixty-six verses, with each letter of the alphabet used for three successive verses. Chapter 4 is similar, but has a pattern of two rather than three verses beginning with each letter.

The Lamentations of the poet-prophet center on the destruction of Jerusalem in 587 B.C. In present-day Hebrew worship, this book is also used to lament the sack of the city by the Romans in A.D. 70. In this sense, therefore, the book is oriented forward as well as backward. The lament over Jerusalem speaks for all men everywhere in time of overwhelming disaster.

First Day *Read Lamentations 1–5*

Here are the outpourings of a sensitive and gifted seeker after God, who is almost overwhelmed by tragedy. Sometimes he seems to speak for himself (3:1–20); more often, the lips of the prophet are instruments for Jerusalem's outpourings.

There are no really new elements here. We have met all the ingredients over and over: flagrant violations of the covenant, a state of spiritual decay so advanced that priests and prophets stand for evil rather than for good, fearful divine punishment, despair, repentance, and new hope in God.

Rooted as it is in a specific place at a particular time, this message is also universal. Substitute any city you please: Babylon, Karnak, Constantinople, Rome, Berlin, Pearl Harbor, Hiroshima, Moscow, Chicago. Read these lamentations as though they were written over the ashes of your own city. Allow enough time, and she who was powerful in the land will become like a widow sobbing in the night.

Here, then, is a timeless warning.

It is balanced and completed with a ceaseless promise. Every individual, every city, every nation can, through war and desolation, be stirred to turn back to God (3:40). All alike can glory in that though nothing that man builds is permanent, God reigns forever, and his "throne endures from generation to generation" (5:19). Thus the potential for restoration is as ceaseless as the certainty of destruction.

Ezekiel

The writings of this prophet-poet, living in exile during the sixth century B.C., form one of the longest and most difficult books of the Bible. Present-day Christians tend to take one of two attitudes toward Ezekiel's visions, warnings, entreaties, and sublime messages of hope.

Many church members, I fear, ignore the book altogether. Because it is hard to read and harder to understand, the temptation to stay out of its pages is hard to resist.

But a minority of Bible readers spend much time with Ezekiel. I wish I could honestly say that I think their time is well spent. Perhaps it is in some cases. For the most part, however, I fear that the fire-breathing evangelist who centers much of his attention upon this book misses the real point of Ezekiel's message. Abstract ideas and elevated poetic imagery abound here. Such material naturally lends itself to almost any interpretation one may wish to read into it. Therefore, for some readers Ezekiel is a book of detailed prophetic statements about national and international events in the twentieth century.

If I seem blunt and stubborn at this point, forgive me. But this most recent rereading of Ezekiel's sublimely dark visions has convinced me that his message is not intended for the twentieth or any other one century. Rather, it is directed to all people in every century. His truths are not centered in the doings of a few Western nations at one period of time. Rather, they are universal. They reveal God in his timeless and unchanging glory, his ceaseless and ever-hopeful courtship of mankind in general and of every person in particular.

Our hasty schedule requires that you go through this book rapidly; and dwelling on minor details is to miss its grand message. Read with eagerness, though with speed, listening for the voice of God as he tells you, through Ezekiel's lips, the meaning of life and of salvation.

Second Day *Skim Ezekiel 1–10*

Reading Ezekiel's account of his visions, filled as they are with strange wheels and stranger creatures, almost makes one's head swim. The dizziness that comes from trying to follow the prophet's imagery is a tribute to his poetic power. He employs symbols and metaphors that are so vivid you and I recoil, bewildered, knowing that we are bewildered.

Ezekiel's visions "say" that God is above and beyond seeing or describing. At its most exalted level the human imagination cannot dimly perceive the Creator in his totality. When we strain most fervently to see God, we are most completely overwhelmed by a sense of divine wonders, mysteries, and marvels.

Yet the invisible and inscrutable Creator can communicate with his creatures. Revelation is real! Man can feed upon the Word of God (2:8; 3:3). It is the special role of the prophet to accept divine truth, then share it with others. The fearful burden of the prophet, son of man, foreshadows the sufferings of the Savior, for the prophet bears the sins of mankind upon his own back (3:16–21).

The heart of Ezekiel's God-given message is: All idols are futile. God alone is great. All humans are limited. They forget this and, in their pride, rebel against Jehovah. Such sin is fearfully punished

(7:1–20) in order once more to convince men—through sword, famine, and pestilence—that God, not man, is supreme (6:13–14; 7:15–27).

Third Day *Skim Ezekiel 11–17*

It is useless, or worse, to pore over the imagery of these chapters trying to treat them as predictions of modern history. The prophet, at times almost intoxicated by his passion for Jehovah, is a poet of the highest order. He uses high-level imagery as naturally as you and I use everyday nouns and verbs.

The breathtaking imagery of chapter 16 gives new depth to the metaphors of the Song of Solomon. Jehovah's beloved having become wanton, God ceases to whisper sweet promises through the lips of his prophet and thunders warnings. "Thus says the Lord …" reverberates through these pages like the roll of celestial cannon (13:8; 13:20; 14:6; 14:21; 16:2). Reduced to its simplest elements, the divine warning is also a promise: wanton Israel, the bride of the Lord, has played the harlot and must undergo fearful punishment; this, however, is but prelude to renewal of the covenant (11:14–20; 14:11; 16:60).

Fourth Day *Skim Ezekiel 18–23*

Responsibility for sin and failure is individual as well as social. Although all persons are shaped by their society and their family, in a special sense they also stand before God upon their own two feet alone (chap. 18).

So for individuals as well as the chosen people in general, the divine-human drama throbs with promises and warnings. God is perpetually rescuing because mankind is perpetually falling and failing. Thus 20:28 becomes a kind of capsule summary of human history. Always, without exception, God's own people drift into idolatry.

If you can succeed in centering upon grand movements of the divine-human drama, and not upon gross details, these chapters will become soul-stirring. Nowhere else in Scripture is there a more vivid description of the faithlessness of Jehovah's chosen bride, Israel. God's own has so thoroughly played the harlot that princes, priests, prophets, and people are alike in their total failure. Not one clean, upright person remains in all the land (22:30).

Always, without exception, the wages of spiritual immorality—idolatry in one form or another—is death (23:46–49).

Fifth Day *Skim Ezekiel 24–30*

God is perpetually engaged in revealing himself to mankind. He uses the lips of devout men as his instruments to pour out his words so that multitudes will hear and understand.

But revelation is by no means limited to words. Much of Ezekiel's work of proclaiming truth is centered in actions, rather than speeches or sermons. His boiling of meat, melting of the pot, and disregard for death (chap. 24) are divinely inspired actions designed to communicate divine things to mortal beings. In this respect, the work of this prophet, who is so often called a "son of man," is strangely prophetic. It points to the work of the Son of Man, whose gospel is communicated not only through what he says but also through what he does and who he is.

When secular history is viewed through eyes made sharp by faith, all the tumultuous risings and failings of nations also serve to communicate great truths. Indeed, they repeat over and over the single message: "God is the Lord" (25:7, 11, 17; 26:6; 28:23, 24, 26; 29:6, 9, 16, 21; 30:26).

Sixth Day *Skim Ezekiel 31–36*

Some of the stirring passages in these chapters have a sweep and grandeur seldom matched even in Scripture. It is a pity that the impassioned and sometimes obscure language of the prophet has caused his book to be neglected by so many modern Christians and distorted by others who twist their own meanings from his metaphors.

Ezekiel's visions are so vivid and overpowering that they are often keyed to the year, month, and day of God's outpouring to this sensitive listener. For his part, he continues to use every possible vehicle of communication to make public what he hears. His reports are in both prose and poetry, and he frequently dramatizes his messages. Revelation is so powerful that it can flow through any channel open to man.

One of the breathtaking revelations of this section concerns the nature of divine justice and grace (33:10–20). Ezekiel has not arrived at his understanding of these matters by logical analysis; truth towers over logic. It is given, not won by striving. Gloriously, incredibly, and victoriously, "the existential now," the present moment is the definitive point in the divine-human relationship! Justice and grace center in this moment—not in the past or the future.

Proclaiming so incredible and difficult a message invites popular misunderstanding (33:30–33). Even the kings (the "shepherds") are likely to be deaf to fresh word from the Lord (34:1–10), so that (incredibly) God must actually rescue the "sheep" (the people) from the "shepherds" (34:11–17)!

God alone, acting personally and not through agents, is ultimate. He alone judges both nations and individuals.

This is a source of absolute, unquenchable hope (34:24–30). Such hope is not rooted in ideas about man or the flow of some impersonal kind of "progress." Rather, it is founded upon the nature of God (34:22, 31)!

Seventh Day *Read Ezekiel 37–39*

Chapters 40–48 are all but meaningless to most modern readers, though they provide a happy hunting ground for those who go to the Bible looking for obscure "proof" of some pet idea. We shall skim through these chapters very rapidly—tomorrow.

Today we are dealing with material of an entirely different nature. These radiant prophecies deserve to be read and reread. Speaking to the exiles in Babylon, the prophet underscores many central warnings and promises later offered to mankind through Jesus Christ.

When a human agent so yields himself that God really speaks to him, Ezekiel sings, all concepts such as "dead" and "impossible" vanish. Graves of whatever kind—physical, intellectual, spiritual—are opened and the dead spring to life (37:1–4).

God's covenant is never annulled. It stands forever. Regardless of how frequently men fail, the divine promise is not withdrawn. God's grace is the definitive pigment in the entire canvas that we call human history (37:26–27).

Because our eyes are often dull, we keep losing sight of this central core of meaning and hope. Thwarted in his attempt to love us into creative union with him, God is not defeated. Over and over, he uses tragedy to open our eyes and force us to see—sometimes almost against our own wills—that he really is the center of meaning and of hope for creatures made in his image (38:23; 39:6; 39:21).

Eighth Day *Skim Ezekiel 40–48*

It is difficult for us in the modern Western world to find a point of contact here. It is also useless to dwell upon minute details of these visions, attempting to use them as keys to national and international events of our time.

The apostle John must have pored over this material until it became meaningful to him, for it clearly influenced many sections of the Revelation.

For most of us, all we can hope to get here is a distant glimpse of the near-ecstasy in which a man lives after he has been given a vision of the New Jerusalem. Details of the city and the temple aside, one who really sees it is thereby made invincible. He lives in the light of the all-powerful God of heaven and of earth, protector of those who have entered into the covenant relationship.

Whether it be Ezekiel or John or a very ordinary twentieth-century follower of the Christ, the person bathed in that heavenly light shakes off some limitations of humanity.

7

Daniel

This strange and fascinating book deals with a man who was the Hebrew prophet Daniel and the Babylonian officer Belteshazzar. His turbulent life hints that every true servant of Jehovah is going to spend a lot of time in hot water—or worse! Whether in modern times or ancient, the notion that piety guarantees a happy and tranquil life is utterly false, if not heretical.

But it is equally false to be gloomy, even in the face of world catastrophe. Whatever we may see when we scan the horizon, it will not be there very long. Our changeless God wove change into his created world partly, perhaps, to persuade a few sensitive ones that tangible prizes are not worth winning.

All that counts is the divine verdict in the judgment. There, princes and kings will loom no larger than other mortals. Regardless of what foes threaten us, we ordinary mortals really can win—by throwing ourselves upon the mercy of our all-powerful God.

Ninth Day *Read Daniel 1–3*

These familiar stories are so colorful that we may be in danger of treating them simply as stories. Here, as everywhere in Scripture, we need to focus upon *salvation history* rather than upon external factors, however exciting they may be.

Daniel and his three friends, symbolizing all who bow to God rather than to a power less than God, deliberately set themselves apart. By so simple and so basic a choice as that of food and drink, they dramatize the fact that they are different from others.

This profound difference accounts for Daniel's ability to see the truth that is hidden from magicians, enchanters, sorcerers, and Chaldeans. Because the Hebrew youth will not yield his allegiance to any idol, he finds kingdom messages in the troubled dreams of a king. God's kingdom alone is enduring, he declares. Using the same figure of speech that Jesus later applied to himself, Daniel asserts that a stone "cut out of a mountain, but not by human hands" (2:45) will shatter all the kingdoms men can fashion.

As though to test that point of view, Nebuchadnezzar—the "golden king"—throws Daniel's three friends into the fiery furnace. They are delivered by a more-than-mortal hand, thus giving a specific illustration of the principle that God indeed sets all the schemes and devices and destructive instruments of man to naught.

Tenth Day *Read Daniel 4–5*

Sometimes we are impatient of the mysterious. We may even fall into the error of wanting a religious faith that is wholly logical, having no halo of the holy unknown about it.

Daniel's experiences remind us that the interpretation of mysteries is a central function of religion. Those who succeed in catching whispers from the lips of God will arrive at meanings that are hidden from the wisest men of the kingdom. Not infrequently, such messages from on high serve to put the prophet of God into the role of an attacker.

With two kings in succession, Daniel fathoms mysteries to persuade them that God alone is great. If not actually "original sin," pride comes very close to being the source of basic human guilt. In all its forms, pride is idolatry—the creature's rebellion against the Creator.

A king with endless dominions (4:22) learned humility through tragedy and as a result extolled God as his Lord (4:1–3, 34–35). If mighty Nebuchadnezzar could change, you and I are left convicted without an excuse when we refuse to bend our own haughty necks.

Eleventh Day *Read Daniel 6–8*

It is easy to get one's feet tangled in the symbolism of these chapters and trip over he-goats and horns, beasts and wheels. This danger is not easily avoided, but it can be overcome.

Remember always, here and everywhere, that the true role of Scripture is to communicate things of God to the sons of men. Therefore, we must always look for the central message. To focus upon incidental details—garments in which that message is clothed—is to misuse the sacred word.

If the motif of these chapters had to be reduced to one word, I think that word would be *victory*.

Human and superhuman forces are at war here. The lions faced by Daniel are insignificant when compared with the "beasts" of nations at war. These, in turn, lose all their terrors when viewed alongside Satan and his legions of demons. Yet Daniel (and mankind) is not overwhelmed! Gloriously, all the terrors of the planet and the cosmos fail to conquer God's children.

Jehovah, the Ancient of Days, rules over all! There is no defeat for him or for those who trust in him through his supreme agent, "one like a son of man" (7:13). All the goings and comings of men and of kingdoms are brief and limited. But God's dominion is everlasting, and his kingdom is one that no force or power in the universe can destroy. To know this with unshakable certainty is to enter into victory!

Twelfth Day *Read Daniel 9–12*

Whether they be prophets like Daniel or simply readers of the Bible like us, all who ponder the meaning of God and of man must deal both with history and beyond history.

Within history, humans are prone to exalt themselves and thereby rebel against God. That is the case with us common folk as well as with princes and kings. But, however splendid it may seem in man's eyes, such a rebellion is always brief. Princes and powers are perpetually rising, only to eventually fall. None lasts; no, not one. Grandeur is fleeting. Power is a vapor that vanishes overnight (11:45).

There is nothing permanent on the finite, created scale. Princes of Persia and of all nations, like ordinary men, must face divine judgment. To recognize that God's absolute rule will bring final judgment is not to gain the skill to analyze it in detail. Absolute, complete, neatly-wrapped-up analyses of the judgment are not given to men (12:8).

Hosea

This little book deserves to be read slowly. You will wish to mark passages that catch your attention and return to them several times to find their deeper meanings.

A stark note of personal tragedy runs through the whole prophecy. Out of a broken marriage, Hosea has come to glimpse the feelings of God at the faithlessness of his own bride, Israel. Sometimes pleading, frequently condemning, and at last hoping, Hosea pours out messages so fervently personal that they are seldom matched in Scripture.

Thirteenth Day *Read Hosea 1–4*

Moral and spiritual decay, such as described in chapter 4, represent a crisis in any society. But in the society of the divine-human covenant, such a state of affairs seems to threaten the very meaning of creation.

What is God to do?

Certainly it will be useless for him to rely upon the officials of the religious institution; they have helped create this crisis. Only an outsider—a religious amateur—can yield himself sufficiently to hear and repeat the divine message.

Then and now, anyone who plays the role of Hosea is likely to be scorned by "bad" people and condemned by "good" ones, for this God-intoxicated fellow enacts in his personal life the drama of Jehovah's marriage with Israel. He enters into union with a harlot, gives his children symbolic names, and through the tragedy of his family, dramatizes the fact that the bride of God has forsaken her husband for the couch of Baal.

Fourteenth Day *Read Hosea 5–8*

Woe unto the faithless bride!

Not only must God punish, for the present he is altogether hidden. It is useless for Israel to go through the motions of seeking him, so long as her heart is wanton. In this state, one cannot search for God (5:3–6).

For the present, therefore, there is no light and no hope. Whatever hope there may be is rooted not in history but beyond history. Matters have become so bad, viewed from the human perspective, that sowers of the wind can only reap the whirlwind (8:7).

Fifteenth Day *Read Hosea 9–11*

To pay homage to anyone or anything except God, to tarnish the divine imprint stamped upon man as made in God's image is to engage in immorality (9:1). Such failure is universal and inescapable. When Israel and all people are not trusting in pagan idols, they are bowing to powerful nations that promise rescue.

The sin of Adam—striving for a way to gain the qualities of God by an avenue other than total surrender to him—is universal and inescapable (10:1). Israel must fall not once but over and over. All people must yield to their humanity by seeking to provide their own rescue through their cunning, their strength, foreign alliances, or some other form of rebellion against God.

Sixteenth Day *Read Hosea 12–14*

Not only the worst of people but the best of people perpetually make the fatal mistake of seeking a savior other than God. A person who bows down before idols (whether hand-carved long ago or mass-produced on the modern assembly line) cancels out any capacity to endure beyond time and space. Because everyone worships some idol or other for some period, it would seem that all is hopeless.

That would be the case were not God able to do more than we can expect or imagine! Regardless of one's shame and infamy, if he will repent and bow down before God alone, he will be restored to the covenant relationship. Such a reunion is a state of ecstatic bliss so wonderful that the tongue can describe it only through metaphors and figures of speech (14:4–7). It is this state of healing, not that of rebellion and idolatry, that is ultimate and finally triumphant.

Joel

Seventeenth Day *Read Joel 1–3*

Nothing is new in this brief prophecy. Its pages echo many voices from the past. It is another interpretation of the unfolding of the covenant, a fresh rephrasing of the old recognition that divine-human relationships produce a cyclical pattern; God's wooing brings about marriage, but the bride proves inconstant so must be punished in order to be restored and blessed afresh.

Old as the story is, Joel manages to make it new and vivid. For he stresses the idea that the day of the Lord must be terrible in order to produce joy; it is a day of blackness but is a prelude to new and glorious light. Regardless of how many times the wheel has turned in the past, in spite of the repetitions of the same cycle, the ultimate triumph of God and his people will be absolute and final! This time, failure and punishment will cease; "And my people shall never again be put to shame" (2:26, 27).

Amos

Much of the Old Testament rings with "official" voices. The religious institutions produced and preserved most of the books about the Law and its applications, as well as psalms and other worship materials.

For the most part, the prophets are lonely outsiders who challenge the religious establishment. Their contact with God has been personal and direct. Their role is to denounce evil in high places and to awaken a society that has been permitted to doze, because religious officials can be comfortable only when their constituents are less than fully awake.

Amos, crying with the harsh voice of a shepherd from Tekoa, criticizes the household of God because he knows himself to be included in the covenant, and he cannot tolerate the way the chosen people have failed to keep their part of the divine-human bargain.

Eighteenth Day *Read Amos 1–3*

Joel was almost exclusively concerned with the day of the Lord— that set of movements on the part of God when history will be given its meaning, and the covenant will be completed beyond history. Amos is almost exclusively concerned with the moral and social ills of his society.

Surely one of these prophets must be wrong!

By the side-by-side placement of these two books, we discover a paradox of *salvation history*. God is concerned with both now and then. It is not a case of either/or, but of both/and. It is as pernicious to focus on heaven to the exclusion of earth as it is to concentrate upon reform and progress on earth so that heaven loses its absolute significance.

Nineteenth Day *Read Amos 4–6*

Official religion flourishes—but is rotten to the core. Instead of bringing delight to God, pious exercises offend him because the people who burn sacrifices and go through ceremonies are not conscious of guilt or need. They are not presenting themselves to God for forgiveness and rescue, but in their pride they strut to the altar as though they were doing God a favor by coming.

Such going through the motions is futile, but no one who is deeply involved in the fate of the religious institution can see this truth. It takes an outsider, a man with nothing to lose, to demand that the people begin to practice love of their fellows before they can expect God to be pleased with their ceremonies and offerings.

Twentieth Day *Read Amos 7–9*

Amos is so intoxicated with God that he finds divine messages everywhere: in a swarm of locusts, a fire, a workman with plumb line in hand. Interspersed with brief visions growing out of everyday experiences, there are longer divine revelations. Because the people of the covenant have grown deaf and blind, God can no longer speak to society. He must pour his warnings and promises into the ear of "a shepherd, [who] also took care of sycamore-fig trees" (7:14) with the hope that this unofficial spokesman can attract the attention of Israel and gain a new hearing for the word of the covenant.

Once more, we find the now-familiar pattern: fearful punishments are coming, but these are not final and decisive. They constitute a prelude to a restoration that will be decisive and final (9:13–15). Like the strange and illogical pairing of time/eternity in *salvation history*, this wedding between judgment and blessing is basic. To emphasize either at the expense of the other is to distort the message of Scripture. To enter into the covenant, to become the bride of Jehovah, is to enter into that state of judgment/ blessing, and wrath/grace that constitutes the Kingdom of God.

Obadiah

Twenty-first Day *Read Obadiah*

This brief prophetic message hardly deserves to be called a book, yet a second or third reading will confirm the judgment of the ancients who considered it important enough to be revered as Scripture.

The prophecy is both specific and universal. It proclaims the fearful doom of proud Edom, a land perennially at war with Israel. At the same time, it depicts in brilliant colors the downfall of every nation and culture whose trust has been in power, wealth, and allies—and not in Jehovah. Verses 15–16, in particular, speak to our own age as clearly as to Obadiah's time. Throughout the vision, substitute present-day names for ancient ones, and the whole is fearfully contemporary. This remarkable double focus is a distinguishing trait of great biblical prophecy.

Jonah

Twenty-second Day *Read Jonah*

What a fearful thing it is to attempt to get away from God! Jonah discovered that it could not be done. Even in the belly of a great fish, he could cry out to God and be heard in order to be rescued.

That his rescue did not make him perfect is clearly indicated by the cycle of events in Nineveh. Judgment belongs to God, not to man—no matter how dramatic that man's experience of divine transformation may be!

Like certain classical books outside the Bible, this brief, strange message can be read on more than one level. Children enjoy *Gulliver's Travels*, while adults get an entirely different message from it. In the same fashion, babes in the faith will not find in Jonah the transcendent and transforming truths that emerge when the book is read by a long-time faithful servant of the all-powerful Lord.

Micah

Twenty-third Day *Read Micah 1–4*

Official religion is silent and impotent (3:5–7). But an unofficial voice speaks with authority that can stem only from personal encounter with God (1:2; 3:8).

The message of Micah is not new. After having entered into the marriage covenant with Jehovah, Israel has become a faithless bride.

Her playing of the harlot centers on that camouflaged kind of idolatry that consists of worshipping money and power. Therefore God has punished her and will continue to pour out his wrath upon her. In the end, however, a remnant will be gloriously saved (4:7–8).

Can there be a subtle message for us in the fact that it is necessary for one prophet after another to continue to shout the same warning/promise? Are there any new truths about God's relationship with mankind? Since failure has always marked man's striving to keep the covenant, why bother shouting of judgment and of grace from generation to generation to people who are sure to fail and fall?

Twenty-fourth Day *Read Micah 5–7*

Socially speaking, human failure is absolute (7:1–6).

So long as one's eyes focus upon one's fellow men and their total inability to deserve God's goodness or respond faithfully to it, it is hard to see anything but evidence leading to despair. Yet, the very fact that at least one inspired individual is capable of reacting to this situation with despair instead of complacency gives a glimmer of light. God has not deserted his own. The end is not yet.

That end involves both history and beyond history, of course. For the punishing, cleansing, and restoring day of the Lord gives life a dimension that is beyond time and space. This day is somehow linked with the coming of a unique ruler, born of travail and coming out of Bethlehem (5:2–3). Therefore, even in the most hopeless of situations, hope flourishes. God's absolute victory, hinging upon forgiveness, is a certainty (7:18–20).

However different they may be in other respects, the brief books beginning with Hosea have a central characteristic. Although they stress failure, evil, and woe, each ends upon a note of victory. Whatever the evidence to the contrary at a given moment in history, the unfolding of *salvation history* is more certain than the movements of the earth and stars. Meaning will triumph over meaninglessness; hope will be victorious over despair; humans, incapable of achieving godlikeness by striving, will receive it as an unearned gift!

Nahum

Twenty-fifth Day *Read Nahum*

Looking back at that part of the biblical story we have already surveyed, it is startling to see how much of it echoes with war and vio-
lence. From the days of Abraham until the time of Nahum, there was
little peace for the people of the covenant. There was always some
dreadful foe crouching on the horizon, ready to pounce and kill. Time
after time, the chosen of Jehovah were actually attacked, defeated,
plundered, and made captive.

Nahum is aware of this aspect of *salvation history.*

Nevertheless, he is convinced that the more recent enemies will
meet the same fate as all the others. Nineveh, too, will fall—and great
will be the fall thereof! In poetic imagery seldom surpassed even in
the psalms, this obscure prophet praises the awe-full God who is
bringing his heavenly hosts to fight for his own. Confronted by such
an army as only Jehovah can muster, the idol-worshipping culture is
bound to fall.

One solemn question confronts the modern reader: what nation
or nations can we identify as modern Nineveh?

Habakkuk

Twenty-sixth Day *Read Habakkuk*

This little book is actually a series of dialogues between the prophet and
God. Habakkuk raises searching questions, then listens and hears God's
answers. Here, then, are illuminating case histories in answered prayer!

Why do the wicked prosper? Their prosperity is apparent rather
than real, for it is contained within time. Sooner or later every wicked

one will fail—but the servant of God will live, will conquer time and space, as a fruit of faith (2:4). There is no question whatever about God's ultimate victory (2:14); the present material triumph of "nations" is meaningless. They will win the prize, of course; but the prize is empty.

This point of view, which the prophet reaches through struggle and prayer, provides a vantage point for him to see more clearly. Regardless of defeat and despair within our time-linked human lives, faith produces timeless victory within the context of God's all-inclusive Providence (3:17–19).

Zephaniah and Haggai

Twenty-seventh Day *Read Zephaniah and Haggai*

These two brief messages are utterly different, yet they have a common point of reference. Both focus upon the day of the Lord, though in different ways.

Earlier, we have seen that this paradoxical day is both within history and beyond history. Haggai stresses the divine acts of judgment, wrath, and reward that shape the destinies of individual nations; Zephaniah is more concerned with universal aspects of the day.

Both prophets fall back in fear and trembling before the terrible wrath of God. Both insist that, regardless of overwhelming evidence to the contrary, God's chosen will somehow be preserved.

Indeed, this terrible day, which is the cause of so much trepidation, will actually become a source of victorious joy for all who know and serve the Lord! To attempt to press beyond the record of the biblical text is quickly to get into trouble. Just when the day will come upon us, we dare not try to guess. Precisely what its specific details will be, only God knows.

7

Zechariah

Twenty-eighth Day *Read Zechariah 1–8*

"Strange" is likely to be the first adjective that comes to mind when one first looks at the message of Zechariah. This fervent seeker after God has so poetic an imagination that he can hardly speak in ordinary terms. He is so filled with a sense of awful and wonderful things that he snatches images from every hand: a red horse here and four horns there, seven lamps each with seven lips, an enormous flying scroll, and women with wings of storks!

How is one to make heads or tails of this?

Certainly not by trying to interpret each individual bit of symbolism. It is the overall effect that we are seeking—not the many ideas that Zechariah uses as building blocks for his mansion of thought.

Clearly, he is asserting that God rules, the divine covenant stands, and a remnant of the faithful will enter into glory. This conviction is voiced with great fervor and attention-catching figures of speech, partly because it is wholly unbelievable. Nothing in the present situation supports the prophet's conclusions. Viewed from the perspective of common sense, the international scene seems to prove that all God's promises are empty. But Zechariah is looking through faith-oriented eyes, so he shouts his convictions through impassioned lips!

Twenty-ninth Day *Read Zechariah 9–14*

This present epoch is not final. Life's meaning is not to be decided on the basis of what can be seen and touched, bought, sold, and captured. History gives some clues to the riddle of our existence, but the past is not a mold into which the future will be poured. Because God is an active agent in ongoing life, the meaning of life is pregnant with capacity for the absolutely new.

Whatever else he may do, Zechariah clearly looks forward and not backward. He is sure, beyond doubt or argument, that God really will do unbelievably great wonders for the people whom he has chosen. As a result of new outpourings of divine compassion, it will be as though faithless ones never had been rejected (10:6)!

Malachi

Thirtieth Day *Read Malachi*

Everything has been said that can be said. Malachi's messages from on high include the same basic strains that have distinguished poetic and prophetic voices of the past. Institutional religion is rotten to the core: the people chosen and rescued and nurtured by God have failed.

Anybody but God would have given up long before now, but he holds firmly to the covenant and continues to insist that his people accept rescue from their sinfulness. In this darkest of hours he promises a new messenger (3:1–4; 4:5–6).

The stage is set! Out of the centuries-long marriage between Jehovah and Israel, a son is about to be born! The new Elijah, so long anticipated, will turn the world upside down, and from the barren soil of rebellious human hearts, he will prepare fallow ground ready to receive divine seed with which to produce a magnificent harvest!

Matthew and Mark

The New Testament

Long ago, God entered into a covenant with Abraham and his descendants. Although active partners in the contractual relationship, these people, "set apart" from the rest of mankind, did not initiate the covenant. The unfolding of their verbal agreement (testament) over a period of centuries forms Act I of *salvation history*. As recorded and interpreted by inspired lawgivers and kings, by priests of the institution, and prophets outside it, the unfolding development in this special divine-human compact forms the literary body we have inherited as the Old Testament.

Act I reaches its climax in the making ready of Israel to bear fruit. The covenant is a marriage contract between God and the people whom he called to be his bride. In due time, a Son will be born—incorporating in one flesh both divinity and humanity, thereby bridging the gap between Creator and creatures. The marriage covenant was drawn up by God as a prelude to the birth of the Son.

Born of a virgin through the agency of God's Holy Spirit, Jesus partakes fully of the qualities of man. In his role as man, he voluntarily gives his life for everyone. Each person who accepts the gift he offers is "made new," that is, enters a radically altered relationship with God the Father.

The challenge to strive for godliness through keeping the law of Moses is withdrawn. Rather, it is superseded. From now on, men may accept the substitutionary death of Christ as a way of "dying" to their sins. The role of the Law shifts to that of an awakener and a convicter, serving to convince people that they need to accept divine rescue.

That rescue is offered and conferred through the paradox, the mystery, and the miracle of the Cross. Although Jesus Christ died upon it, all people may make that death their own, so that he and the world are "crucified" to one another (Gal. 6:14). Such a severing of ties between an individual and the world is a particular instance of the general cosmic victory won on Calvary, in which the God-man "disarmed the principalities and powers and made a public example of them" (Col. 2:15). Freed from sin through participation in the death of Jesus Christ (Rom. 6:6), his followers become literally and not simply figuratively *new persons*.

It is for the production of such new persons that the Good News is proclaimed. The story of the coming into the world of the Son of the covenant, together with witness about the meaning of that coming by a few who were close to it in history, forms the literary amplification of the New Covenant that is commonly called the New Testament of our Lord and Savior Jesus Christ.

Abraham's blood descendants are human partners of God in the original covenant, or testament. The new one radically alters the terms, so that belief in Jesus Christ is the condition for human participation—all believers now playing the role that was formerly reserved for Abraham's seed. Precisely what tangible human system is formed by all believers is a vexatious central question of the faith. Clearly, the ideal spiritual church is not identical with any visible church or body of churches. Yet these finite systems are the guardians, transmitters, and interpreters of the New Testament, just as the historic Israel was the guardian, transmitter, and interpreter of the original covenant.

To read the New Testament as literature is instructive but not necessarily fruitful in more than surface fashion. Faith, in the inclusive sense of recognized spiritual guilt blended with eagerness to accept unearned divine rescue, is essential to meeting the Savior in the pages of the Book that centers in him. Hence, the Book that is for all mankind is also, in another sense, private and secret. The depth and duration of the dialogue depends upon what each reader brings to the meeting—the self presented for encounter with the Savior to whom the entire Old Testament points and of whom the entire New Testament witnesses.

Although the New Testament contains fewer words than the Old Testament, we shall devote five of our twelve months to it. On occasion, you will wish to reread Old Testament passages in order to get an entirely new message; again, you will wish to discover fresh relationships between the message of a day's passage and other portions of the New Testament. Comparatively brief readings in the biblical text itself, therefore, invite you to look far and wide for correlations, fresh revelations, and new interpretations of passages upon which you center for a day.

Matthew

For this gospel writer, Jesus of Nazareth is supremely and superbly the King, before whom all believers prostrate themselves. Although born in obscurity, Mary's son is also the Son of David. This title, established by Matthew's elaborate genealogy, is used more frequently in his gospel than in any other. From the cradle to the grave, literally and not figuratively, persons and circumstances proclaim the royalty of Jesus. He is revered as King by wise men from the East. Jesus deliberately uses the language of authority to assert his supremacy over the law of Moses. His triumphal entry into Jerusalem is that of a conqueror. Even though it is bestowed in mockery, he accepts the title of King in his encounter with the representative of Roman power. And it is as King that he dies upon the Cross.

Matthew's special interpretation is an appeal to the Jews that they hail Jesus of Nazareth as their King. More than any other, this gospel deserves to be subtitled "An Appeal to the People of the Covenant." The Jewishness of Matthew's report is basic to its structure and content. More than a dozen times, the evangelist specifies ties between prophetic voices from Israel's past and events or emphases in the proclaiming through Jesus.

Faithfully reporting the rejection of Jesus by leaders of Israel's religious institution, Matthew yet believes that Abraham's descendants can be persuaded to see and to know. Therefore, his account is more closely related to the approach of a teacher than of an evangelist. More than any other gospel writer, Matthew has organized large bodies of instruction by Jesus, so that they come to us in the form of lengthy sermons and messages: the Sermon on the Mount (chaps. 5–7); responsibilities of apostles (10); parables of the kingdom (13); qualities of the New Life (18); and a foreshadowing of Act III of the divine-human drama—the coming of the kingdom (24–25).

To be most effectively prepared for response to Matthew's outpouring of the Good News of the New Covenant, readers must approach it in precisely our present mood—satiated, almost, with the story of God's dealing with his chosen people and almost bursting with impatience for the coming of the long-promised Son who will unite, in one person, the spirit of God the Father and the flesh of all mankind.

First Day *Read Matthew 1–2*

Although some modern persons find it hard to accept, ancient thought saw no difficulty in using numbers as well as words to convey meaning. More than any other gospel writer, Matthew is skilled in such ways of expressing complex ideas. He reports three messages to Joseph, three temptations of Jesus, three denials of Peter, three prayers in Gethsemane, and three questions of Pilate. There are three crosses, three hours of darkness, and three days of guarding the tomb. Although each expresses other ideas as well, every such occurrence of "three" also points to the Holy Trinity—God in three persons.

In addition to the number three, Matthew makes great use of the perfect number, seven. He reports Jesus' warning that an evicted evil spirit will bring seven others back with him (12:45) and specifies his Master's use of seven loaves (15:34) to yield seven baskets of fragments (15:17). Chapter 13 gives seven parables of the kingdom, while chapter 23 lists seven woes. So whether the twentieth-century interpreter can find it there or not, there is a hidden message in the fact that the genealogy of Jesus is reported in three sections, each of which includes twice seven generations.

Lacking written vowels and employing letters of the alphabet for numerals, the Hebrew language indicated "David" by DWD. Taken as numerals rather than letters, this cluster of symbols has the meaning "14." Therefore, in order to express the hidden truth that Jesus of Nazareth is the Son of David, Matthew lists ancestors in groups of fourteen—divided to form a trinity of witnesses!

That the materials of Matthew's history should lend themselves to such testimony about his King is to be accepted rather than explained. Anything that is explained is thereby reduced to human dimensions— so it is faith rather than logic that rejoices, because everything in Israel's history testifies that Mary's son is also the Son of David.

Jesus Christ, entirely divine and altogether human, is a fruit of the covenant. Biologically, however, he is generated by the Holy Spirit. That such would be the case, Isaiah announced long ago (Isa. 7:14). Full understanding of the prophet's message did not come until after believers made a radical reorganization of their belief, in the transforming light shed by Calvary and the empty tomb.

Yet it is not simply a genealogy (history) that identifies Jesus of Nazareth as the King. Men from a distance—wise ones from the East—have keener vision than most close at hand. Jerusalem's dedication to the covenant and the absorption of her wise and good ones in the minutiae of interpretation, cloud her eyes with a cataract. Those most adept in handling an inherited system may be the slowest to find in it radical new patterns of meaning. The fulfillment of numerous Old Testament prophecies shouted, "This is the long-promised Savior!" Yet functionaries of the established religious institution looked and looked and saw only a carpenter's baby.

Second Day *Read Matthew 3–4*

One or two announcements (genealogy and wise men) of God's supreme work are not enough. There must be proclamations through every medium likely to convince the people that Jesus of Nazareth and the Christ of God are one and the same.

Chapters 1 and 2 make that identification through genealogy, visitation by divine messengers (angels), fulfillment of prophecy, and recognition by wise men. It would seem that God has done more than we could reasonably expect, but no avenue can be neglected.

Accordingly, God sends a special herald, John the Baptizer, whose great central role is to arouse public interest, then point to Jesus. His announcement, sealed by baptism, is confirmed by still another supernatural messenger—the Spirit of God who appears to human eyes in the form of a dove.

With identification of the Savior completed so that even the dullest hardly fail to recognize and venerate their King, the drama of his work is interrupted by the brash intrusion of that chief antagonist: Satan. This is his last chance. Unless he can persuade Jesus to turn aside from the path that leads to Calvary, evil will be defeated, and the battle for the souls of men will be permanently decided. Satan therefore exerts his supreme effort (in a trinity of temptations). He appeals to the human needs and wants of the God-man but absolutely fails to sway him.

This hurdle passed, the Jesus of history formally launches his work by the calling of disciples and starting a visible crusade.

Third Day *Read Matthew 5–6*

The Sermon on the Mount is the largest organized body of formal teaching by Jesus. Because it seems so practical by comparison with visions and angels and miracles, it has been elevated in recent centuries of common-sense religious faith. Many have treated the sermon as the heart of the gospel, and from it have extracted a social gospel of change on the human level designed (however disguised) to enable us to build the kingdom here on earth with our own hands.

Viewed from some perspectives, the sermon actually seems to present a sensible pattern of moral and ethical conduct, conformity to which makes it possible for us to live up to the requirements of Jesus. That is to say, the new code of conduct here defined by Jesus is adopted as a substitute for the law of Moses. Though the two patterns differ greatly, they are alike in that each is viewed as offering a way to spiritual victory through discipline and regulated conduct.

Beautiful and instructive though it is, in the context of Matthew's account of the King's coming, the Sermon on the Mount is not offered as an amended version of the law of Moses. No substitute for the requirement that sinners surrender as a prelude to acceptance of divine rescue, the sermon itself echoes throughout with impossible demands. Instead of comforting, it convicts—persuading us that we cannot possibly meet its terms, so we must accept grace rather than achieve goodness.

Murder, adultery, divorce, profanity, justice, and love are radically redefined here. The demand is for perfection, according to a divine rather than a human standard. Total commitment to God, with absolute loyalty, is required. Here is no call to imitate an ideal man, but a challenge to measure one's self by a divine, and hence utterly impossible, standard. All those who see themselves in the light of that standard can only kneel before their King and cry, "Have mercy on me, a sinner!"

Fourth Day *Read Matthew 7–8*

It is not pious mouthing of "Lord, Lord," that opens the door to heaven—but a surrendered life. Always, the direction of that surrender must be toward a high and holy God who demands the impossible.

So paradoxical and astonishing is the demand/promise of the Sermon on the Mount that "insiders" are likely to reject it automatically. So Matthew describes a series of "outsiders" who act in surrendered obedience and thereby become recipients of supernatural power. These outsiders are a leper, a fisherman's mother-in-law, a Roman centurion, and a pair of Gadarene demoniacs. Meanwhile, scribes and disciples alike betray their lack of capacity to accept the highest and best gifts of the King. This perpetual failure on the part of those whom human logic judges as the best of men is part of the scandal of the Good News proclaimed in the life and through the words of Jesus Christ.

Fifth Day *Read Matthew 9*

Mighty and unexplainable demonstrations continue. All distinctions between physical and spiritual healing, "making whole," vanish. Jesus demonstrates his capacity to rescue any part-person and restore him to wholeness. Recipients continue to be common folk and out-siders such as tax collectors and rank sinners, while upright and devout leaders of the community and the religious institution stand back, challenging Jesus and rejecting his offer of mighty works.

Surveying the evidence and unable to refute popular claims that wonders are being worked, the Pharisees reject Jesus' claim that he represents God. They are therefore left with but one alternative: this worker of wonders must be a representative of Satan.

"Who is this man?" remains a central question to which every-one who encounters Jesus of Nazareth must give his or her own per-sonal answer.

Sixth Day *Read Matthew 10–11*

From an informal beginning, the Jesus movement has become an organized campaign. There are no strings attached to Jesus' promises or qualifications limiting the recipients. At first look, this seems strangely inconsistent with a clearly defined mission to the Jews. In spite of the fact that Jewish scholarship and piety are offended by Jesus' claims and performances, it remains true that Israel constitutes the fertile soil that was cultivated for centuries in order that it might be ready to receive the new divine revelation embodied in Jesus Christ.

All these things—and all events whatever—are included in the context of Providence, not chance or blind fate. For a disciple to rec-ognize this is to enter a state of absolute confidence. Defeat is not an alternative; whatever may occur, the will of the Father is actively at work, moving forward. Victory is guaranteed and can sometimes be seen dimly from a distance even through the feeble eyes of mortals.

Thus, the imprisonment of John and the rejection of Jesus by the scribes and Pharisees and entire cities are no causes for despair. Of course, only those wise with the wisdom of God can hear the truths proclaimed through the voices of mockers and challengers. But to listen with the inner ear is to hear promises of the covenant with Abraham repeated and reinterpreted in every aspect of the human life of the divine-human Son, whose coming marks the drawing up of a New Covenant.

Seventh Day *Read Matthew 12*

Christians find it easy to become self-righteous by condemning Jewish legalism. Laws of the Temple and customs of the synagogue, seen from the perspective of a Christian culture, are obviously man-shaped even though adopted in obedience to divine directives. Jesus' creative and spontaneous reshaping of customs and laws, seen from our point of view, is so laudable that it is hard to discover how anyone could fail to applaud.

But matters are not quite the same when our laws, our traditions, and our institutions are involved. Authorities today are no more eager for disruptive and threatening change than were authorities then. You and I are prone to cry "Beelzebub!" when it is our system of values, our set of standards, that is challenged.

This chapter uses specific practices rooted in a particular culture to illustrate the universal principle that encounter between the human and the divine is *necessarily* disruptive. Whenever individuals or their social institutions really and not theoretically meet God, the alternatives are clear: traumatic change or rejection of the divine revelation.

Eighth Day *Read Matthew 13*

As a way of expressing God's truth so that ordinary people can understand, a parable illustrates the paradox that it always presents. Thus, a parable is uniquely fluid. The meaning conveyed through it is not automatic and constant. Rather, it is a variable, shaped largely by the human recipient, the personality who constitutes soil into which seeds of divine revelation are tossed.

Concepts uttered through parables are revealed only to those whose minds are prepared to receive highest truth. For this reason, misunderstanding is a recurrent gospel motif. Recipients of bread from heaven fail to understand the meaning of the miracle (16:5–12). The disciples themselves completely disregard the concept of children (18:1–6; 19:13–15). Zebedee's wife asks rewards for her sons right after Jesus' statement about the Crucifixion (20:20–21). Scriptural messages about resurrection are meaningless until after Jesus has demonstrated victory over death (22:29).

Truth proclaimed may become truth distorted by the recipients. It is a high-level message of this sort, perpetually proclaimed in public but often widely misunderstood, that is offered through Jesus' private instruction of members of the inner circle. Discipleship is a continuous program of discipline calculated to increase capacity to receive the messages of God.

We modern Americans are prone to think of discipleship in terms of *doing*. But here (and everywhere in the New Testament) it is *being* that comes first. The chief work of a disciple is to seek eagerly and obey joyfully, in order to grow in capacity to produce a crop from seeds that are scattered from above, without the disciple's doing anything to initiate the shower.

Ninth Day *Read Matthew 14–15*

Events in the career of Jesus the Teacher, absolute revealer of God the Father, move forward with the relentlessness of a Greek tragedy. Whatever may happen must contribute to the climax, that is, every incident reported in the Gospels is keyed to the announcement and interpretation of the New Covenant. From the womb, Jesus Christ is headed for self-sacrifice. He came to give himself as a divine-human sacrifice, providing rescue for all those who will participate in the marvelous feeding that he provides in the wilderness of society.

It is futile, therefore, to speculate what the outcome might have been had events been ordered otherwise. What if Herod had not been so weak a king? What if John had lived to head a movement whose growth might have kept Jesus in obscurity? What if Jesus' move into the spotlight made empty by John's death had resulted in acceptance by the authorities instead of their rejection?

All such speculations are empty. Every development and each encounter underscores the basic message that God was in Christ, who came into the stream of humanity to effect reconciliation between the Creator and creatures made in the divine image. Always, such reconciliation is accepted only by the consciously alienated: "the lame, the blind, the crippled, the mute" (15:30).

Tenth Day *Read Matthew 16–17*

It doesn't matter if one is a scribe, a Pharisee, a Sunday school class teacher, or an executive of a denomination, anyone who sets out to "test" Jesus Christ is restricted to a single result. The conditions of the test preclude the recognition and the acceptance of the transforming truth from God. In this sense a vigorous, not a passive, faith is essential to grasping the Good News. Not simply skepticism but absence of vital faith renders the soil of the personality sterile and incapable of multiplying the seeds scattered on it by God's perennial messengers.

Every "sign" is fluid and paradoxical, conveying one meaning to the skeptic and various other meanings to believers of various levels of faith and experience.

Much of the time, Jesus' most intimate ones are far from understanding! Even the great confession of Peter represents but a momentary interlude of fertility; there will be future periods in which the "rock" will be sterile—incapable of nurturing seeds and causing them to sprout. Indeed, Peter's moment of illumination is followed by what (to us) seems almost unbelievable blindness.

Let every seeker beware of adopting a patronizing attitude toward Peter. He represents not the worst but the best of which humanity is capable. To reduce the New Covenant to a system that is wholly understandable, so that it makes sense by our human standards, is to repudiate it—voluntarily to be counted among this "unbelieving and perverse generation." God chose to offer salvation in an utterly incredible fashion; failure to register distress (17:23), to act as though the self-giving of the God-man is reasonable, is to substitute our own system of achievement for the divine rescue that gives life to the New Covenant.

Eleventh Day *Read Matthew 18–19*

Jesus the King offers citizenship in a realm so alien to any human system that direct description of it is impossible. Its nature is dimly hinted at by the fact that its values and conditions of human existence are turned inside out in complete reversal of the established order. In the kingdom, it is not princes and rulers who are great, but those who are as humble as children.

Because the kingdom defies human power to analyze and master, candidates for citizenship must meet conditions that are demanding to the point of utter absurdity. For example, instead of exhibiting "perfect forgiveness" through seven instances of it, seekers for the kingdom must forgive "seventy times seven." Instead of meeting the letter of the law concerning divorce, they must go to the radical extreme of regarding a perfectly routine divorce action as adultery—punishable by stoning. Instead of striving for goodness through living up to the commandments inherited from old, pilgrims toward the eternal city must exhibit absolute love in all of their relationships.

It is this basic factor of the *impossible* in Jesus' call that upsets everything reasonable and causes the (seemingly) last to be (actually) first, while those regarded as first are really last in the kingdom. No system of values that society can devise is exalted enough to remain stable in the utter transformation that characterizes the society of the redeemed.

Twelfth Day *Read Matthew 20*

To say what the kingdom of heaven *is* puts upon language a strain it cannot bear. The most that can be done is to suggest what the kingdom *is like*. As reported by Matthew, Jesus consistently teaches that the kingdom is so absolutely different from human society that many conditions will be totally reversed and "the last will be first, and the first will be last" (16, 26–27).

Similar "reversals" reported elsewhere in this gospel involve substitutions between the destitute and the prosperous (5:3), mourners and the comfortable (5:4), things hidden and things revealed (10:26), prosperity and want (25:29). This kind of scandalous logic is involved in the crucifixion of the King. Everything in these ideas jars us. They may so repel us that we refuse to accept such notions, repeating the conduct of Zebedee's wife who listened to Jesus' description of his glory in verse 19 ("to be mocked and flogged and crucified") and promptly begged him to give her sons temporal power in the kingdom. She, who had so many opportunities to hear and understand, failed utterly. Reversing that situation, two blind men seized upon a chance encounter to succeed absolutely in accepting the most sublime gift Jesus can confer: divine mercy.

Thirteenth Day *Read Matthew 21*

Paradox, contradiction, and scandal continue.

For a king to ride on an ass is unheard of; the horse is the animal of royalty. Hence the triumphal entry witnesses that the King of whom Matthew writes is no ordinary one—but a King whose sovereignty will be demonstrated to all the world through his death as a malefactor.

Hailed by the masses and rejected by religious leaders, Jesus demonstrates his authority to exceed that of the Temple. Verbally, he underscores the paradox by which "children and infants" can speak more wisely than learned men (cf. Ps. 8). Dramatically blasting a barren fig tree that stands for fruitless official religion, he underscores the vital role of faith as a factor in human dialogue with God.

Through every medium—direct words, parables, and dramatic lessons—he underscores the warning that those in the best position to recognize God's supreme messenger are likely to be last to the identify and revere him. This basic human blindness (inherent in our status as creatures and no more potent in ancient Israel than any other era, including our own) once more demonstrates our need for a Savior. We cannot save ourselves; the institutions and processes that we develop in our zeal to know and serve God always become stumbling blocks.

Fourteenth Day *Read Matthew 22*

The kingdom of heaven, that spiritual realm in which the Lordship of Christ is definitive, is the goal toward which all creation moves. This is the destination of every Christian pilgrim. Yet even our Master himself cannot directly communicate its nature to us because of our limitations. Even the basic human institution, the family, does not carry over into the kingdom in anything like its present form.

No wonder religious institutions are arch foes and bitter critics of God's supreme messenger! By nature, institutions (of whatever type, not just the religious ones) are conservative. They exist to develop and perpetuate structure and system. Society could not continue for one generation without the conserving and directing influence of its institutions. In one form or other, men must pay taxes to some Caesar; that is one of the prices of being human.

Nowhere is the basic dualism—the dividedness—of people more vividly demonstrated. We are made in the divine image but have feet of clay. Our heads are lifted toward the clouds, but our feet are firmly planted on the earth.

We cannot get along without religious systems that include the law of Moses or some equivalent. We cannot function as corporate seekers for God without a temple or its equivalent. Scribes and Pharisees and Sadducees of some variety are absolutely essential. Nevertheless, whenever and wherever the divine stirs in the souls of men, the religious experience comes into conflict with institutions and authorities whose work is vital to the engendering of such experience.

Whether by means of the temple or revival meetings, we cannot save ourselves. All the bridges that we build share the limitedness of the builder. Ideally, the church is of God—but in all its concrete manifestations, absolutely essential though they are, the institution is finite. Each of us is a creature; our most sublime religious systems partake of our creaturehood. If we are to reach the kingdom, it will not be along any highway of our construction but through divine salvation that makes of us what we can never become through striving.

Fifteenth Day *Read Matthew 23*

Pride in its many forms is an inescapable human weakness; indeed, it may be that, if original sin can be named at all, it is best entitled "pride." Not even in "the highest and best" religious circles, but especially there, pride takes root and flourishes. Those who ought to be fully occupied prostrating themselves before God inevitably take their eyes off divinity long enough to compare themselves (favorably) with the rest of humanity—ceasing, in the blindness of pride, to become candidates for rescue and elevating themselves as having achieved righteousness.

This unparalleled chapter of woes pronounced upon the most godly people of Jesus' day is among the most misunderstood in Matthew. You and I are prone to commit the very error Jesus condemns. We find it dreadfully easy to measure ourselves by these ancient blind ones and congratulate ourselves on our keener eyes. Arrogant in our certainty of twenty-twenty spiritual vision, we are ready to kill and crucify once more—in the name of Christ.

Until we center our attention upon the Father, whose glory reveals us tarnished, we lack that eager humility that is prerequisite to recognizing the Son when he is met face to face.

Sixteenth Day *Read Matthew 24–25*

In the drama of *salvation history*, Act I is the period of the marriage covenant through which a particular people, Israel, become the bride of Jehovah. Act II deals with the coming of the Son of that union—combining divinity and humanity in one person in order to effect reconciliation between the Creator and fallen creatures. Act III concerns the spiritual kingdom where God rules supreme over a society of redeemed souls.

Although this climax of the process for which the world was created has its roots in history, it cannot be contained here. Because it is spiritual and not material, heavenly and not earthly, the most that mortals can do is dimly grasp a few vague outlines. We know from passages such as these something of the principles that will prevail—but we are here repeatedly warned against too great concern with details of the kingdom. We know that justice will be done, but not how. We know that there will be rewards and punishments, but we cannot even imagine what specific ones God has prepared for souls without bodies.

Nevertheless, a cardinal aspect of the Good News emerges here: THE MOST IMPORTANT BUSINESS OF THIS LIFE IS TO PRE-

PARE FOR THE LIFE TO COME. Nothing that one can win or do or achieve on this earth is of more than fleeting consequence—while, through the work of our Savior, the eternity for which this life is a prelude offers meaning and glory and enduringness to once-finite creatures.

Seventeenth Day *Read Matthew 26*

Outraged religious leaders press their demand for blood. Here is a supreme paradox of the Good News—so incredibly creative that it scandalizes all who have status to defend. Man cannot long be at peace with the divine Savior. Confronted by his challenge, we must either accept transforming grace or send the God-man to his death. Even the most intimate disciple cannot, in his own strength, go for even a day without denying him.

All these factors and the specific events that reveal them are necessary and inevitable in the sense that they are basic to the divine-human situation. *Salvation history*, clearly delineated in the Scriptures that form the Christian's Old Testament, reveals man's alienation from God and moves toward a reunion. In order that the Scriptures should be fulfilled (54), (i.e., their essential message revealed in such fashion that we can see and understand), it was necessary ("written into the stars") that divinity should suffer and die for the sake of humanity.

Eighteenth Day *Read Matthew 27–28*

The son of Mary—flesh of her flesh, bone of her bone, and therefore brother of every mortal—is sold into death. At the same time, the Son of God, wholly divine, mounts the cross on Calvary. If the incredible story of Matthew had to be condensed into a single phrase, it would be the charge on which his Lord was executed: "THIS IS JESUS THE KING OF THE JEWS" (27:37).

Divinity incarnate in humanity suffered and died in order to accomplish for mortal creatures those results open only to the Creator.

This is the glory, the mystery, the paradox, and the miracle of events that produced the New Covenant between God and his children.

In the fearful events of the day that ushered in the new epoch for all humanity, not simply Israel, one outsider suddenly saw that Jesus of Nazareth was truly God's Son (27:54). For most, however, including his apostles, it took the empty tomb to reveal that their Master actually could not be restrained by death. Even dimly seen from a distance, this central fact of existence literally ushers each believer across the threshold into a new age—a radically altered order of existence, prepared before the foundation of the world to receive and shelter those who dare let God do the impossible for them through Christ.

Mark

Mark's account of the establishment and meaning of the New Covenant is often considered the least difficult of the Gospels to understand.

It is true that this evangelist uses short words and brief sentences. It is the shortest of the Gospels and employs fewer technical symbols than any other. It is far less "Jewish" than Matthew's account.

However, any notion of simplicity in ideas vanishes as soon as a reader ceases skimming familiar words without really noticing them. The first words announce Mark's purpose: to tell "the gospel [Good News] about Jesus Christ, the Son of God."

The gospel according to Mark, thought to be the earliest, tells the story of Jesus of Nazareth, who is also the everlasting Christ—the same story told by Matthew, Luke, and John. Because Mark's gospel is less poetic, more plain and direct, it stirs us differently than the other Gospels, even though the rescue we are here offered is identical with that of the other accounts.

Nineteenth Day *Read Mark 1*

Jesus of Nazareth, whom a few clear-sighted ones recognized and hailed as the long-awaited Christ of God, served as an inlet through which the Spirit of God could pour into human society. Nothing that the Son does is apart from the will of the Father. It is the Holy Spirit who serves as active agent in the baptism that identifies a man as God; it is the same Spirit who launches the temptation in the wilderness.

Action and urgency are basic in this account; there is no time to lose. Centuries of preparation are coming to fruition; the meaning of human existence must crystallize, not simply in the life of one man, but in a few years of his life. Everything moves forward in relentless fashion. The word *immediately* occurs nine times in this brief opening chapter; notice the occasions and what they mean.

Urgency is the keynote because " 'The time has come...[and] the kingdom of God is near' " (v. 15). The challenge of John must be acted upon now or the opportunity to repent and believe will forever be lost. Neither individuals nor societies have all the time there is. None can believe and be made whole yesterday or tomorrow, only now. The meaning of my life—and the significance of the whole creation—trembles in the balance *now*. In the moment of my encounter with Jesus Christ, I can be freed from the tyranny of evil spirits and cleansed of the spiritual leprosy that makes me loathsome to myself as well as to others. But the time of decision cannot be prolonged at my pleasure; Jesus is moving swiftly toward a predetermined goal. Nothing can persuade him to stop or even to pause longer than the Spirit prescribes; I must act in the light that I have now, if I expect ever to act at all.

Twentieth Day *Read Mark 2–3*

Jesus' mighty works, of which forgiveness of sins is chief, are without parallel. No one—then or now—has ever seen the like. As clearly as any section of any gospel, these chapters challenge the whole concept of "growing more like Jesus." The gulf between the Son of Man and all humanity requires the believer to accept rescue rather than simply strive to be Christlike. Yet this central truth of the Good News is not acceptable to all who hear it; only the spiritually sick who know they are sick are capable of responding.

For those who represent established patterns of piety, the mighty works of Jesus offend and disrupt. No age-hardened wineskin can expand enough to keep from bursting. We are quick enough to see that Sabbath customs of the ancient Pharisees restrict rather than liberate, but we are slow to apply this conclusion to ourselves and our codes.

Given the creative and disruptive impact of divinity upon humanity, it is no wonder that friends and foes alike should be aghast. Confronted by Jesus Christ but unable to see him as Son of God, we conclude that the poor fellow must be out of his mind.

Twenty-first Day *Read Mark 4–5*

All of us are potential citizens of the Kingdom over which Jesus Christ reigns, but it is not easy for those who want citizenship to meet the terms. Chapter 5 consists of case histories that have one feature in common. Each underscores the paradox that the unlikely candidates, humanly speaking, have the best chance of acceptance. Outsiders who are conscious of their alienation from God are most likely to understand and act upon the divine offer of rescue.

Chapter 4 has made it abundantly clear that states of "understanding" and "misunderstanding" (acceptance and rejection) are not automatic or constant. Instead, the organized system of experiences, values, beliefs, and hopes that makes up a human individual is variable and fluid. Even when a message comes directly from the lips of Jesus Christ (perhaps especially when this is the case), the meaning of the message depends upon the outlook of the hearer. The most likely candidates for great gifts, the disciples, center their attention on the riddle of who their wonder-working Master is, while a master of the synagogue, whom logic would label a foe of the Good News, seeks in such eager belief that he finds the gift of new life.

Twenty-second Day *Read Mark 6*

Urgency and mighty works mark the witness not only of Jesus but also of his disciples. The confident expectation that great things are going to be done by God for his glory, right now, is a necessary condition for driving out demons and healing souls and bodies.

John the Baptist, coworker and herald of the Messiah, was sometimes regarded as the long-anticipated deliverer. His death heightened the climate of crisis and made it imperative that Jesus plainly announce himself as the new Moses. He did so both in the dramatic feeding of the five thousand that reenacted the feeding during the Exodus in the wilderness and in his demonstration of mastery over the sea, that ancient symbol of death.

As a result of these two spectacular acts, multitudes of common folk understood the message. In mingled joy and expectancy, they rushed to accept divine power made tangible through marvelous healings.

Twenty-third Day *Read Mark 7–8*

Official religion always finds it hard to continue paying homage to God the Creator. Instead of seeking enlargement and transformation (for self, the institution, and society) it is easy for the priest—by whatever title he is called—to center upon guarding and transmitting good things from the past. Many Christian groups fall into this error, by glorifying the first century (as seen dimly through the glasses of time) and thus making it, rather than Christ, the goal of religious experience.

Regardless of how much heavenly bread may be offered by Jesus Christ, all the proud who have status to defend will continue to test and question. Signs from heaven do not communicate divine truth to persons who see themselves as inheritors and guardians of all truth. Such "yeast of the Pharisees" (8:15) ferments and rises through the whole personality, creating the only incurable kind of spiritual blindness—that variety which persuades the afflicted one that his vision is keener than that of other folk.

Twenty-fourth Day *Read Mark 9*

Mighty portents continue. Elijah and Moses add their voices to those of men and events witnessing about Jesus. Still apostles do not grasp the meaning of the forthcoming victory over death. To make matters worse, they hesitate to ask for more explanations.

169

The tongue-tied disciples are in sharp contrast with the father of a demon-possessed boy. This man wavers, too, but his wavering is positive and that of the disciples is negative. Their reluctance to ask questions seems to stem from pride rather than devotion, since Jesus gives them (and us) an indirect rebuke by elevating the importance of childlike dependence and trust.

Twenty-fifth Day *Read Mark 10*

Laws are given, not as standards of righteousness, but as points of departure in striving for righteousness. Measured by the higher standard of Jesus, those who succeed in keeping the letter of Moses' law still are dismal failures. Even warned of this, the disciples once more fail the test of ambition. They remain greedy and blind.

The healing of a blind man, after another warning against materialism, shouts that spiritual blindness is not cured by striving but by believing in Jesus as Christ, in order to accept the great gifts he offers.

Twenty-sixth Day *Read Mark 11*

Eagerness for the Messiah's coming, as a prelude to an earthly state of peace and prosperity, is a guarantee of disappointment. For Christ came into the world to bring a sword rather than a dove. Both by word and example, he demonstrated that prayer is powerful, working to transform people's hearts and society's institutions.

By nature, the Savior confronts and challenges. He requires men to take a stand for him or against him. Neutrality, complacency, satisfaction with the status quo, all are human defenses against the disruptive, traumatic, and challenging effects initiated by the Savior.

Twenty-seventh Day *Read Mark 12*

Part of the paradox of the Incarnation centers in the differences between our own reactions and our judgments about the reactions of others. It is always easy to see the blindness and folly of others. Surveying the actions of first-century leaders, it seems impossible that they should have failed to recognize and revere the Christ. As participants instead of observers, we are prone to engage in the very rejection that we so readily denounce in others.

Because in God's realm life rules death, it is the spirit—the living principle—of the law that we must seek. This precludes any fixed and final interpretations, any ethical and moral standards that are absolute for all times and conditions. We must perpetually welcome reevaluation of values, creative transformation of attitudes and practices as a fruit of encounter with our Creator.

Twenty-eighth Day *Read Mark 13*

The accomplishment of God's purpose for mankind, in such fashion that finite creatures can perceive and understand this fruition of creation, is necessarily a source of marvel and bewilderment. No aspect of Jesus' message is more important than the proclamation that human existence is meaningful and not meaningless, because it is rooted in a heavenly kingdom. No phase of his promise lends itself to greater diversity of interpretation.

Watch is the key word here. By cultivating a mood of attuned expectancy, believing seekers prepare themselves to receive whatever it may please God to send, whenever it is God's will to send it. This is the most that anyone can do to hasten the coming of the kingdom—personally, or in society.

Twenty-ninth Day *Read Mark 14*

By her dramatic action at dinner, Mary of Bethany proclaims Jesus of Nazareth to be the long-expected Anointed One—the Messiah. In some respects this marks the end of the series of events through which Jesus Christ is announced to the people whose covenant served to prepare them to receive him.

Yet lack of understanding—or partial understanding—continues even among the disciples. Fresh from the supper that is to stand in relation to the Passover meal as the New Covenant stands to the Old Covenant, Peter and James and John fail and fall.

At the height of the dramatic interlude leading up to the divine self-giving that offers salvation to all, the chief apostles demonstrate that they still need rescue. They are mortals, prone to all mistakes of mortality. After walking with the Savior for months, they remain incapable of saving themselves. Mercy, not justice, is needed if any expect to hear, "Well done, good and faithful servant!"

Thirtieth Day *Read Mark 15–16*

The chief priests, who are chief among the mockers, succeed by a perverse kind of genius to emphasize a central aspect of the New Covenant. They offer to believe in Jesus of Nazareth as the Christ, provided that he come down from the Cross and save himself. That is precisely what the Savior could not do and still be true to his saving role.

Without comprehending that the voluntary death of Jesus Christ has begun the new age, a handful of faithful ones remain to pay a last tribute of love. At the empty tomb, however, their Master looks different—and everything under the sun has changed. For these new persons, there is a new universe whose most incredible feature is that the Savior does for them what they never could do for themselves. To accept the conditions of citizenship and enter the kingdom by faith is to become a cosigner of the New Covenant.

Luke and John

Luke

Luke, a gentile physician writing for gentile readers, has a style and an approach all his own. He tells the same story as Matthew, Mark, and John, but because the man through whom the story comes is different from other gospel writers, his report differs from theirs.

Traditionally, the calf has been used to symbolize Luke's gospel. It is the animal used in major sacrifices, and for Luke the supreme fact about Jesus Christ is that he voluntarily gave himself as a sacrifice for all people.

This gospel is, in a special sense, a book of Jesus' parables. Luke not only reports many more of them than do Matthew and Mark, he deliberately emphasizes this special medium through which deep spiritual truths can be explained simply. Throughout your reading, notice that Luke repeatedly stresses the vital role of the listener. The precise message that one gets from a parable, Luke shows us over and over, depends upon the background from which that parable is approached.

Jesus Christ himself, truth incarnate, means many things to many people. Part of the work of the witness—whether New Testament writer, Protestant reformer, or twenty-first-century evangelist—is to select and shape the vehicles through which he attempts to pour the truth that is inside him but which must be translated into words or musical notes, or visual patterns before it can be made public.

In his ardor to pour out for mankind the universal message that Jesus Christ, Lamb of the World, offers salvation to all who will accept it, Luke makes prodigal use of symbols. While his literary style is not so scintillating as that of John and his metaphors are not so blinding, it takes but a few hours to see the grandeur of his words on two or three levels of meaning.

Whatever the means used—history, parable, symbol—the end purpose is the same: to point all eyes to the central cross on Calvary and persuade the viewers that God proposes to let them see (in a spiritual sense)…themselves. It is to foster the *sympathetic identification* between Christ and man, between Savior and saved, that Luke writes.

First Day *Read Luke 1*

Luke the physician, whose experience with human frailties makes him especially sensitive, preserves here some of the most lofty poetry of the human race. The Magnificat of Mary (46–55) and the song of Zechariah (68–79) express messages beyond those conveyed through their literal words.

Poetry "says" a great deal about God and man. Made in the divine image, humans cocreate their own world. True religion involves not monologue, but dialogue. Thus their upward thrusts meet God's downward thrust. The gospel story is the climax of the centuries-old romance between God and man. Supremely and superbly, the child, who is flesh of Mary's flesh while generated by the Holy Spirit, unites God and man in one person. It is this that enables him, in his substitutionary dying, to "make amends" in a fashion that no mortal could do.

However good the intentions of an interpreter, every attempt to explain Luke's report in order to make it rational is an exercise in futility. For he has set out on a wholly irrational task—that of persuading us that the limitations of mortality disappear when we believe in Jesus Christ and thus "identify ourselves with him." Therefore, the only suitable prelude to the heavenly symphony is precisely what Luke gives us: beautiful stories of incredible events working together to produce a God-man.

Second Day *Read Luke 2*

God has given us a physical body that requires tangible things, such as air, water, food, shelter, and a narrow range of temperature. But for us to be human in the full sense, a social as well as a physical environment is required.

For this reason, even God could not send his own Son without a context into which he could be received. The existence of some kind of civilization and preparation by some of the chosen people were necessary before the Christ Child could enter the stream of human history. Therefore it is appropriate that Luke, the gentile physician, should go to great pains in stressing the Jewishness of his Savior's human background. Lacking a prepared and expectant people, the actual coming of God's Son would have gone unnoticed.

Both in this literal sense and in figurative ones, the arrival of the Savior attracts the attention and commands the reverence of a select company—those who ardently seek encounter with a Savior and are attuned to the evidence about him.

Third Day *Read Luke 3–4*

The Word of God offers solace to the troubled. It is balm for the wounded heart, and it gives strength to the weary. But stress upon its healing functions must not blind us to the fact that the divine Word is also a weapon with which God attacks the Evil One and all who support his cause or give him shelter.

Metaphors in the Old Testament make the word of truth function as a weapon, as "the sword of the Lord." Now slashing, now stabbing, it is a disruptive influence in society and the lives of individuals. In this sense Jesus came to bring a sword rather than a dove. Yet precisely here, by a shining paradox of the gospel, lies good news (3:18).

The role of John the Baptist was to wield the sword of the Lord in such fashion that men, made aware of their danger, would seek a protector. His divinity attested not only by marvels attending his birth but also by visible and audible witness of the Holy Spirit, Jesus steps forward to champion the cause of doomed mankind. Demonstrating his power to function as Savior, he disarms and humiliates Satan at the outset of his public ministry.

Nevertheless, many who hear him persuade themselves that they can fight their own battles and do not need a divine substitute. Such persons, as seen in the rejection at Nazareth, are the only ones for whom the Savior can do nothing. The hands of God are tied, so long as mortals take the attitude that they are able to stand on their own feet and meet every foe that threatens their (spiritual) lives in this world and the world to come.

Fourth Day *Read Luke 5–6*

Nothing can withstand the power of God's supreme agent, who came into the world to strike the word impossible from the vocabulary of believers. All limitations vanish before the power of his presence. The sea, the ancient symbol of the frontier man cannot conquer, gives up its treasures. Leprosy is overcome, paralysis is vanquished, and the heart of a tax collector is warned!

Why does the story not come to a quick climax right here? Why is it that those confronted by such evidence scan it and remain unmoved? How could they deceive themselves into thinking they could win God's approval by their own efforts following the law of Moses?

After twenty centuries, it seems incredible that men who were good and holy by the highest of human standards should have been the chief opponents of Jesus. But, now, as well as then, the tendency to resist and rebel is basic. We, too, want to work out our own salvation. We, too, are prone to demonstrate by our lives that we feel we must make our own way to some destination that will give meaning to our lives. So we, too, need the spiritual slap in the face that is offered by messages Luke preserves such as the Sermon on the Plain (6:20–49). Instead of being the spiritual soothing syrup we often try to make it, this collection of Jesus' sayings offers an opportunity for genuine encounter with the living Word. Here, readers are first confronted and then convicted, persuaded that they are unable to achieve the approval of God, so that they must have divine help if they are to be acquitted in the judgment.

Fifth Day *Read Luke 7*

Part of the recurrent note of scandal in the Good News stems from the fact that while salvation is offered to all, there are those who cannot be saved, namely, all who fail to see themselves as desperate men for whom no human help will avail.

Were it not so fearfully tragic, I think there would be an almost comical note in the fact that the elders of the Jews serve as emissaries on behalf of a Roman centurion—but they themselves reject Jesus' offer to confer new life!

It is not difficult here to understand the eager acceptance by outsiders of God's good gifts through Christ. It is much harder for us to survey the contemporary scene and decide what persons and what groups are sufficiently conscious of their alienation to be receptive.

Our real business in reading Luke's account of the watershed of *salvation history* is to make personal application of his challenge and promise. We need to pose personal questions: Are there respects in which I am a modern Pharisee, blind to my own nakedness and indignant at the suggestion that I should accept God's offer to clothe me? Have I been busy serving causes which, however pious they appear on the surface, represent camouflaged instances of idolatry? How can I become aware that I am blind, lame, unclean, deaf, and dead, so that in recognizing my poverty, I may become rich (21–22)?

Sixth Day *Read Luke 8*

Luke not only reports the parable of the sower, but he is careful to include Jesus' own interpretation of it and to set it in a context to illustrate the truths of the parable. In this respect, his eighth chapter is without parallel in the New Testament. Here we have a delineation of the central role that is played by the hearer of the Word.

It is not from witnessing but from an encounter between witnesses and the recipients that transformation stems. Even when the person offering his witness is the Son of God—divinity lodged in flesh—no automatic results can be expected. Always, the harvest is radically affected by the nature of the human soil upon which the seed of the Word falls.

Luke reports the bewilderment of Jesus' own disciples. Their reaction to the parable is a mirror of the reaction of the world when confronted by the enigmatic promise that constitutes the offer of salvation. In quick succession, we see the negative principles of the parable illustrated by the reactions of Jesus' mother and brothers, his disciples, and the people in the country of the Gerasenes. In sharp contrast, positive principles are illustrated by the reactions of an outcast woman and, incredibly, an important official of a religious institution.

Seventh Day *Read Luke 9*

The message of the gospel is that there can be no salvation without a Savior. Because of the limitations of humanity, we mortals are incapable of recognizing and accepting the divine bounty in wholly spiritual form. We must have something or someone tangible. Through Christ, God became incarnate so he could appeal to our eyes and ears and not simply our capacity to think abstract thoughts.

Consequently, a vital aspect of the New Testament story is the recognition of Jesus as Savior. Of the multitudes who see and hear him, a few succeed in connecting Jesus of Nazareth and the Christ. For them, and for all others who manage to stand where they stood, salvation is real, because it is an item of personal experience.

We must not get discouraged if we are puzzled by this aspect of the Good News. Peter did not leap to his great confession in one bound. And even after other disciples heard it with their own ears, they continued to misunderstand the work of their Master. Whether on a personal Mount of Transfiguration or among hostile Samaritans of our own time, we are prone to fall and fail! *Were this not the case, we might need a guide and helper—but not a Savior.* It is our limitedness, our fallibility, our feet of clay, that require the gospel of rescue through the divine-human Son of the covenant.

Eighth Day *Read Luke 10*

Kingdom truths are simultaneously revealed and hidden. No amount of proclamation will serve to convey the Good News to any person who is incapable of recognizing and accepting it. Always the pride of wisdom leads to failure, while the humility of ignorance is likely to be a prelude to success.

The gospel must be proclaimed by his disciples. It is the real function of the church (and perhaps the only real function of it) to propagate the faith by multiplying opportunities for encounter with the gospel. Whether disciples are in a modern Sodom or some counterpart of Capernaum, they must be true to their mission—and leave the results to God.

Ninth Day *Read Luke 11*

It comes as a shock to realize that the chief formula Jesus offered his disciples is a pattern of prayer. The entire history of the covenant relationship points to a two-way dialogue between God and man, and the Bible exists to foster such exchange. But we are not really prepared to see prayer as *the* religious life.

Note the sequence here. Jesus provides a pattern of prayer. Then he exhorts his disciples to be urgent in their seeking, and by casting out a demon, he gives a dramatic illustration of the power that stems from relationship with the Father. All these things are wasted on the Pharisees and lawyers. These men do not know how to pray, in any vital sense. Their yearnings and longings turn inward upon themselves. Instead of being involved in dialogue with God, accepting all the dreadful risks and glorious opportunities that dialogue includes, they spend their lives talking to themselves and to one another.

I cannot think that the consistent blindness and failure of the Pharisees and lawyers is emphasized in order to condemn first-century Jewish leaders, only. Rather, these unredeemed ones are symbols of those men in every age who trust themselves in lieu of seeking salvation so urgently that they demand it of God.

Tenth Day *Read Luke 12*

How dumb can you get?

Jesus gives a sermonette on the dangers of concern with material goals, and a listener immediately pipes up asking for divine help in gaining an inheritance!

You and I may smile in patronizing fashion, but then we proceed to urge upon Jesus our own yearnings for tangible blessings! To enter the mood symbolized by careless lilies, is not only desirable, but essential. This involves centering upon the kingdom in such fashion that eagerness to greet the Master causes all other goals and concerns to fade into the background.

Eleventh Day *Read Luke 13–14*

Repentance is a turning inside out of the self. Through it "the natural man" becomes spiritual, his surrender enabling God to work such a transformation that he is literally no longer the same person. It was to call us to such repentance and to provide avenues along which we may move toward it, that Jesus Christ came into the world.

Through repentance, in its inclusive sense, barren trees begin to bear fruit and bent persons become straight. It would seem that all of us would want this transformation so eagerly that we would "assault the gates of heaven" to get it. But that is not the case. Many—perhaps most—are willing to settle for a degree of satisfaction and status within the context of human society.

For this reason, the altogether positive Good News becomes threatening and negative when rejected. To eliminate the element of dread from the encounter with God is to reduce him to human dimensions. The fearful prospect of being shut out from the banquet is as live an alternative as any vision of ecstasy. Here trembles the meaning of human existence: acceptance or rejection of God's overtures has both personal and cosmic consequences.

Twelfth Day *Read Luke 15–16*

Chapter 15, with its three parables of the lost, is among the most radiant of the New Testament. God is eternally on the offensive, these stories say. There are no impossible situations, except those concerning the lost ones who are comfortable and satisfied in their lostness and do not wish to respond to divine overtures.

This is not to say, however, that the pilgrimage to the New Jerusalem is easy. For if God is perpetually bidding for surrender, so is the world. Our space- and time-bound physical selves easily fall prey to that all-pervasive kind of idolatry that consists of making some type of "riches" the goal of life. In a special sense, this captivity to the material is the "far country" to which each of us flees but in which no prodigal (whether Pharisee, rich man, or ordinary church member) need stay long enough to die and be buried in a lonely grave.

Thirteenth Day *Read Luke 17–18*

Although salvation is free, in another sense it is costly. Including as they do warnings about the terrible day of the Lord, these chapters also stress that the price of rescue is a totally dedicated life in which belief in Jesus Christ is dominant. The fact that, of ten lepers cleansed, only the Samaritan gave thanks is enough to warn us; the realization that a Pharisee, whom his fellow men considered holy, was rejected while a wretched tax collector was approved is enough to frighten the wits out of us—if we will apply the warning to ourselves. Once more, we are confronted by the fearful announcement that salvation is impossible by human effort. To be proud or casual or complacent is to create a mood that encourages rejection of God's offer to do for us what we cannot do for ourselves.

Fourteenth Day *Read Luke 19–20*

Paradoxes are strewn through these pages like boulders along a mountain road. The one who is conscious of being lost is likely to be saved. Those who have much (spiritually speaking) are sure to gain more, while poor wretches with nothing (spiritually speaking) will surely lose what they have. Escorted into Jerusalem in triumph, Jesus does not exult—but weeps. Entering the temple, the chief holy place of God's chosen people, the Son of God does not soothe and commend; instead, he condemns. The rejected stone, he says, becomes the foundation on which an edifice rests.

Surely this clustering of apparent contradictions on the eve of Calvary is not accidental. It challenges all notions of an easy or "simple" gospel. We expect too much if we hope to grasp all the subtleties and nuances of the Good News by giving it only part of our attention during a single proclamation. Here is a soul-absorbing quest that demands undivided attention throughout life!

Fifteenth Day *Read Luke 21–22*

The reversal of ideas is as characteristic of the kingdom as is the paradox of the Good News. The day of the Lord is so transforming that no established conditions will prevail. Our great task is to "be always on the watch" (21:36) to avoid being entangled in worldly pursuits, so that the explosive impact of the kingdom will not destroy anything that is important.

Judas' betrayal illustrates the results of failure in this respect. For the sake of a tangible trifle, the disciple disposes of his own soul. In a special sense, he sells himself rather than Jesus for thirty pieces of silver.

Through that act, Judas unwittingly implements the flow of *salvation history*, for on that day of unleavened bread, the new sacrifice, God's Son, plays the role of Paschal Lamb.

Sixteenth Day *Read Luke 23–24*

As a man condemned by due process of law—however barbaric that law may seem as viewed through twentieth-century eyes—the Son of Man goes to Calvary. He is found guilty of being King of the Jews. The punishment is absolute, and Jesus of Nazareth pays the price for his offense against the society of his day.

In a special sense, the sequence of events is necessary, for the grand theme of Luke is Jesus' taking upon himself the sins of the world and meeting for us the demands of the law. So the working-out of human justice is a prototype of the working-out of divine justice, under which everyone is sentenced and must receive the death penalty.

Only the condemned who succeed in seeing themselves as condemned and who, in faith, accept Jesus Christ as Savior are released from claims of the law. They are already "dead," already "punished," because the Savior mounted the Cross for them. This incredible series of events is true, authenticated by the empty tomb.

Salvation history reached its climax on Calvary when divinity that came into flesh rescued us from the sentence of death.

John

Even first-time readers sense a new mood when they turn from the last chapter of Luke to the first chapter of John. Because there are many types of men—varied kinds of soil, if you please—the likelihood of a maximum harvest is increased by using a variety of methods to sow seed. John's sowing, altogether different from that of any other gospel witness, has dynamic impact upon some persons who are left unconvinced by Matthew, Mark, and Luke. He conveys the same message they offer, but he transmits it through a different channel: his unduplicated self.

It is commonplace to speak of John's gospel as "poetic." That label is valid, but it does not convey the depth and height of his message. Essentially, it is an impassioned personal testimony, a confession of faith.

Consequently, John is unconcerned with things that interest the historian. Not only does he bypass every single incident of Jesus' first thirty-three years, he also ignores the whole matter of his Savior's human lineage. For John, the fact above every fact is that God the Creator is totally incarnate in Jesus Christ.

Hence, for him, the supreme vehicle through which the Savior teaches is action. John reports many miracles but not one parable. Every act is communicative. Each mighty work is a divine proclamation! As a result, the gospel of John is both easy and difficult. More than any other body of Christian witness, it has the power to stir men into belief-powered surrender. Yet the testimony that makes converts never ceases to yield fresh insight and to heighten the conviction of long-time Christians. Here is a book not so much to be read, as to be encountered—growing more powerful and more intriguing with each meeting.

Seventeenth Day *Read John 1*

Jesus Christ is to reveal God to man so that they may gain power to throw off the limitations of their finite nature. Hence, the experience of knowing God through Christ is the most creative event into which a human can enter. In "listening to the incarnate Word," man becomes cocreator with God. For this the world was created, and in it the divine work of creation is as vital as that described in Genesis. Notice that, in Genesis 1, God the Father *speaks* the world into existence. Now speaking "in these latter days" through the Word made flesh, God fosters the creation of transformed persons. Each instance of such a transformation is a cosmic event on the scale of the creation of the world.

John the Baptist raises his voice to catch the attention of men, to prepare their hearing of the divine Word. In his work as Savior, Jesus serves as the Lamb sent down from heaven to be offered up by those who do not know the import of their action in a once-for-all sacrificial ceremony. The effect is to atone for the sins of all who believe that this unbelievable thing has been done for them.

Eighteenth Day *Read John 2–3*

At the outset of Jesus' public ministry, we discover that he is going to use dramatic action as a means of communication. Through his turning of water into wine, he not only demonstrates divine power, but he also announces the marriage feast celebrating the union of God and his people in the New Covenant.

This message was not fully understood by those who heard it; they were puzzled and uncertain. The same reaction followed his verbal announcement of the coming demonstration of victory over death (2:19–21). Later, disciples encountered divine truth through a nonverbal message proclaimed by the empty tomb. So transforming was

184

this encounter that their total systems of understanding were reorganized. They then looked back on past events and reinterpreted them, finding meanings they had overlooked at first (2:22).

Such a pattern of religious experience can mark the life of every believer. It is partly because John's gospel so clearly exhibits this process in action and yields itself to it, that this account both appeals to the beginning Christian and continues to enlighten the developing one. Nicodemus' experience is an example of the apparent failure to see light when confronted by the Light. Yet John is careful to show (19:39) that this man, too, was led to reevaluate and reorder his house of belief in the Light shed by the events of Passion Week.

Nineteenth Day *Read John 4–5*

Those outside the covenant relationship, who lack Nicodemus' disadvantage of seeming to have gained spiritual security by birth, do not have to make so radical a readjustment as he. Therefore a Samaritan woman and her fellow villagers join a Roman official in recognizing divinity incarnate, without the necessity of the Cross and the empty tomb as proof.

In Jerusalem, the center of true worship, it would seem that everyone would be ready and eager for the healing power offered by the Savior. But that was not the case; only those really wanting to be made whole were capable of receiving the gift freely offered to them, thereby passing from death to life (5:24).

Once more, the danger is underscored of considering oneself to be spiritually secure. Experts in the interpretation of the written law so trusted in their superior virtue that they felt no need for rescue, and they lacked the capacity for receiving the transforming belief in the new law that was proclaimed by God through the Son.

Twentieth Day *Read John 6*

Remember that deeds as well as words serve as agents of the Word made flesh. In the light of this fact, it is not hard to see that the feeding of the five thousand is communicative and revelatory. Here is a reenactment and reinterpretation of the ancient feeding in the wilderness provided for the children of the covenant as they moved from Egypt to the land of promise. Jesus of Nazareth, the second Moses, delivers from captivity to sin and self.

His absolute and unqualified lordship is demonstrated in his mastery of the sea, but the multitudes do not understand. They look and look but fail to see. Stumbling over literal meanings of symbolic formulas, "the Jews" scoff at the notion that the son of Joseph should be regarded as "the new manna"— bread from heaven. Even the apostles find sayings of this sort to be hard to understand. But when many once-ardent followers withdraw their allegiance, Peter is inspired to witness in sublime fashion. Not only in our own day, but also in first-century Judea, the disciple who demands a neatly ordered set of understandings makes all the doors of his house too small to admit a Savior.

Twenty-first Day *Read John 7*

Though Jesus exhibits power and confers healing, he also brings about divisions among people. Many causes and interests are challenged by the Good News; incredibly, the religious institution and its functionaries are high on the list, if not actually at the top of the list, of opponents. The reason for this is that pride, status, self-interest, and materialism take root in organized religion as readily as in any other soil.

Twenty-second Day *Read John 8*

When one is incapable of accepting evidence, it is as though that evidence did not exist. No power on earth can stuff proof into a person as sausage is packed into a casing.

Much of the New Testament deals with the nature of knowledge, meaning, and communication. Few chapters, however, face these issues so directly and continuously as does John's eighth. For here, "the Jews" flounder and thrash about; they seem to almost wallow in their attempt to find a point of contact between their ordered systems of belief and the disturbing one who demands that belief be oriented toward him.

Early in the Christian era, religious thought was distorted so that Jews were regarded as natural enemies of Christians. The basis of this was the kind of verbal literalism here demonstrated to be sterile. Although Jews actually were Jesus' opponents in the historic situation, they also provided the cultural seed-bed necessary for the coming of the God-man in the flesh. Lacking a people with the sense of covenant, which we traced through the Old Testament, there could have been no Incarnation.

So, it is precisely here that the self-styled Christian needs to make a leap of faith and recognize that any person secure in his own sense of righteousness actually is a "Jew" in the sense of this chapter. Pursued to its depths, this issue becomes very personal. I have no business standing in judgment of others; judgment belongs to God alone. My sole business is to "continue in the Word" with such ardor that I am constantly increasing my capacity to receive and nurture seeds sown in my life by God.

Twenty-third Day *Read John 9–10*

All of us are blind from birth, but only those who know it are subjects for healing.

Like many other mighty works that took place on the Sabbath, the opening of the blind man's eyes created a new occasion for bickering. The Sabbath controversy itself has deep symbolic meaning. For on the day intended to point us toward God's work as Creator, guardians of the religious system insisted that an outburst of creative power constituted an offense against God! That raises the question (now as well as then): Who is it—really—that is blind?

Ask such a question, seriously seeking an answer, and you will either take a trembling step toward transformation or you will pick up stones to hurl at Jesus Christ.

Twenty-fourth Day *Read John 11*

I think this is the longest of all New Testament accounts of a miracle, with its antecedents and aftermath. Here is a chapter to be read, reread, and then read once again. It could be used for a month's pilgrimage, rather than that of a day.

Surface meanings center on Jesus' demonstration that he has power over death. The exhibition of this power, however, is utterly unconvincing to his opponents, who go right ahead with their plans to seize him—at the very season when, in ancient Egypt, the angel of death passed over the firstborn of God's people.

Like all the other mighty works of Jesus, this one is performed in order to convey messages calculated to attract and to convince in a fashion that words alone cannot do. Fully to plumb the depths of meaning here, it is necessary for us to seek to enter into the experience of Lazarus—over and over being raised "from the dead" (spiritually, intellectually, physically) through the power of the divine Word as uttered in the words and deeds of the Son of God.

Twenty-fifth Day *Read John 12*

Although subsequent events challenged tributes paid during his triumphal entry to Jerusalem, the fact is that Jesus, who died as a malefactor, really is a King. Like so many other truths, this one is too sublime for any disciple (ancient or modern) to incorporate into a personal system of experience, until that system has been transformed by encounter with the glorified Savior.

God trumpets from heaven—and bystanders nod to one another in agreement that it has only thundered.

How, then, can anyone hope to gain capacity to hear?

Every pilgrim must use what light is available, be it bright or dim, to see to move forward. In this state of moving toward the goal, not in the arrival at some terminus, disciples increase their capacity to be seed-beds in which belief can flourish. Those who wait for total illumination in order to run with all their might will never start. "Put your trust in the light while you have it, so that you may become sons of light" (36).

Twenty-sixth Day *Read John 13–14*

One of the "secrets" of the kingdom, proclaimed so loudly that we often tune the message out, centers in the relative importance of men and of Providence. Especially in modern times, we deceive ourselves into thinking it is our job to "bring the kingdom in." When we talk of that, we actually claim the ability to use our minds and our muscles and our time so that we achieve results that God could not accomplish if left to himself.

This view comes close to heresy, for the truth is that the fermenting divine work proceeds whether a single human being responds to it or not. It is my job and yours to try to make ourselves fertile soil in which divine seeds may flourish, but we may be sure that God will scatter seeds in society and his harvest will come to maturity if we do nothing whatever to help him.

These chapters, like so many others, reiterate the promise/warning that "likely candidates" (humanly considered) are poor risks in the sight of God. It is the humble ones who are receptive enough to receive seeds and nurture them. Bent old women, along with "the poor, the crippled, the blind and the lame" (Luke 14:21), can only hobble—yet, in the end, they always outdistance Pharisees and rulers who run at top speed!

Twenty-seventh Day *Read John 15–16*

Bonds between the Savior and the saved are organic. There is a continuous two-way flow, a spiritual dialogue. Precisely such a relationship is basic to that identification between him and us, by which the suffering and death of Christ serve to wipe out the guilt of his disciples. That is to say, when the vine-branch relationship is taken seriously, we begin to see how it is possible to say that you and I suffered and died on Calvary.

Jesus' invitation into the role of friend, rather than that of servant, and his promise of the Counselor's coming are sources of strength and comfort. They will be sorely needed, he warns, in time of conflict and apparent failure.

Of course, much that he is saying is falling upon deaf ears. Never mind. Listen and treasure and remember in spite of lack of understanding, he urges. There will come a climactic moment of spiritual-emotional-intellectual experience in which the crucible of experience will reach such a temperature that everything in it will melt and assume a new structure when it crystallizes upon cooling. This aspect of knowledge and faith, stressed so strongly in John's report, is basic to our entering into a life of discipleship. However comprehensive it may be, religious education is not enough. It must be extended and transformed by religious experience. Then and now, the definitive ingredient in vital religious experience is an encounter with a personal Savior, recognized as God in human flesh. When disciples experience such an encounter, all their accumulated meanings and values and beliefs are reorganized. The empty tomb will catapult disciples into the hour of encounter whose dramatic results might be called "spiritual travail" (see 16:1–23).

Twenty-eighth Day *Read John 17–18*

Jesus' long priestly prayer in chapter 17 is oriented toward that select company which makes up his true followers. It is the destiny of these persons, "given to him by the Father," that concerns him. Although his actual moment of physical self-giving has not yet come, here Jesus gives himself as absolutely as upon Calvary.

The contrast is vivid, therefore, when chapter 18 is read. The concern of the Savior is totally directed outward in chapter 17, while the motives and actions of the people described in Chapter 18 make them totally self-centered. Notice that the whole spectrum of humanity is involved. From Judas the traitor to Peter the rock, we are confronted by rejection of the Savior because of selfish motives. The best of men, as well as the worst, fails and falls.

Nowhere in the Gospels is there a sharper and more dramatic piece of evidence to help convince us that we all need not merely help but *salvation*. Our nature is such that we cannot long focus upon the highest and best. Even in religious service (sometimes especially here), it is easy to become self-centered, concerned with what rewards are in prospect. Before the Master's utterly unforgetful prayer has ceased to echo, the chief apostle finds himself concerned only with saving his own life.

If the Good News invites you and me to identify ourselves with the Christ so that we are "crucified with him on Calvary," it also warns that we cannot escape running the gamut of denial that extends from Peter to Judas. In the hour when we should rise to sublime heights in the strength of Jesus' complete love for us, we stumble and fall. Try as we may, we can never follow our Master's good example for long; we must turn to him for rescue.

Twenty-ninth Day *Read John 19*

For the fulfillment of the unfolding New Covenant, it was necessary that the Son of God pay the supreme penalty. Moreover, for the New Covenant to come into being, he had to be executed as a felon. Guilt (humanly speaking) was a necessary ingredient, for only through his entering into a state of guilt was it possible for Jesus Christ to become a substitute for guilty men (spiritually speaking).

We are prone to get sentimental about the indignities heaped upon our Lord. It certainly is true that the events of Passion Week stir us and convict us. It is equally true that the condemnation and death of Jesus Christ can be viewed in more than one light. In spite of these factors, it yet remains a paradox (and a stumbling block) of the Good News that no agent of God who lived and died as a hero could have played the role of Savior. To provide a way by which mankind could be offered rescue from the inevitable consequences of mortal deeds, divinity had to be condemned to death.

Thirtieth Day *Read John 20–21*

Christian principles could hardly have been grasped by even a few, had not the Resurrection served to reorganize their beliefs. The apostles themselves, in spite of months spent with their Master, did not grasp the miracle of the Incarnation until the first Easter demonstrated that he is fully divine as well as so completely human that he died as an executed felon.

Such concepts cannot be seized intellectually; they must be encountered in the crucible of experience. For them to come alive in a more than academic approach to Christian thought, they must become a part of the believer. There must be a fusion between the self and the Good News, so that the scandalous and paradoxical, glorious and transforming ideas lead to identification with Christ. Such a state, in which the follower so surrenders that he cannot clearly determine boundaries between the organized self and the divine Savior, constitutes redemption. It was for this to come into being that God entered history in the person of his Son.

Acts and Romans

Acts

As the title indicates, this vibrant book deals more with deeds than with ideas. Nevertheless, beliefs and loyalties are the foundations on which outward actions rest. This is indeed an account of the actions of the apostles, who are obedient to an inner compulsion that makes them do wonderful things. But, because it is an incredible story dealing with accomplishments that any sensible person would consider impossible, it is also a book about Jesus Christ.

His indwelling power, conveyed through the Holy Spirit, literally transforms those men whose acts fill this book. A bewildered and defeated group of obscure followers of a village visionary are suddenly welded into a band of dynamic witnesses, who will be satisfied with nothing less than the conquest of the whole world!

Read in isolation, the book of Acts can be seen as almost ordinary, in spite of the incredible impact of a single apostle who has to be guarded by Roman soldiers. Read not simply as a follow-up to the Gospels but as in organic connection with the Old Testament, Acts emerges as one of the most explosive documents ever penned. It deals with nothing less than world revolution.

Although men are essential instruments of that revolution, it is unlike any other political or social upheaval. It is a transformation worked by God the Father among men made in his image who have been impacted by the Good News, brought by Jesus Christ. Not simply individuals, but also institutions, cultures, and eventually nations and ideologies are affected.

In these pages we recognize that God-oriented change (often unpleasantly disruptive) is basic to ongoing Christian development. God does not want or expect our day to be a reenactment of the first century. He does not call us to duplicate the precise outward effects of the day of Pentecost or the great church conference in Jerusalem. But through his Son, the Creator does expect—demand—creative enlargement on the part of those who now call themselves his own.

It is death for any individual or group, any class or congregation, to reach an intellectual-spiritual peak, however high, that permits ease and complacency. Struggle and growth and God-oriented enlargement are the most precious gifts that can be conferred on a soul still enmeshed in a physical body. With the soul, as with that body, life retreats and death reigns the instant two-way interaction with the environment ceases.

First Day *Read Acts 1–2*

For Luke, the physician-historian, Jesus' death and resurrection mark not the end but the midpoint of history. Although it is approximately the same band of followers with whom he deals throughout, his account in the gospel of Luke depicts men and women who are noticeably different in the second half of the story found in Acts. Here all their values and ideals are in the process of being reinterpreted in the light of the system-shattering recognition that Jesus of Nazareth was the Son of God.

Notice that their reinterpretation extends not only to personal experiences but also to Scripture. In the light of the Good News as communicated in Jesus' life and words, they find radical new meaning in familiar passages. A case in point is the long passage from the Book of Joel, which Peter quotes on the day of Pentecost (2:17–21; see also 2:25–28, quoted from Ps. 16:8–11).

Not only familiar Scripture, but *everything*, is new. The personal transformation of the disciples is so great that they are literally *new persons*.

A major aspect of the transformation centers in the potent "gift of the Holy Spirit." These disciples do not pay homage to their old goals; they are now so dominated by zeal for the kingdom that they are "possessed"—dominated, controlled, and owned—by the indwelling divine personality. Inevitably, social structures are as radically affected as are individual lives.

Second Day *Read Acts 3–4*

Not simply holy boldness, but marvelous new power, marks the daily life of the transformed disciples. These are not the same men who floundered and misunderstood and hesitated so recently. Something tremendous has happened to them, and it has come to a climax in the period between the Crucifixion and Pentecost. Before, these quite ordinary men and women would have made little impact upon society. Now, they are so potent that they quickly begin—almost in spite of themselves—such mighty works that they "turn the world upside down."

For the faithful today, these tumultuous events have a vexatious set of questions. Shall we try to recover first-century Christianity, seeking to duplicate experiences and patterns of the emerging church? Or shall we seek new outpourings of the Holy Spirit, calculated to bring new Pentecostal experiences whose fruits will be appropriate to conditions of the present age?

The crux of the question is the direction of creative transformation by divine power. Does the first century exhaust its potential, so that the Christian ideal is reenactment of events in Acts? Or is the ideal divine-human encounter, calculated to have such creative impact that no one can predict or channel the explosive results? If the Holy Spirit takes possession of lives today, will our generation spontaneously return to practices and patterns of Peter and Paul? Will we find totally new ones whose shape cannot be predicted in advance but must be accepted as they emerge in mighty works of continuing divine creation?

Third Day *Read Acts 5*

You may take this as a basic principle: whenever the power of God is actively at work, strange and fearful things will take place in the lives of individuals and in the corporate life of the church. Today, we who name the name of Jesus Christ tend to commit, I think, one of two grave errors.

Frequently we approach our faith as though we could be in a transforming relationship with God through Christ; yet we live in a way calculated to win social acceptance as good and upright people who are "normal" by prevailing secular standards. This fearful error, by which the transforming impact of being in the stream of salvation is rejected, is balanced by an opposite one. If we regard the Christian pilgrimage as the focal point of continuing divine creation, so that radical transformation is expected, we are likely to insist upon guiding the flow of that transformation. That is, we may expect neither more nor less than the outward effects which are described in the Acts of the apostles.

Actually, it may inhibit God's creative power to expect him to strike down a new Ananias and a fresh Sapphira every time men and women seriously seek the Holy Spirit. Authenticating "signs and wonders" (12) there will be aplenty, when we really put God first. Precisely what these will be we cannot possibly know in advance, nor can we measure any group or movement by the degree to which it conforms to accepted patterns. Like Gamaliel, we must insist upon open-mindedness and willingness to let time and events challenge or support the validity of all claims that God is presently working in mighty ways among those who believe themselves to be guided by him.

Fourth Day *Read Acts 6–7*

Is it inevitable that mighty outpourings of divine power should create divisions and arouse opposition? Probably so. It may be argued that when no opposition is being aroused, little creative work of God is taking place. Notice especially the near-automatic antagonism to Jesus' own message and ministry.

Viewed in this light, the martyrdom of Stephen is an index to the explosive impact of divine power, released through Peter and his comrades. It is a perennial fallacy, however, for God-seekers to pursue martyrdom on any scale for its own sake.

Stephen's great defense, in chapter 7, is among the most illuminating of all New Testament passages in its power to show the interdependence of the Old Testament and the New. While it is true that the New Testament can be read by itself with profit, it is also true that familiarity with the Old Testament will serve to give new dimensions to the New Testament and each of its parts. Stephen here summarizes *salvation history* in its entirety and shows the organic bond that stretches, through the chosen people, from Abraham to Jesus Christ.

Confronted by so great a challenge, Stephen's hearers could not be neutral. In a sense, their unwillingness to accept his invitation to bow at the feet of Jesus Christ required them to stone Jesus' messenger. No middle ground was possible.

Fifth Day *Read Acts 8–9*

In its solemn unfolding, *salvation history* requires continuous creative encounter between God and his people. Humanly speaking, the plot thickens when we recognize that the creature who moves toward the Creator must participate both socially and individually. That is to say, both an Israel and a Saul of Tarsus are essential factors. There is a unique human group, the chosen people, whose marriage contract with the Creator leads to the birth of the God-man, our Savior. The fruition of the covenant, however, does not eliminate the need for new human partners of God. On the contrary, the New Covenant involves both a social group (the church) and hosts of individual men and women willing to surrender in such fashion that they become agents of God.

Chief among such individuals in the emerging church is Saul, who becomes Paul. In somewhat the same sense that a betrayer was necessary, so that, had Judas not functioned, God would have had to raise up a substitute for him, so a theological spokesman—a man of keen mind—was needed to put the new faith into systematic form. Had the versatile and disciplined Saul not responded to the divine call for a theologian, God would have had to provide another.

Peter's vision and Saul's conversion are two sides of the same coin; both men were instruments of the divine purpose, by which the

Good News would burst out of Judaism and offer new life, in Jesus Christ, to the whole world.

Sixth Day *Read Acts 10–11*

Whether in a biological organism, the spiritual-intellectual realm of an individual, or the structured group that constitutes a human institution, there is a state of continuous change. The individual pilgrim toward the City of God who ceases to engage in conscious struggle has forfeited the opportunity to let the stream of divine creation use his life as a channel. The group or church or society that centers upon zealous preservation of what it has attained and received thereby says no to God's ceaseless invitation to grow toward him.

We applaud the decision to send the Good News to the gentiles but are in danger of rejecting our own opportunities to engage in the transforming experience of letting God send us into virgin territory.

Even for Peter—especially for Peter—the "bursting out" into the gentile world was fearfully demanding. He found himself in a state of dialogue with God, so attuned that events "spoke" to him with persuasive power. This served to erase the thin line between everyday sensory experience and divine revelation through an agent of God. So long as he remained in this exalted state, Peter actually found it hard to determine just when he was seeing a vision, and when he was involved in mortal experience (see 12:9).

No one can make neat explanations of such phenomena. But anyone can read of the utterly transforming events of these months and be very sure that—somehow—God's creative power was manifest in unusual fashion through the lives of a few dedicated men who were very ordinary mortals.

Seventh Day *Read Acts 12–13*

Peter's visions convey much the same message as Stephen's long defense (chap. 7) and Paul's exhortation in the synagogue of Antioch (13:16–41).

In the intellectual-spiritual heat of his new personal authority, Paul reinterprets the whole history of the divine-human covenant. His tremendous speech is a key passage in which to discover the organic bond between Israel and the church, the essential connectedness of the Old Testament and the New. Here are early stirrings of the mind and spirit of a one-time Jewish scholar who, as Christian evangelist, is destined to write spirit-filled letters that will speak of salvation through Jesus Christ in such powerful fashion that he will communicate with those born two thousand years later.

It is significant for our pilgrimage through the Bible to find underscored here this warning: familiarity with words of Holy Writ is no guarantee of valid encounter with its spirit (13:27). This basic factor is a key to both acceptance and rejection of the gospel; the outlook and goals of the hearer are vital ingredients in understanding words "that are read every Sabbath."

For a modern Christian (whatever the degree of his commitment to the Savior), it is almost pitifully easy to congratulate one's self on the capacity to hear with understanding in order to act with obedience. A crucial question is: To what degree do I actually play the role of a "jealous" devotee of the Old Covenant (13:45), while persuading myself that I am listening with the eager ears of a Gentile hearing a first invitation to accept salvation and glory in the riches of the kingdom?

Eighth Day *Read Acts 14–16*

Suppose you were required to summarize these chapters in a few key words. It will be a fruitful exercise to attempt just that.

For my part, I think I shall have to list these basic factors in the swift-moving events here described: action...power...marvels... struggle...division.

Looking through rose-colored glasses, as we usually do when we read about the doings of the apostles, we tend to magnify the place of teaching, preaching, healing, and evangelism. At the same time, we tend to minimize opposition and defeat suffered in the glorious first century.

Actually, these chapters suggest that then, as well as now, a fundamental spiritual law of physics can be seen at work. This principle might be that every God-oriented flow of power creates a powerful contrary force. To pour energy into service of God is automatically to arouse opposition on a proportional scale.

Whatever gives us modern Christians the notion that things are going well when nobody resists, nobody attacks? Perhaps because we have deceived ourselves into thinking that we live in a Christian society, we have too often equated piety with tranquillity. Fearing the condemnation that may be an inevitable accompaniment of stirring up a commotion, we have (in practice if not in theory) valued the way of compromise, the route of least resistance. To read of Iconium and Lystra, Antioch and Jerusalem does not encourage any zealot to put a premium on controversy for its own sake. However, it fortifies modern disciples to know that any flow of divine power through them is likely to stir up the conventionally pious and may even precipitate new stonings, beatings with rods, and imprisonment in the name of law and order.

Ninth Day *Read Acts 17–18*

In the months that you and I have spent with the Scriptures, we have repeatedly seen that interpretation is variable. God's power to reveal himself (through the Bible or any other medium) is affected by our willingness to accept divine truth. I suppose, therefore, it is both a consolation and a source of alarm to discover that Paul himself failed in his attempt to persuade devout people that Jesus Christ is offered through the holy books of Israel. Temporary success in Beroea is as notable as failure in Thessalonica—underscoring the realization that it is the work of the witness to sow in obedient faith and leave the increase to God.

In all his encounters, whether with pagans in Athens or devout scholars of Israel in Corinth, Paul was concerned with pouring out a single incredible message: Jesus of Nazareth, who died on the Cross, was the Savior for whom God took a chosen people as his bride and through whom God makes salvation possible.

Then, as well as now, this hard teaching defied intellectual analysis. It was not difficult to accept the Jesus of history or to trust in the

Christ of God. Difficulties centered in achieving the leap of faith by which Jesus Christ may be encountered as the God-man: divinity joined with humanity to offer unearned rescue to those made in the divine image. It is the Incarnation that serves as the enigmatic building piece of the Good News—a stumbling block that becomes a cornerstone for everyone willing to use it so.

Tenth Day *Read Acts 19–20*

Explain the events of these turbulent months; no one can. Accept them; every believer may.

Part of the intriguing riddle of Paul's life and witness lies in the fact that this man of keen mind was also subject to deep emotion. He clearly displayed charismatic gifts, himself experiencing ecstasy in various forms and, by his laying on of hands, inducing it in others (19:3). Yet he was no "Holy Roller" who elevated emotion above intelligence. He had not only a warm heart but also a keen mind.

In practice, you and I tend to emphasize one of these gifts at the expense of the other. Some people and groups give such emphasis to the intellectual side of Christianity that they tend to squeeze out emotion. Others make the opposite mistake, cultivating an ecstatic state for its own sake, rather than accepting it as an unsought side effect of being captured by the Holy Spirit.

Somewhere between the two extremes (or in a synthesis of them) lies what might be called "Pauline Christianity"—potent, transforming, utterly unpredictable, yet utilizing every resource that is available to a trained and disciplined mind.

To the degree that you and I succeed in moving toward personal enhancement of a faith that demands warm heart plus keen mind, our reading of Acts will put us, with John Wesley, into the mainstream of that salvation in which the divine work of creation is continued and completed. Possessed as he was by so disturbing and enlarging a faith, it is no wonder that Paul created turmoil nearly everywhere he went, even though the Holy Spirit warned him "that prison and hardships" were facing him (20:23).

Eleventh Day *Read Acts 21–22*

Why didn't the apostle Paul settle down in Ephesus or some other fine city and devote his life to making a long-term impact, instead of wandering hither and thither and staying nowhere for any great length of time?

The answer is that he felt himself under divine compulsion. Because a central aspect of his Christian experience was continuous change—participation in the flow of divine creation—geographical moves were necessary. Because, being under compulsion to accept enlargement through Jesus Christ, he literally could not keep still!

Not every other disciple must follow the path of this footloose Apostle. The response to an encounter with God is as individual as the human soul whose surrender puts the sinner in the process of being rescued. Transforming response must, however, be there—a process as well as an act of commitment. This process requires change, flow, growth, enlargement, and movement—all a spiritual "unfolding," which is likely to have tangible and visible effects. These may center in one's prayer life, use of the Bible, relationship with neighbors, treatment of family, or any other aspect of experience.

One does not have to push restlessly from Cos to Rhodes, and from Patara to Ptolemais, to be a disciple. It is not always necessary to go back to Jerusalem against the dictates of common sense. But the concept of follower of Jesus Christ implies spiritual-intellectual movement. When that ceases for any length of time, when there is such adjustment to life conditions that stirrings cease and no foes agitate the crowd, it is hard to think that any seeker can continue to be a pilgrim moving toward a destination. In this connection, reread Paul's speech in self-defense (22:3–21) and notice how it is dominated by action verbs.

Twelfth Day *Read Acts 23–24*

Talk about turmoil in the church! Anyone who feels that peace at any price is the route to spiritual power in the life of an individual or a congregation or a culture, needs to read and reread these chapters.

Notice that the force of Paul's witness was so powerful that the proportional and opposite force created in reaction to him sent forty men into ambush, under oath. Notice that the Roman official called out 470 men to escort a little tentmaker from one jail to another. Notice the symbolism in the prisoner's transfer from Jerusalem (the city of David) to Caesarea (the city of Caesar).

Reading this stirring story from the perspective of twenty centuries, we see quite clearly that God was at work in and through the troubles that descended on Paul's head. Can we—dare we—make a great leap of faith to the conclusion that, if we honestly continue our process of surrendering to God through Christ, our own troubles and turmoil may be sanctified, and we may play vital roles in the ongoing flow of Providence?

Thirteenth Day *Read Acts 25–26*

After two years, the foes of Paul still seek his life. Far from having turned aside to other interests, they hate the prisoner so much that they are eager to arrange an ambush, since legal machinery has not served to send him to death. One of the first official acts of the new Roman governor is to reopen this sensational case.

If any additional evidence concerning the dialectical movement of the young church is needed, here it is! Evangelistic success has engendered opposition on a life-and-death scale. The strange back-and-forward alternation of direction, the emptiness and impotence of human justice, sends the most eloquent of evangelists into the capital city of the world!

Once more, we are persuaded that nothing can defeat the purpose of God. Providence pervades every aspect of existence. Ultimate victory is guaranteed—"written into the stars." Nothing—not even the Roman Empire—can stop God in his ceaseless, creative work of elevating reborn men to heights no natural man can attain.

Paul's impassioned evangelistic plea, hardly a "defense" in the accepted sense, is a reiteration of one claim and one only: in Jesus of Nazareth divinity entered the stream of humanity as a fulfillment of the covenant whose unfolding constitutes *salvation history*.

Fourteenth Day *Read Acts 27–28*

Characteristically, Paul is soon the dominant personality in the band of travelers! In a vivid example of a paradox of the Christian pilgrimage, the prisoner of Christ directs men whose human status is that of power and authority.

Visions, providential care, mighty works, and radical transformations continue. Paul arrives in Rome imprisoned "for the hope of Israel" (28:20). Nearly everywhere he is being accepted by Gentiles "outside the Old Covenant" in a fashion not matched by Jews conscious of their special blessings under that covenant.

The outsiders, the aliens, the consciously outcast ones, accept God's offer of rescue. In Rome, as in Jerusalem, the insiders, the established ones, the favored of God reject salvation because they are offended at the suggestion they need it.

As a central issue in the Jewish-Christian struggle, the paradox of salvation is destined to remain vital, but it takes new forms as an ostensibly Christian culture establishes new categories of "insiders" and "outsiders."

Romans

Toward the close of his third missionary journey, sometime around A.D. 56 to A.D. 59, Paul paused for a period. Writing from Corinth or nearby Cenchreae, he addressed a congregation whom he had never visited, Christians in the capital of the mighty Roman Empire. This letter, then, is a sort of visit by proxy. This might well have been the evangelist's only contact with fellow Christians in Rome, and it contains the distilled essence of his entire witness.

Not only the most important of Paul's writings, this letter is also the first and, by many standards, the greatest of Christian theological tracts.

If it stood alone, it would be insignificant if not actually unintelligible. To read it without linking it with the entire body of Scripture—not only the Gospels, but also the writings that make up our Old Testament—is to distort the nature and to overlook the purpose of the letter. It is written by a one-time Jew who wishes to show that in Christ the age-old promise of God to his chosen people was fulfilled. In many respects, consequently, the letter is as intensely Jewish as it is ardently Christian. More than any other one document of Christianity, it provides a theological foundation for our total missionary and evangelistic enterprise.

The impact of this letter, buttressed by a prior acquaintance with the rest of the Bible, has been without parallel. Space permits me to mention only a few all-time notables who linked their conversion or intellectual-spiritual awakening with passages from it. Saint Augustine, Martin Luther, and John Wesley are among those who found Romans to be the torch that set their lives afire.

We shall spend a day with each chapter of this letter. Even so, we shall hardly do more than take a quick look at a few of its themes. Many readers have spent years with it. Donald Grey Barnhouse, for example, concentrated much of his life upon verse-by-verse and word-by-word study. His commentary on chapter 1 occupies 301 pages, while that on chapter 5 runs to 418 pages.

Perhaps our quick passage through the entire Bible will persuade you to devote long periods to meditative reading of special portions of Scripture. If so, you can do nothing better than to spend a year with this epistle and other years with each of the Gospels, Psalms, Genesis, Revelation, Acts, 1 and 2 Corinthians, and so on.

Fifteenth Day *Read Romans 1*

In Jesus Christ two streams met. One of them was that biological stream that constitutes the story of the chosen people. The other was the direct spiritual encounter between God and man. Through the first stream, the Son of David entered history. In the power received from the second, Jesus Christ rose from the dead to display the unlimited and unqualified effects resulting from the impact of the Creator upon the creatures made in his image.

In the first sentences of Paul's letter, we discover a new clue to the significance and power of the name Jesus Christ. Simply to breathe that name is, in faith, to link humanity with divinity, to witness that the God-man is the pivot on which all of man's existence turns.

It is as a captive to this faith that Paul writes. He is not his own master. On the contrary, he has entered such a state of surrender that he cannot fully think his own thoughts or write his own words. Using his life as a channel, God flows through him in such fashion that it is God's thoughts and God's words that are made public when God's apostle writes and speaks. Of course this is the ideal in all prophecy and evangelism. It is no new relationship but simply a fresh instance of what prevailed with those whose messages make up much of what is now the Old Testament. On lower levels and for briefer periods, it is the state of impassioned surrender that every preacher, teacher, evangelist, missionary, and witness tries to achieve. Partly because Paul exemplifies a relationship with God in its finest form, his letters are unique in their capacity to help others move toward such a relationship.

Speaking through his servant Paul, God warns that there are two paths that we can follow—and only two. One of them leads to God and to life; the other leads to less than God and to death. Everyone must choose one of these paths, and there is no middle ground. To vary from true north by even a fraction of a degree is to follow a course that will, over a period of years, take the pilgrim far from the one destination where abundant life may be accepted as a divine gift.

Whatever else it may do, this stirring chapter explodes the modern myth that the comfortable road of compromise and easy conformity is the way to life on the part of the institutional church, a local congregation, or an individual seeker after God. The religious quest is rigorous, demanding, exacting—and the tension never eases. Always, those who seek their Creator are confronted by a cosmic choice, an either/or they cannot escape for a single instant of their existence.

Sixteenth Day *Read Romans 2*

Judgment is the prerogative of God, who will assess every soul. It is both rebellious and impious for us to usurp the divine role and try to sit in judgment upon our neighbors. To survey our shortcomings is to become involved in so absorbing an activity that there is no time left for criticizing or condemning others.

It is not life under the law of Moses, or outside it, that will determine the fate of the soul, but the individual's relationship with God. Whether reared within the fellowship of the people of the covenant or among pagans who never heard of that covenant, one who sins (and everyone does) is sure to be condemned for that sin.

Once more we modern Christians discover, as we frequently did in reading the Gospels, that it is easier to make first-century applications than twenty-first-century ones. We are prone to condemn the blind and rebellious Jews who trusted in an inherited status and so rejected the rescue offered by Jesus Christ. But we find it hard to see that one who has grown up in Sunday school and church, who may take an active part in the official life of a congregation, can be playing the role of the "Jew" whom Paul castigates here (17-29).

The heart of this chapter is a challenge to come into a personal relationship with God through Christ, rather than to rely upon an inherited status or the favorable judgment of our neighbors. Regardless of the name—the temple or the church—by which it may be called or the century in which it flourishes, such is the nature of the religious institution that we are perpetually in danger of paying homage to instead of the God to whom both only point.

Seventeenth Day *Read Romans 3*

If you have never examined a New Testament that indicates quotations from the sacred books of the Jews, this is a good time to do so. Verses 10–18 represent a mosaic of brief passages from the Old Testament, with Psalms being most heavily represented. Weymouth's modern-language translation of the New Testament shows such quotations in capital letters; with it, you can thumb through the Gospels and the Epistles and quickly discover the interrelatedness of the Old and the New Testaments.

Using the sacred writings of his people as the authority to support his arguments that are also rooted in dynamic personal encounter with God through Christ, Paul here presents the chief idea of the entire letter. We are "justified" (acquitted in the sight of God the Judge) in only one way, he insists. It is futile to seek righteousness through keeping the Law, however exalted that law may be. Justification comes as a gift, made available through the self-giving of God through Christ. We cannot earn or achieve or win such a state of justification. We enter it only through the door of belief-powered participation in the cosmic sacrifice performed at Calvary.

"Justification by faith" became the battle cry of the Protestant Reformation. If you find it difficult to see why anyone should become excited about so abstract a theological idea, I must warn you that the indictment rests upon you and not Romans 3. The unqualified verdict of the ages witnesses that here we have the distilled essence of Christianity. Neither Paul's letter nor his central doctrinal proposition is subject to serious challenge from the Christian perspective. Should you be inclined to object to the line of thought presented in today's reading, or if you find it dull or irrelevant, here is proof positive that you are in great need of deeper acquaintance with the Bible and a more transforming personal encounter with the God-man through whom we may enter a state of rescue and accept righteousness that cannot be achieved by any other means whatsoever.

Eighteenth Day *Read Romans 4*

Virtually the whole of first-century Jewish thought rested on confidence in the Law. It was through keeping the letter of the law, insisted the great religious teachers, that one achieved righteousness. Since the Law was regarded as the royal road to divine approval, it was natural that scholars should devote their lives to interpretation of it.

At least to his own satisfaction Paul did away with the whole legal structure with a single new interpretation. Abraham, symbol of the God-seeker who lived under law, had always been presumed to have gained his righteousness through the Law. He did nothing of the sort, according to Paul. Rather, he became righteous through faith, before he acquired that legal righteousness symbolized by circumcision (marking him as a member of the covenant people).

Viewed from the distance of centuries, Paul's argument is not especially strong, nor is it easy for us to see why he, or anyone else, should become excited about so academic a question.

Rephrase the issue in modern terms, and it takes on a different character. Do we become righteous by being born to churchgoing parents, who see that we are baptized, enrolled in a membership class, and eventually led to take the vows of the church? Or is something less tangible required? Is church membership the royal road to heaven, or is it simply an outward process through which to seal and communicate inward changes? Cast in such terms, the issue of Abraham's claim to righteousness becomes strangely pertinent!

Nineteenth Day *Read Romans 5*

By faith and faith alone do we enter into the state of righteousness that makes us "just" in the sight of God, Paul asserts. Although this faith is spiritual and wholly intangible, it needs as substantial a channel as possible. Put in another fashion, we require a handle we can grasp in our hand even though the door we seek to open is spiritual.

Jesus Christ, wholly divine and entirely human, is God's answer to human need. Because he was flesh of our flesh and bone of our bone, we can reach out our hands and touch him—grasp hold of the divinity incarnate in him. Because Jesus Christ was the creative agent of the Creator, "very God of very God," the Father himself was involved in the world-changing events of Calvary.

Every human can identify with Adam and take part in his sin and its consequences. By the same token, every human can so believe in Jesus Christ that he "pours himself into the life of the Savior" and *thereby suffers and pays the penalty of sin himself by death upon the Cross.*

Theologians refer to this line of reasoning as "the doctrine of redemption." It is only one of several historic ways of trying to put the mystery of redemption into words and thought-forms that seem reasonable to the human mind. Useful when employed as a tool, this doctrine (and all other theological systems) becomes barren or even pernicious if elevated to first place in the religious quest. Like the Jewish legal system, theology loses its power when treated as an end in itself instead of a means to the greater end of transforming personal encounter with the God to whom law and theology haltingly witness.

Twentieth Day *Read Romans 6*

Belief-oriented identification with Jesus Christ extends to the special events of his life: his baptism, death, and resurrection. Provided that we surrender to him, his victories become our own—literally, not figuratively.

It is here that we catch a glimpse, from a fresh perspective, of the supreme significance of the empty tomb. For in his mastery over death, the Savior, who was fully human as well as completely divine, "opened the door" for everyone who will enter it. He proved himself victor over sin, and thereby invited all people to shed the limitations of humanity and enter the state of justification (righteousness in God's sight).

Of course, the offer of rescue through Jesus Christ is not to be taken as an invitation to engage in flagrant sin! Here we find one of the great danger zones of Christian thought. Many a zealous and eager person who has been transformed by encounter with God has been tempted to feel safe for life. We could devote not just this month but an entire year to the discussion of positive and negative concepts of sanctification, the second blessing, and the gift of the Holy Spirit. Whatever the language used, it is spiritually dangerous to conclude that one who has been rescued is thereby made invulnerable. It is some consolation to find that instead of this being a modern heresy, the first century saw the rise of this persistent tendency toward error on the part of persons who had deep and genuine religious experiences and, as a result, distorted the whole idea of salvation.

Twenty-first Day *Read Romans 7*

The capacity of the believer to participate in the life of Jesus Christ extends even to his relationship with the religious law. One who has died and been raised into new life, as is the case with all who truly yield themselves to their divine-human Savior, is actually a new person. Old relationships have dissolved, and former bonds no longer hold. Therefore, it is foolish as well as dangerous to give too great a place to the observance of the law. Every elevation of good works through the law is a way of reducing one's absolute trust in the redemptive work of Jesus Christ.

Paul's tortuous arguments at this point are not attractive to the modern mind, but his conclusion is as fresh and startling as the day it was penned. You and I, along with his first-century readers, know from experience that the religious quest actually is warfare. We know, too, that neither our own strength nor the power of a socially accepted set of approved practices is adequate for victory. In order to win, you and I must have help—divine help. We must accept rescue rather than work frenziedly for achievement. Once we accept that verdict and yearn for the gift of grace, in the act of yearning we gain it through our great deliverer, Jesus Christ.

Twenty-second Day *Read Romans 8*

God is Creator and sustainer of all that is. In this sense, the universe and all its parts are a coherent whole. It is a universe and not a multiverse. Within the ordered system and all of its parts there is a state of tension revealing double or divided relationships. For example, humans are both flesh and spirit at the same time. In the same fashion, the unified flow that constitutes all time may be seen as divided into this present time and the time to come.

Part of the glory of Christianity, Paul asserts, lies in the fact that belief in Jesus Christ helps us tip the scales in every divided situation. By our own power, we are incapable of elevating spirit above flesh; through identifying ourselves with the divine-human Savior, we can leap the chasm and succeed in centering our minds on the spirit. In precisely the same fashion, God's work of rescue serves to lift us out of "present sufferings" (18) and transport us into a realm of glory that, strictly speaking, is yet to come.

It is this strange and more-than-logical work of rescue through Christ that enables humans to rise above all the stresses and tribulations of our mortal existence. Nothing in the world—no member of any pair of opposites, "neither death nor life…neither the present nor the future…neither height nor depth" (38–39)—can defeat or even hinder one who lives "in Christ." Through Christ Jesus our Lord, we puny space- and time- and flesh-bound mortals burst all bonds and scale every barrier to become "more than conquerors" (37). Here—right now—is the glorious reward for surrender!

Twenty-third Day *Read Romans 9*

Chapter 9 represents Paul's radical reinterpretation of the idea of the covenant. Grieving over the failure of his people to accept the long-awaited Savior, he arrives at a startling conclusion. It is not the Israel of biology, but the Israel of the spirit to whom the promises of God pertain. This point of view lifts the whole covenant relationship to a new level. It makes the divine-human bond potentially universal, rather than local and national.

Viewed from this perspective, neither the covenant nor relationships deriving from it may be explained. Our role is to accept what God has graciously established. That is to say, faith and not works must be pursued in order to enter into righteousness. We come into a state of creative union with God by following the route of surrender, rather than by clawing our way upward until, by virtue of our own effort, we stand shoulder-to-shoulder with him.

Twenty-fourth Day *Read Romans 10*

All the old distinctions between Jew and Gentile have now faded away, Paul insists. Doubtless the sharp lines between the two groups were essential to God's purpose of sending his Son through a prepared people, but now that divinity and humanity have become one in Jesus Christ, every human is in the same situation. All who enter belief-oriented surrender and who call on God through the Savior will be saved.

Now and always, God requires messengers and witnesses who will stir people into listening and responding, but no one has any excuse not to do so. The very heavens are evangelists who shout the glory of their Creator day and night through all the ages! (See Ps. 19, whose total message is suggested by Paul's brief quotation in verse 18.)

Twenty-fifth Day *Read Romans 11*

Israel's failure, though real, is neither so absolute nor so lasting as it appears from a surface look. There are some from within the people of the covenant who have accepted Jesus as the Christ. Indeed, without such a response, the divine breakthrough would have failed for lack of heralds.

Again, rejection of Jesus Christ by institutional Israel served as the lever with which God could thrust his Son into the gentile world. Let gentile converts take heed at this point and guard against the fatal error of spiritual pride. Instead of boasting over their superiority to stubborn Jews, zealous adherents of the new church must recognize that God is using them as instruments of his larger purposes.

Sublime movements of Providence are upon so large a scale that we cannot perceive them and tend to get caught up in those few details we can distinguish. To avoid the idolatry which stems from making comparisons between ourselves and others, we need to focus our attention upon the almighty and inscrutable Creator whom we can never fully know but whom we can praise with all our hearts and minds!

Twenty-sixth Day *Read Romans 12*

Paul's reasoning is upon a high level. This letter is intensely theological, in the sense that it deals largely with issues that human beings cannot resolve by experiment or logical analysis. It is also very practical, for our beliefs govern our actions every time.

Those people who think they can get to heaven by living a better life than their neighbors will deal with them in the light of that belief. And those who are convinced that both they and their neighbors must depend upon God's unearned grace cannot avoid conforming their daily life to this theological position!

In dealing with a document like Paul's letter to the Romans, it is a temptation to center upon such "practical" passages as this chapter, which is a spontaneous by-product of Paul's primary message. It does not stand alone but has organic bonds with earlier chapters. To really grasp his interpretation of love in action, we must first glimpse the height and depth of his love for Jesus Christ as redeemer.

To begin with good works and move toward deeper surrender is to proceed along the spiritual highway in the wrong direction. Much of the emptiness of many modern Christian movements lies precisely here. We have tried to persuade people to love their neighbors for the sake of those neighbors; however, they must surrender to God first before they can love their neighbors. It is the act of surrendering to God that automatically establishes new relationships.

Twenty-seventh Day *Read Romans 13*

The gulf between the flesh and the spirit is absolute, Paul insists. To place any value upon things of the flesh is thereby to reduce one's devotion to things of the spirit, and hence to fail in life's grand quest.

If this line of reasoning is accepted, it follows that the successes and failures, comforts and sufferings of our material life are trifling and transient—not worth fighting over. Instead of agitating ourselves over such issues as conduct of masters, civil authorities, and tax collectors, we need to elevate the law of love into such prominence that everything else becomes unimportant.

Did Paul anticipate the long debates that would rage over this chapter? Perhaps he did, for he undoubtedly recognized that he was making impossible demands by insisting that Christians "not think about how to gratify the desires of the sinful nature" (14). Once more, by a roundabout path, we are face to face with a trumpet call to justification by faith! Those of us who try to subdue the flesh completely are bound to fail; in this failure, they can look up and out and, in a flash of intuition, recognize that righteousness cannot be won or achieved and is reached by the road of surrender rather than striving!

Twenty-eighth Day *Read Romans 14*

Tolerance of others' views and practices, like many other everyday attitudes, is not an end product but a by-product. The people who see themselves standing under divine judgment will recognize that God is the judge who sits over every case. Conscious of being the accused and guilty one, they will not presume to pass judgment upon their fellow culprits—and tolerance will develop as a by-product.

Instead of condemning others in order to praise ourselves, we need to be spiritually sensitive, so that we may avoid doing things that cause others to fall. Even when I feel that no moral issue is involved, I need to abstain from any practice that raises moral problems for other persons. To guard my conduct in this respect is a full-time job that leaves no time for sitting in judgment of other people.

Twenty-ninth Day *Read Romans 15*

The pilgrimage toward the city of God is a lonely one. Everyone must pursue it alone, and no substitutes are permitted. Belief in the redemptive power of Jesus Christ and identification with him as Savior is so highly personal that its deepest meanings cannot even be communicated.

Yet the pilgrimage is also as fully social as it is individual. (Here we discover one more instance of the double nature, or dualism, that God has woven into his creation.)

No one, not even Paul, makes his journey without contact with others. Some of them went before him. By their influence, and the legacy they left behind, they helped shape the course of his life. Other persons are fellow pilgrims to whom the apostle gives a helping hand, gaining greater strength every time he assists some fallen one to his feet. Still others will come in other centuries, inspired and guarded by the religious experience of a first-century tentmaker who excelled nearly all men in his capacity to make public the fruits of his quest for God.

Fully as much as they need him, Paul needs the Gentiles to whom he writes. Witnessing is the other side of hearing, and a rounded pattern of spiritual growth requires that the pilgrim be involved in both.

Thirtieth Day *Read Romans 16*

One almost wonders why this chapter is included in the New Testament. It deals with persons whose names are labels for compartments of ignorance. Except for the fact that they appear here, most of these names mean nothing at all to us. Clearly, we are tempted to say such a passage has no significance; it is simply an appendage—and an almost unintelligible one—to the body of Paul's letter.

But reflection suggests another verdict.

Here is proof positive that the "author of Christian theology" is deeply concerned with *persons*. This is the most convincing piece of evidence in any of his letters to witness to the fact that he sees himself as a bridge over which specific individuals (and not a vague humanity in general) can walk in order to find a transforming encounter with the Savior who is in the process of making Paul a saint.

This evangelist is daily—hourly—concerned with the immortal souls of Junias and Ampliatus, with all their faults and failings. His one life-dominating concern is to persuade them to enter new life, through the divine-human Savior. All his theological arguments, fine-spun as they sometimes are, have emerged as by-products of his passionate desire that folks like Aristobulus' family and Paul's relative Herodion should surrender to God, through Christ, so that the Creator will enable them to trample Satan under their feet!

Individual men and women, made in the likeness of God and having potential for godliness as a fruit of divine rescue have evoked the letter to the Romans. It is for precisely such persons that God sent the supreme messenger to whom Paul points. The Old Testament and the New Testament exist so that ordinary mortals—namely, you and I— may be impelled to enter that state of faith through which God can provide rescue of such order that we may become blameless in his sight.

From Corinthians through Philemon

Corinthians

After being destroyed by the Romans (146 B.C.), Julius Caesar restored the city of Corinth (46 B.C.) in the province of Achaea located at the end of a narrow isthmus that links central Greece with the Peloponnesus. It was one of the oldest and most powerful cities of ancient Greece and was an important trading center under the Roman empire.

Paul made his first visit to the city about the year A.D. 50 and remained for eighteen months. He returned at least once, five or six years later, and wrote at least four letters to the congregation he had founded there.

Partly because they are highly personal, the little "books" of 1 and 2 Corinthians are as vivid as they are direct. Paul makes no effort to organize a systematic treatise like his letter to the Romans. Instead, he deals with whatever practical issues happen to occupy him at the moment.

Filled with everyday advice about personal Christian service and the organized life of the church, these short documents dispel the myth that all early Christians were saints! These Corinthians were folk like us. Had it not been for their arguments and dissensions, theological errors, and abuses in public worship, Paul would have had no occasion to rebuke, correct, and encourage them in the letters that also speak directly to us in our present-day attempts to follow Christ individually and as members of congregations.

First Day *Read 1 Corinthians 1–2*

Individually, those whom Paul addresses here are persons consciously engaged in pilgrimage toward the city of God. Collectively, they form a church that is an outpost of the kingdom. In spite of their high calling, these men and women are weak, prone to fail and fall, that is, they are exactly like the persons who make up congregations today!

The divisions among the Christians grow out of the fact that many of them have elevated human leaders to first place in their thought, thereby reducing the fervor of their devotion to Jesus Christ. They have tried to master the secrets of the faith, to reduce the sublime promises of the Good News to human dimensions. In doing so, they have turned their backs upon the goal to which the Christian pilgrimage leads and have actually walked away from the Cross, which is never comprehensible.

There are two realms of knowing, Paul reminds his readers. In doing so, he simply repeats in fresh language an emphasis that runs through the Bible from beginning to end. Worldly wisdom is distinct from spiritual sensitivity. Consequently, the meaning and value that a person discovers in any situation will depend upon the mood and goals with which he assesses it. Spiritual truths constitute "God's secret wisdom" (2:7), which can never be reduced to the level of ordinary flesh-oriented knowledge without major distortion. That is why paradox is the language of faith.

The problem is somewhat like that of making maps. In order to project a round globe upon a flat piece of paper, an orderly method of distortion is necessary. When the geography involved is that of the solar system or the universe, the problem is even more complex. There is no way to devise a map of the solar system that is accurate for more than a few selected factors. Just so, it is impossible to put the glorious truths of the gospel into logical and prosaic language; in order to "know" the good gifts of God through Christ, one must turn his back upon human wisdom and rely upon seeing spiritual things with the eye of the spirit.

Second Day *Read 1 Corinthians 3–4*

To call oneself a disciple of Paul (or any other man) is to insist upon remaining in the childhood of faith. All missionaries and evangelists and pastors are merely agents—spokesmen proclaiming a message not their own. Ideally, witnesses empty themselves so that they can function as a channel for the flow of continuing self-revelation by God. Such an exalted state, however, is rare and brief, for witnesses themselves are caught up in the stream of humanity. That is precisely why Christians need to avoid forming parties and putting their trust in mere men (or their doctrinal systems or religious organizations or patterns of religious experience) instead of the Savior to whom their leaders only point.

A leader—even Paul—is to be regarded simply as a steward who, for a little while, has been entrusted with a few of the mysteries offered to men by God. He is not a master of knowledge. On the contrary, in order to function at his highest, he must himself be captive of his message—directed by it, rather than controlling it.

To discover this fundamental aspect of human knowledge and leadership and live in the light of that discovery is to conquer pride and the flesh and "live according to Scripture" (4:6).

Third Day *Read 1 Corinthians 5–7*

Paradoxically, these chapters are both chastening and encouraging. They warn us that human nature is the same in every epoch. Just think! Men and women whose ears throbbed with burning words from the lips of Paul himself descended from their mountain peaks of religious experience to engage in lawsuits and immorality!

At the same time, these chapters offer hope. For it was from such weak vessels as those who are chided here that God forged the mighty apostolic church!

Clearly, the church partakes of the double nature of humans who form it. It is of God and dedicated to God; yet men and women are

MONTH
11

the only raw material from which God can form saints, through the church. So it is at one and the same time the most sublime and exalted of all institutions and also a context in which humans can offer proof positive that sin is indeed universal.

The church echoes the impossible demands of the Savior whose message she seeks to transmit and to whom she points. The church calls people to live in a fashion impossible to flesh-bound creatures. For this reason such matters as sex and marriage are basic. To stress Christian doctrine in the abstract and to neglect to emphasize practical purity and control, is to pervert the Good News. The high demands of the church serve to convict us of our sins and failures and call us, once more, to seek divine grace in order to be lifted into that state of perfection that we can never enter by dint of our own efforts. Always, the church must require of its own more than they can possibly expect to achieve.

Fourth Day *Read 1 Corinthians 8–9*

Knowledge, in the sense of consciousness of being an expert, is exceedingly dangerous! Possession of it is likely to persuade us into a state of pride, in which we trust ourselves instead of divine grace. If "wise" people do not fall into that error, they may commit the sin of ignoring their influence upon other persons.

A modern parallel to this first-century issue is the use of tobacco by persons who consider themselves good followers of Christ. Can you succeed in following the Pauline reasoning as it applies to the present-day controversy? In the light of Paul's analysis, regardless of whether or not you accept the apostle's conclusions, do you think a minister of any faith can be blameless in using tobacco? What about a church officer, an "ordinary" church member who holds no office but is under a vow of fidelity to Christ?

No matter what your conclusions may be, you will probably find a personal challenge in Paul's personal confession. As a witness who speaks under divine compulsion, he never achieves a state of complacency, or even ease. His Christian life is a constant struggle. He never finds it possible to rest on his laurels. He is continually revising his judgments and reexamining his personal conduct.

Anyone who adopts the apostle's attitude in this respect will be perpetually bombarded with questions and problems. When the tobacco issue is settled to his satisfaction, an equally vexatious one of a different sort will take its place!

Fifth Day *Read 1 Corinthians 10–11*

It is simple to see the fallacies involved in idolatry as practiced by someone else. But it is fearfully hard to escape paying homage to less than God. Regardless of its form, prostration before any finite goal or set of values constitutes idolatry.

All people of every epoch are tempted and tested. It is a temptation to look back to some period which seems to constitute "the good old days" and to conclude that it was comparatively easy to seize the prize of life in such a simple, pious period. This is nonsense. Christians of first-century Corinth faced problems just like ours today. Specific ways of falling away from God differ from one epoch to another, but the ultimate choice between serving God and serving other-than-God is the same in every generation.

As with individual seekers, so it is with the church. Every age has its own pressing issues. In a day when the question of headgear for women seems trivial, the matter of gay rights is not. Whether in the first century or the twenty-first, the highest and holiest heritage of the church (no less than the Lord's Supper) invites abuse as well as use.

Once more, we are reminded that even in the house of the Lord—perhaps especially there—we retain our human limitations. We are creatures upon whom the divine image has been stamped. We have feet of clay, but our hearts yearn for the heavens. Perpetually dissatisfied with ourselves, we are prone to try to win victory by striving, instead of by accepting divine rescue. To see ourselves as poor, blind, and naked, even in the band of pilgrims that forms the Church, is to recognize anew that something must be done for us as well as *by* us. Although the term does not occur in these chapters, here is a vivid example of the necessity for "justification by faith"!

Sixth Day *Read 1 Corinthians 12*

Because we take our humanity with us into the worship and work of the church, we are prone to engage in idolatry before the very altar of the Lord. We find it difficult or impossible to avoid putting God in second place, because we concentrate our interest and attention upon such matters as forms of worship and varieties of spiritual service.

If one person likes formality and solemnity in worship because it seems to him to be the most effective path toward God, he is easily persuaded that he should insist upon use of this path by all his fellow pilgrims. If his insistence reaches the level where he attaches more importance to ways of worship than to the God who is worshipped, he has become an idolater. Worst of all, he may feel that any person who refuses his form of idolatry is a blind and stubborn sinner who will be condemned in the judgment!

This monumental chapter is a prelude to the more familiar chapter 13. Beautiful as the latter is, and comforting, in some respects it is less important for Christian thought than is chapter 12, for many of the sad divisions in Christianity stem from the very errors that Paul underscores here. A limb or an organ of the body that makes up a congregation or a denomination becomes proud and self-centered. Soon there is a demand that the rest of the body pay homage and come into conformity. Fresh division is the inevitable result.

Tolerance is demanded here, of course, but it is not tolerance for the sake of tolerance. Rather, it is tolerance that grows out of unswerving concern for continuing divine rescue. Those persons or groups who are consciously under the judgment are not likely to sit in judgment upon others. Those who know themselves to be perpetually failing and falling recognize that they are no better than those who have stumbled over other obstacles and fallen in different ways.

If we unite in our zeal to serve God through Christ, our individual differences become unimportant. This applies not only to spiritual gifts, but also to racial, educational, and economic factors. When we become truly united in our surrender to God through Christ, all of our differences will dwindle into insignificance, and we will cease our squabbling.

Seventh Day *Read 1 Corinthians 13–14*

The thirteenth chapter of first Corinthians is among the most favored for memorization. Like the greatest of the psalms, it is powerful in its own right, but like every other passage of Scripture, it is most meaningful when read in context.

The early Christians who broke away from the restraints of tradition and religious law were impelled to give great weight to religious experience. Personality makeup is so varied that men and women of equal piety gave quite different expression to their surrender. Those who succeeded in reaching such a state of ecstasy that their speech became incoherent began to boast of their superior devotion. It was this practical problem, the merits gained by speaking in tongues, that stirred Paul to write about the superiority of love over all other spiritual goals.

Here is an inescapable dilemma. Institutions cannot function without structure. People who throw off the rule of religious law— ancient or modern, Jewish or Christian—find themselves having to establish a new system of authority. Enthusiastic over some potent gift of the spirit, such as speaking in tongues, devotees confuse cause with effect and begin to seek spiritual ecstasy for its own sake, rather than as a by-product of encounter with the risen Christ. The end result—another variety of idolatry, which is centered in the practices of a given group of seekers—becomes pernicious. The last state of these people is worse than the first.

Eighth Day *Read 1 Corinthians 15–16*

Neither speaking in tongues nor any other gift of the spirit is important unless the seekers continue in a state of surrender to Christ. It is what Christ has done for them, not what the disciples accomplish, that is paramount. Having given himself into the power of death and having risen again from the dead, the divine Christ offers life to every human who will accept it in him.

No one can offer an acceptable intellectual exposition of this mystery. Paul himself is not under the delusion that he is here explaining immortality. Rather, he is using metaphors that point toward aspects of life that, seized through faith, defy all our attempts at full explanation. This mystery gives mortals the potential for transcending all the limitations of mortality. Here is the grand prize of the Christian endeavor, the reward for entering into surrender that makes rescue actual instead of potential. For this the whole of *salvation history* has been ordained.

However, the glory over cosmic victories and ecstasy at the prospect of achieving enduringness like that of the Creator do not relieve the creature of present responsibility. Instead of reducing the importance of practical good works in this life, the sure hope of heaven magnifies them. Nowhere in Scripture is there a more vivid example of the fact that individuals who stand alone before God are also in organic relationship with their fellow man. Chapter 16 affirms that to be human means to have a set of bonds with other humans who form social systems, organize churches and other institutions, and depend absolutely upon one another as well as upon God. A person must enter the kingdom in company with other Christians, or not at all.

Ninth Day *Read 2 Corinthians 1–3*

Humans, including those who band together in the church, are at the same time totally individual and completely social. It is therefore not strange, but natural, that the society of the redeemed should reflect both the limitations and the glory of humanity.

For the church to exist, there must be an evangelist and a group of converts; the relationship between pastor and people is analogous, but not identical. In the pastor-people as well as in the evangelist-converts relationship, mutual interdependence is the rule. Each depends heavily upon the other. Paul could never have become what he was in a spiritual vacuum. Lacking the influence of those to whom he witnesses in general, and of the Corinthians in particular, he would have developed along quite different lines.

As a witness, he never forgets the urgency of his divine commission (1:21–22; 2:17; 3:6). He is sent to persons who are so typical that they become involved in quarrels and divisions, but they also form a "divine letter," a sort of "living epistle" written by God to the world (3:1–3).

In practice, therefore, the church is as paradoxical as the gospel from which it springs. It is headed toward heaven but walks with feet of clay!

Tenth Day *Read 2 Corinthians 4–6*

Paul, the witness, sees himself as a channel through which divine messages may flow. He is convinced that they actually do proceed through him, in the sense that his words are not fully his own. This is the source of his power—and perhaps a key to some of his clashes with converts and fellow workers.

Were absolute victory possible, he consoles himself, we should cease to depend upon God. However, even our failures and afflictions can be turned to good ends. Through dedication to eternal spiritual goals, all temporal and finite issues—including health versus sickness and affluence versus poverty—become secondary.

Notice that the closing lines of chapter 6 again reveal a man shaped by lifelong absorption with the Scriptures. He does not so much quote sentences and phrases as he spontaneously uses biblical language to express ideas he wishes to convey. Few of us in the modern church will ever achieve such unstudied skill, but every one of us can facilitate the life-giving work of the Book of Life.

Eleventh Day *Read 2 Corinthians 7–9*

It is comforting to discover that Paul himself has to give considerable attention to the vexatious problem of church administration, namely special offerings! His letters, which soar so high into the heavens, are yet linked with Earth. Instead of serving the risen Lord in an ideal situation where there are no mundane problems to vex him, he is working in a "normal" context. The congregations are plagued with frictions, and the need for money is so great that the evangelist is forced to put on the pressure!

The life situation in which Paul works plays a vital part in his transmission of the Good News that has made a new man of him. Because the goals and values linked with that Good News are wholly spiritual, all material barriers are temporary hindrances only. On that basis, the much-troubled and always-beset evangelist can exult, "in all our troubles my joy knows no bounds" (7:4).

Here the disciple of the risen Lord offers a convincing case history. The radiant faith that is reflected in many of the psalms is actually an achievable way of life. In and through the search for holiness that comes "out of reverence for God" (7:1), we puny mortals actually can achieve peace, victory, and joy here and now!

Twelfth Day *Read 2 Corinthians 10–11*

Who is this impassioned witness whose words still ring after twenty centuries? Why did God choose to use this special channel through which to pour messages that form about one-third of the New Testament?

His name we know well enough: Saul who became Paul. Fragments of his personal history are preserved here and elsewhere, but what of the man himself, his inner self? Clearly, he does not think of himself as eloquent. He is not "a trained speaker" (11:6) and stands a bit in awe of some noted colleague "who is praised by all the churches for his service to the gospel" (8:18).

Measured according to any material scale of values, the messenger named Paul, who feels himself commissioned by God, has made a very poor showing. His familiar summary (11:23–33) reads like an account of failure rather than of success.

In the whole history of the Christian movement, however, Paul stands above every other witness. Why? Because of the depth of his surrender, the unqualified passion of his ceaseless search. It is not so much what he *does* that counts, as what he *is*. Failing and falling, he yet remains true to his purpose of so serving God through Christ that he is an instrument of *salvation history*. He manages to empty himself of self so that he becomes a vessel through which grace may be conveyed to the world. He is a human agent in the divine-human process for which the world was created—the marriage between God and man (11:2), by which the creatures made in the divine image are lifted to the level of the Creator himself.

Thirteenth Day *Read 2 Corinthians 12–13*

Contradiction is the theme of these closing pages. In *salvation history* whose stream includes Paul of Tarsus, you, and me, there is always an intermingling, which sometimes baffles us. Power comes through weakness rather than strength (12:9, 13:4). Victory is won only when the smell of defeat is strong in the air (12:20–21). "A thorn in the flesh" may prove to be a potent instrument of grace (12:7).

Conscious dependence upon God is essential to spiritual growth. Israel's history provides many instances of conspicuous failure on the part of the chosen people during times of peace and prosperity—and numerous cases of reentrance into the covenant in times of failure and defeat.

As with nations, so it is with individuals. It is foolish and dangerous for seekers to boast about their victories. Incredibly, weakness, which requires us to accept grace, is the only valid ground for spiritual pride! This grace, which Paul invokes in his benediction, marks finis to his correspondence with his so-human converts in Corinth.

Paul's Short Letters to Congregations

Like the longer letters of the missionary evangelist, Paul's short letters to the churches grow out of life situations. For the most part they are evoked by problems. Had all gone smoothly with Paul, he would have had no reason to put into writing the arguments and exhortations and promises that make up the bulk of these documents.

The fact that these brief letters reflect the kinds of crises and opportunities that still confront congregations and individual seekers for God through Christ is a source of great consolation. We are perpetually tempted to think that we have fallen upon evil times, that the clock of history is running backward, that people are getting worse and worse. Such a pessimistic verdict concerning God, man, and the universe is thoroughly demolished by a sensitive reading of the messages sent by Paul to the Ephesians, the Philippians, the Colossians, and others of their day. Even when the glory of the resurrection was still bright in the eyes of many, those who heeded God's call and tried to obey it were still…human!

Reading of the first-century situation, we discover a fresh opportunity to dwell upon the central message of Paul. Without exception, all of us, in every epoch, need something done *for* us as well as *by* us. We must strive with all our might to live as God demands, but in the midst of our striving we must also be forever in the act of yielding. Not one of us—now or then—stands blameless in the sight of God. But each of us can accept from him through Jesus Christ, the righteousness we can never earn. In the first century as in the twenty-first, the unfolding of the covenant requires a belief-powered turning to God for mighty acts that transform and literally make new those mortals who succeed in accepting what the Father offers.

Galatians

Fourteenth Day *Read Galatians 1–3*

Never fall into the error of thinking that the gospel is easy to understand and simple to follow. Its ease and simplicity are accompanied by its difficulty and profundity. Its truths are not so much to be learned, as to be accepted (1:12). Even a band of first-century zealots who are converted by the preaching of the apostle Paul quickly begin to pervert the gospel (1:6–7; 3:1–5). Even Peter and Paul find it impossible to agree with one another on all major issues (2:11–14).

Paul's own spiritual biography reveals the fact that God confers his best gifts only to those who are forever seeking and struggling, never complacent. Indeed, it is essential to identify oneself with the Savior, even to the point of participating with him in the fearful agony of Calvary (2:19–20).

Through acceptance of divine grace offered by God's own Son, the ancient covenant is fulfilled, not canceled, as logic would indicate. Rather, it gains new depth and invites participation by a new and larger "chosen people." Thus, the way faith supersedes law is the key not only to the work of Christ, but also to the centuries-long unfolding of *salvation history* in its entirety. For this, the events recorded in the Old Testament took place. For this, God created the world and put in it creatures shaped after his own image.

Fifteenth Day *Read Galatians 4–6*

Saul, so long a zealous student of the Law, has become Paul, who is convinced that nothing anyone does will cause them to earn or win the commendation of God. The old Covenant of the Law, symbolized by Hagar (4:24) was not so much "false" as incomplete or immature. It was a preparatory stage—and an essential one. Without it, men could never have been made ready to enter the New Covenant constituted from elements that included both the Old Covenant and Jesus' death upon the Cross.

Now that men are invited to enter the New Covenant relationship, the choice is not between law and freedom, but between the flesh and the spirit. To enter into a state of continuous striving for larger surrender to the spirit is to accept the invitation to covenant. Those who do that participate in the events of Calvary, so that they are in the process of "crucifying" flesh-born yearnings (5:24). To do this is to sow eternal life (6:8).

This is the victory. It is for this—and nothing less—that you and I were born. Here is our reason for being.

11

Ephesians

Sixteenth Day *Read Ephesians 1–3*

God's choice is the central fact of the universe. That choice was made "in the beginning," but it includes human freedom. Therefore, the primeval choice of God becomes actual, rather than potential, only through purposeful responses of individual men and women.

Exercise of the option to "choose God" involves acceptance of unearned grace. Through the act of acceptance, the mystery we call *salvation* occurs (2:4–10). This salvation is offered to all people who will accept it, not just to the physical descendants of Abraham. Therefore, since Calvary the chosen people are all human beings. Without exception, God yearns to confer grace.

To proclaim this radical message, Saul of Tarsus was seized in the hand of God and made "a servant of this gospel" (3:7). Through lips that no longer belong to him but are "captive to God," he pours out a message not his own. For that reason the letters of this missionary-evangelist to his converts and colleagues rank as Holy Scripture. They are shaped by God himself for the purpose of imparting divine things to mere men who, responding and accepting, form a society of the redeemed that we call the church.

Seventeenth Day *Read Ephesians 4–6*

Continuous radical change is the hallmark of surrender. We must perpetually be in the process of discarding our "former way of life" (4:22) in favor of a radically different "new self" that is more a gift than an achievement (4:24).

There are radical implications for everyday life as well as the goal of life, and practical issues for the first-century Christians are discussed (4:25–6:9). Because Paul's exhortations are directed to specific persons in a definite cultural context, "the letter of the law" does not always apply in other situations. It is the spirit that matters.

If you and I can succeed in achieving the state of continuously transforming surrender/rescue of which Paul witnesses, we will make our own practical applications.

Let us not be under the delusion that such surrender/rescue is easy or once and for all. Rather, it involves a ceaseless fight against both visible and invisible forces of evil (6:12). Victory does not mean the overthrow of Satan so that he never again threatens. Rather, it means continuous faithful resistance with every defensive and offensive weapon available.

In this sense, personal salvation simply echoes *salvation history*. Struggle, by both God and man, is the essence of it. Continuous divine-human interaction, of such nature that the work of creation unfolds thereby, is the context in which salvation becomes tangible and mortals put on immortality.

Philippians

Eighteenth Day *Read Philippians 1–2*

God's continuing act of rescue, oriented toward individual human souls, takes place "within history." Grace can be, and is, conferred within time and space. Yet there is also a sense in which the work of salvation—which alone gives meaning to human existence—centers beyond history. To surrender to Jesus Christ is to seek to be blameless both today and in the "day of the Lord."

Never fall into that pernicious and perennial error—if not, indeed, actual heresy—which asserts that salvation is easy and cheap. Attempting to live a life "worthy of the gospel" (1:27) is to be forever striving, failing, and yearning for a fresh act of divine rescue. It is almost laughably easy to mouth pious words about "having in ourselves the mind of Christ Jesus"; it is fearfully hard to apply those words to actual decisions we face in our daily life and to actual relationships in family, community, and congregation.

Nineteenth Day *Read Philippians 3–4*

Here, and in the two preceding chapters, we catch an illuminating glimpse of the relationship between Paul and those who felt indebted to him for their knowledge of Jesus Christ. Both Paul and members of his congregations were very, very human! Clearly, individuals and groups sometimes brought great sorrow to the evangelist. Just as clearly, he sometimes spoke and acted a bit hastily, if not angrily.

Paul's ceaseless stress upon personal surrender to Jesus Christ and continuous spiritual growth are essential to the creative relationship that exists between the evangelist and his converts. Although he prods and challenges and scolds them, he never does so in pride or self-righteousness. Always, he goads himself more zealously than he urges those to whom he witnesses. Whatever else he may be, Paul is a man with a burning consciousness of commission who never flags in his zeal to serve his Savior better. He stands as an all-time challenge to preachers, teachers, witnesses, parents, church officials, and all others who seek to influence their fellows for good.

Colossians

Twentieth Day *Read Colossians 1–2*

Paul here presents a poetic and impassioned plea that also forms one of his most vivid theological tracts. Here within a short space, he deals with many facets of the universe and life to a degree seldom approached in other letters. While the treatment is not orderly and systematic, it approaches a complete bundle of truth, instead of offering only fragments.

This world, he insists, is pervaded by the principle of dualism. While it has unity, it also has diversity. God is perpetually opposed by forces of darkness and evil. It is in this context of cosmic conflict that people live as free agents whose choices and acts of surrender will affect not only themselves, but also the fate of the whole world.

All the creative work of God, not simply in the beginning but also in the living present, centers in the God-man whom we revere as Jesus Christ. Nothing that has ever existed did so apart from Christ. In this principle, we find a new door into the Old Testament. Those who enter that door can never again read the Old Testament as merely a pre-Christian document. Jesus Christ permeates it as truly as he does the New Testament, though in quite different fashion.

Christ the Creator, who makes and sustains all that is, has a special role of effecting the transfer of human souls from the kingdom of darkness to the kingdom of light. Through two-way "identification," or mutual yielding and surrendering, Christ and his followers "become one." In and through this grace-powered act of salvation, the rescued make the latent divine image real, AND THE PURPOSE FOR WHICH THE WORLD WAS CREATED IS REALIZED!

Twenty-first Day *Read Colossians 3–4*

There are earthly, flesh-linked consequences of spiritual victory through Jesus Christ. He who has "been raised with Christ" (3:1) out of death into life must act accordingly. He must live as a citizen of the Kingdom of light, no longer being enslaved by darkness.

This radical transition as a consequence of rescue affects the whole person and every compartment of life—hopes, goals, conversation, family relations, daily work, prayer life, and all other activities and relationships.

Although he does not specify such a conclusion, the evangelist implies that "the social gospel" is a by-product—but an essential one—of individual surrender to God. Those persons or congregations or societies claiming to be Christian must show it in every aspect of daily life. We cannot have our eyes "on things above" (3:2) and not be noticeably different from our neighbors still captive to Satan. Of course, to concentrate upon social reforms and a high moral-ethical code, without having entered into the surrender which alone gives life a new goal, is futility compounded.

Thessalonians

Twenty-second Day *Read 1 Thessalonians 1–3*

Some emphases and ideas that occur everywhere in Paul's letters are here especially prominent. Perhaps partly because of its brevity and intimacy, this letter reveals the organic bond between the evangelist and his converts. Two-way intercessory prayer—Paul's praying for his converts and their praying for him—is high on the list of factors affecting all who are in this relationship.

These chapters especially echo with a note of radiant joy (1:2; 2:13; 3:9) so clearly linked with struggle that one wonders whether it could be evoked by a calm and placid life. Paul is never at ease. He faces abuse (2:2), disappointment (2:17), and affliction (3:4, 7). Not so much "in spite of" these factors as because God's continuous deliverance is made vivid only in a context of struggle, the apostle's joy frequently rises to the level of ecstasy.

Twenty-third Day *Read 1 Thessalonians 4–5*

Paul's life vividly illustrates one of his chief emphases. Having had some intimation of what one should do in response to God's call, it becomes the believer's lifelong task to "do this more and more" (4:1, 10), ceaselessly keep awake (5:6), and "hold on to the good" (5:21). Ceaseless growth is a condition of the Christian pilgrimage.

Once more, we glimpse a delineation of *salvation history* in its entirety. Abraham, chosen by God for special instruction and a unique covenant relationship, does not reach a terminus. Instead, he launches a movement destined to become wider and deeper throughout history.

There will be a climax, or consummation, to the entire process. God has ordained a day of judgment and that day will be entirely good. Then all wrongs will be made right and every inequity wiped away. In that prospect, the Christian can rejoice. But time and thought and energy needed for today's pilgrimage should not be wasted upon idle speculation about the day and the hour or the specific details of the day of the Lord. Our task now is to believe, accept God's mercies, and move forward. This is salvation!

Twenty-fourth Day *Read 2 Thessalonians*

In the first century as in the twenty-first, one of the sugarcoated temptations of Satan is the offer of secret knowledge. Oh, how it appeals to our pride to be able to say with assurance that we know hidden things of God that have not been given to other men! Especially in regard to the mysterious and near coming of our Lord Jesus Christ (2:1), there are riddles and obscurities we cannot fathom.

Therefore, urges Paul, take care. Avoid the temptation to loaf with the excuse that the coming Judgment Day makes all human effort meaningless (3:6–13). Guard with your life the tendency to question God's goodness in sending present suffering (1:5–8). Never forget that forces of evil are at work, namely, the minions of Satan himself. They must and will be overthrown by God.

In this assurance, believers can face whatever comes and triumph. This task demands much of our energies—indeed, all our time, thought, and effort—and leaves no place for idle speculation about the day and hour, or empty boasting of secret knowledge. God is faithful, and his living word is potent; to know that, and to live accordingly, is to pursue the path that leads toward the kingdom.

Paul's Personal Correspondence

Four of Paul's letters to his colleagues have been preserved. Like the letters to his congregations, they are intensely practical, and yet they are soaked with theology. Paul can hardly write about problems of daily life without also offering profound theological ideas.

He is an example of the effects of his message. He is so dominated by his goals and loyalties that he cannot take up his pen without betraying where his heart lies. He is a man under orders, and though he several times acknowledges consciousness of this role, his indirect witness is actually more convincing than the direct. Of those whom he instructs, the missionary-evangelist demands no less than the devotion he exhibits. So absorbing is his orientation toward God through Jesus Christ that his every act and each of his words serve as witness.

Timothy

Twenty-fifth Day *Read 1 Timothy 1–3*

The organization and functioning of a church always involve problems—human problems! For a group of men and women to band themselves together as pilgrims toward the kingdom, some kind of structure is essential. Structure means a division into various levels of leadership, along with ordered categories of followers. When the raw material for leaders and followers is mortal, there is no escape from the tendency to quarrel at public prayer and the temptation to appoint a bishop or elect a deacon from less than the noblest motives.

Is this a cause for despair? By no means! Once more we are confronted with the challenge/promise of justification by faith. In the church as in the world, men and women cannot save themselves. It is my task and yours to recognize ourselves as "foremost of sinners" (1:15) in order that, confronted and convicted, we may join Paul and Timothy in continuously accepting divine mercy, while we do our poor best to serve as worthy churchmembers.

Twenty-sixth Day *Read 1 Timothy 4–6*

In all times and places, it is imperative that we use the head as well as the heart in the service of Christ. Every age has its own set of godless myths and old wives' tales (4:7) that are hard to distinguish and repudiate.

The work of church administration should not be taken casually. Any person in a place of responsibility—an evangelist, a preacher, a teacher, or a congregational leader—must be firm and gentle, ardent and patient when dealing with people. In every congregation there are many different needs. There are those in need and those with abundance, those who are patient and those with short tempers, those who are forgiving and those who have a fondness for quarrels (6:4, 20–21) and controversy of every shade and hue.

The person who thinks of himself as God's man, not his own, must aim impossibly high and strive with more than mortal strength. This is the call to discipleship. Each runner in the race for life must snatch the baton from the hand of some elder brother in the Lord and dash forward to seize defeat in order that victory may be conferred upon him.

Twenty-seventh Day *Read 2 Timothy 1–2*

Paul is imprisoned because of his faith, helpless to do anything but watch from a distance. One by one, the structures he erected begin to topple, until it seems that everyone in the province of Asia has deserted him (1:15).

Is this defeat a cause for despair, for ceasing to strive?

By no means! On the contrary, this situation illustrates that being a disciple of Christ is similar to being a soldier, an athlete, and a farmer (2:3–6). Struggle is the context in which discipleship must mature!

If the struggle is within endurable limits, the disciple, with Christ's help, continually grows stronger but is never overwhelmed. The disciple gets support in his certainty that he is indeed "one with Christ," sharing with him in his triumphs and glory.

Twenty-eighth Day *Read 2 Timothy 3–4*

So personal are the exhortations here, that they apply directly to every one of us today. If Paul's analysis is taken literally, we can always regard our own epoch as "the last days," for the conditions he describes in 3:1–7 are universal! So are human tendencies to exalt false teachers whose doctrines are more pleasing than convicting (4:3–4).

It is under precisely such circumstances as these that the church unfolds and displays her glory. For in a context of misunderstanding and difficulty, God provides young Timothy.

What if the next generation of the Church should fail; what other plans does God have for the salvation of the world? God has no other plans. He is sovereign, so his plan will work.

Titus

Twenty-ninth Day *Read Titus*

In this short book, there are enough challenges and suggestions to keep any Christian worker busy for the rest of his or her life. Just as in the first century, in the twenty-first century people are the only raw material with which God has to work in building his kingdom. He always sends his messengers and envoys into impossible situations. Without exception, God commissions his representatives and then requires them to live as angels—all wise, ever faithful, ceaselessly true.

Obviously, no man can do that. Neither Titus, nor Paul, nor you, nor I can go through even one week as leader of a congregation and not fall short of the perfect man. What, then, shall we do? Shall we lower our standards for ourselves and for others? Shall we compromise and accept some lower level of accomplishment?

God forbid! The fate of *salvation history* is at stake here. Whether within the framework of the Jewish legal system or the Christian code of morals and ethics, the seeker who adjusts the demands of God to his own capacity is doomed. The answer is to recognize defeat, admit failure, and enter the remnant of rescue that God wove into the fabric of the universe—the remnant that men (especially those with a reputation for wisdom and piety) are perpetually reluctant to accept.

Philemon

Thirtieth Day *Read Philemon*

There is no situation or condition from which Christ is absent. Regardless of the human dilemma, faith will find a firm answer.

Here is part of the glory of discipleship! Those who surrender their lives as Paul surrendered his are no longer masters, but servants. They belong to Christ and look to him for solutions and answers. Out of this surrender one gains power. By abasing himself, Paul receives a dynamic sense of authority. Therefore, he can speak boldly and unequivocally upon any issue whatever. It is not his own wisdom that he offers to a slave owner with a valid claim for redress, but the wisdom given by his Master—Jesus Christ.

Precisely here, in the briefest of Paul's letters, we find the source of his dynamic authority. He is never baffled, never at a loss. He is always confident. He always has a message, but it is never his own!

Hebrews, Brief Letters, Revelation

Hebrews

Except for a few favorite passages that are often memorized, this brief book is much neglected in the modern church. Actually, it is among the most important and illuminating guides provided us in the entire Bible.

The very title is symbolic and suggestive.

Addressed to "Hebrews," this work may be confusing to those who have not soaked themselves in the fruits of *salvation history* so that they understand the vocabulary and metaphors concerning the Law and the prophets. Modern Christians must study the entire Bible, as all the parts are related to the whole.

The "Hebrews" who are addressed here are not only the recipients of a centuries-long stream of revelation, they are also the human agents upon whom God is depending to receive, interpret, and transmit the definitive message he has given through his Son. Therefore, the "Hebrews," whether first-century inheritors of Jewish things or twenty-first-century inheritors of Christian ones, stand in a special position. They are "in" the doorway that is Christ. They have one foot in the past and one in the future. They must balance their weight upon both feet in order to maintain their equilibrium in the living, creative present.

Although this figure of speech is artificially simple, it is this "creative equilibrium" that the letter to the Hebrews seeks to establish so that all seekers may find in Jesus of Nazareth the long-awaited Christ of God.

First Day *Read Hebrews 1*

To gain the full sweep of this chapter's glory, you must read it not once, but many times. Turn to Genesis 1 and John 1 because they may help you enter the secret door so artfully fashioned by today's reading.

Jesus of Nazareth, the Son of God, is "the last word of God." He is ultimate, absolute, and final. God has no more to say to man than what he says through the Son. For him and through him, the covenant came into being. In him, it finds its meaning.

Jesus Christ is totally communicative. Not just his words but also his every act and deed constitute revelation at its highest. Anything divine that humanity is unable to receive through Jesus Christ is forever hidden. He offers God in his totality, and each seeker receives portions according to his ability.

Jesus Christ is the essential central Person in the total divine-human relationship for whose unfolding God called the world into being. Everything before him flows into him and through him. Everything after him has proceeded from him. Human history, of which salvation is only a portion but the portion that gives it meaning, is like a beam of light. Focused so that it falls upon a lens, Jesus Christ, it is thereby totally transformed. All that was, is, and will be, gains its meaning—indeed, its very existence—from this relationship.

The angels of heaven and the kings of Earth are as nothing before Jesus Christ, altogether human and entirely divine, embodying absolutely in himself that creativity which transforms everyone who surrenders in order to be rescued.

Second Day *Read Hebrews 2–3*

Whoever first suggested that the gospel is simple did mankind a great disservice. It is simple, but at the same time it is profound. The gospel partakes of the paradoxical nature of Jesus Christ, from whom it flows. Even those moments of revelation which convince us that we have been visited by angels are not to be taken as definitive. Jesus Christ alone is definitive. Although he is simple on his human side, he is unutterably mysterious on his divine side. Therefore, even when they are offered to men and women through the lens of the divine-human Savior, the things of God must forever remain obscure, while at the same time clear and understandable.

Having entered into suffering and death, Jesus Christ, who forever creates and conquers, serves as a human-divine doorway through which mere mortals may penetrate a little way into divinity. It was for the coming of Jesus Christ that God entered into covenant with his faithful servant Moses. Only a prepared people, self-conscious in their special relationship with God, though blindly unaware of the consequences of their contribution to *salvation history*, could provide a social womb to nurture and yield a Babe at once man and God. Moses and the Law were essential forerunners of Jesus Christ and the gospel.

Belief is the key that unlocks the door. It, too, is paradoxical, for it is both easy and hard. Only vital belief, pulsating through our souls in the living present, enables us to appropriate the gifts offered through Jesus Christ. Regardless of what ecstatic victories lie in the realm of the past, pilgrims who expect to reach their destination must be perpetually in the process of believing more deeply. It is therefore the chief work of the church to provide a context in which those whose appetites are whetted by feeding may "encourage one another daily, as long as it is called Today" (3:13).

Third Day *Read Hebrews 4–5*

Make no mistake, the going is hard here, intellectually. Fibers of thought and of faith are interwoven in complex patterns. None stands alone. Each requires all the others to form the fabric that interprets the Good News, which is the motif of Scripture in its entirety.

Notice that today's reading begins with the word *therefore*. Skim hastily through chapters 4–5 and observe the word again and again. Now turn back to chapters 1–3 and focus your attention upon this key word until it jumps out at you from one hiding place after another.

The word *therefore* in the letter to the Hebrews almost overthrows the widely held notion that one can know the Bible by centering upon scattered verses and phrases. No accumulation of disconnected fragments, the Bible (and the gospel it pours out) is an organic whole. Each grand theme and every exalted concept is essential to all others. Because God has performed mighty acts through the Hebrews, *therefore* the whole world is the beneficiary!

Precisely here, near the end of our year-long journey through the pages of Holy Writ, we begin to gain new understanding of the fact that the New Testament yields its richest treasures only to those who have dug faithfully in the Old Testament. When we catch a glimpse of the way in which David contributed to God's unfolding purpose, we see the Son of David in an entirely new light. Given some understanding of the way Aaron and the Jewish priesthood helped to level mountains and fill valleys in the human mind and heart, we achieve a new dimension in our personal encounter with our "great high priest who has gone through the heavens, Jesus the Son of God" (4:14).

Fourth Day *Read Hebrews 6–7*

God's oath confirming his promise to Abraham constitutes the nucleus about which the history of the Hebrew people clusters. It is impossible to glimpse the idea of *salvation history*, to say nothing of beginning to understand it, without having been personally captured by the grandeur of this initial act. Through Jesus Christ, God entered history—absolutely, without qualification or reserve. But this pouring of divinity into humanity was no isolated act. Rather, it actually had its organic beginning in God's promise to a patriarch. Calvary was foreshadowed at Mount Moriah.

For twenty-first-century Christians not soaked in the Scriptures, the role of Melchizedek and the Jewish priesthood is not so compelling as that of Abraham, Moses, and the Law. Many contemporary worshipers have no firsthand experience with holy mysteries solemnly guarded and transmitted by men whose chief work is to offer God to man by way of sacraments, rites, and ceremonies. Therefore, we find it difficult to magnify Jesus Christ as one "like Melchizedek" (7:15).

First-century seekers, steeped in the customs and traditions of Israel, never could have accepted the idea of a Savior who did not have as one of his chief functions the work of an ideal high priest. Many of today's disciples may be much the poorer for their lack of handles with which to grasp this idea. Lifelong habits of Bible reading will do much to raise one's level of receptivity at this point. Here we see, although dimly, the benefits from skimming the book of Leviticus.

Fifth Day *Read Hebrews 8–9*

In his role as great high priest, Jesus Christ functions somewhat like earth-bound priests who serve as intermediaries between God and man. He offers sacrifices to God to atone for the sins of men. By giving himself, he became an eternal sacrifice, establishing a means by which everyone may escape the death penalty that is invoked because of our being born.

So viewed, Jesus Christ is the mediator; he serves as the sacrifice (offered upon Calvary) which he presents before God to make up the deficit in our final rendering of accounts. So important is this work that Jesus Christ's performance marks a radical new point in *salvation history*—no less a peak than that which reveals the ratification of a second covenant between God and his people.

The very idea of a covenant—or solemn agreement—suggests the necessity of orderly procedures. There are certain things required of the contractual parties, and these must be clearly understood on both sides. Among the chief stipulations of the covenant with Abraham was the provision that God would permit his people to make sacrifices to him in order to make up for their failings. Interpreted and reinterpreted by generations of the faithful, growing in complexity and obscurity, ceremonial rites and laws concerning them came to dominate the life of Israel. Always the concept of blood sacrifice remained central. Once a year, the high priest went into the holy of holies and poured blood upon the altar in order that his people might be washed of their sins.

Jesus Christ, the great high priest who presided over the most solemn sacrifice of all, poured out his own blood upon Calvary. This continuing act of sacrifice enables his followers to rejoice that they are "washed in the blood of the Lamb." This self-giving of the divine-human Savior is the watershed of both *salvation history* and of the whole unfolding universe. Participating as humans in the sacrifice of the man on the Cross, mere creatures enter into the victory of the Son of God and thereby find meaning for themselves and this world.

Sixth Day *Read Hebrews 10*

Noble as it was and essential as it was to the developing of God's purposes nurtured within the covenant, the law of Moses was not the final Word of God. Instead, it was the base from which that Word might spring; the foundation upon which God's finished structure might rest. God's people had to slay bulls and goats for centuries before they could be made ready to conceive of God's blood being poured out upon Calvary in a once and for all sacrifice.

We must not be too impatient with ourselves if we do not gain from such a line of thought the heady inspiration that comes from following, say, John's interpretation of the life and message of his Master. At the same time, we must not be too quick to turn aside from such passages as this, rejecting them as barren for present-day Christian life and thought. After you have read the letter to the Hebrews, Paul's letter to the Romans echoes and reechoes with new overtones that combine to form subtle harmonies that you may have failed to hear when you listened there a few weeks ago.

As one who would quench his thirst from the living water of Scripture, "you need to persevere" (10:36) and hold fast to your confidence in God's great rewards. Discipline is essential. To stay with your purpose, not simply of reading the entire Bible this year, but of rooting your life in it, is in some degree to achieve your goal.

We cannot begin to cultivate an appetite for God's most tasty gifts until we have read, pondered, reread, and assimilated the whole Bible in such fashion that we can, in faith and trembling, step forward and ask that the shed blood of Jesus Christ be accepted by God in lieu of the Godlike lives he demands of his children.

Seventh Day *Read Hebrews 11*

Faith is essential to any grand enterprise—whether that of journeying through the Bible in order to meet God or of desperately hanging on for God to bestow victory in despair.

Faith, moreover, is an essential ingredient in that sublime salvation. It serves as the magnetic field which puts together the human pole and the divine pole. Nothing can substitute for it. No other glue will hold the components together.

All the grand achievements and noble exploits of the past are monuments to faith. Name the heroes one by one, and they all are seen to have reached their niche because they believed in ideals and values they could not see with their eyes. Yet all the most radiant hours of the past were but prelude. Each is a lighted highway sign that pointed forward. Through the whole torturously sublime struggle that constituted the period of the first covenant, and indeed before God brought into existence a world that could nurture a people of the covenant, God had something better in mind: the sending of his Son.

Eighth Day *Read Hebrews 12–13*

You are surrounded by heralds who shout to you of God's ceaseless creative striving on your behalf. Therefore, it is time to stop attending to distractions and hesitating over difficulties. Having been assured of victory through our divine champion Jesus Christ, "let us run with perseverance the race marked out for us" (12:1).

The race will never be easy. Thank God that this is so! It is through the faithful, if sometimes painful, work of discipline that flabby muscles become hard!

However long and rough the road ahead, you must not ask to be excused from running this race. You are under a divine imperative. God, whose voice shakes Earth itself, has called you. It is for this that you were born. It is for this that all previous history, pouring into you as though through a funnel, has run its course. It is for this that the world was created!

Nevertheless, the vision of eternal and invisible rewards laid up for you at the end of the race must not make you contemptuous of this present life and your neighbors. Acts of love are not to be scorned, for there is no way to reach the world to come except by passing through this world. Be obedient to God, therefore, in your daily life. Put faith to work here and now!

Brief Letters

Some of Paul's brief letters are more important because of their having come from the apostle than for their contents. Judged by the standard of sheer capacity to evoke dedication to Jesus Christ and aid the seeking pilgrim, 2 Thessalonians, for example, falls short of the peaks attained in Thomas à Kempis's *Imitation of Christ* and other classics that do not have the authority of Scripture.

Much the same thing can be said of the miscellaneous brief letters that are grouped after Hebrews and before Revelation. They are priceless treasures from the experience of men who either walked about Palestine with our Lord or absorbed inspiration from his life and teachings at second or third hand. Yet even the most ardent advocate of biblical literalism will not go so far as to suggest that 3 John is on a par with Psalms or Luke.

In a sense, therefore, the structure of the Bible serves here to remind us that we are dealing in history with a gospel that transcends history. Because the Word was made flesh, the drama of salvation was enacted in a particular place at a specific period. It was not some vague humanity but particular men who were, in the flesh, permitted direct encounter with Jesus of Nazareth. God used these men, and those whom they infected with the contagion of their own discipleship, as agents through whom to offer the New Testament to the world. Thus, in a sense, the Book that is the vehicle for transmitting the power of the New Covenant is also limited by the humanity of the contracting parties.

If, therefore, Jude yields less direct inspiration than any chapter of John, with its cluster of companions it still serves to persuade us that in Jesus of Nazareth, God entered humanity and history.

James

Ninth Day *Read James 1–2*

Testing is the fire that hardens the metal of faith, producing an alloy that cannot exist without having been heated! It is the divine alchemy through which trials are transmuted into joys!

This, indeed, *is* the victory—no less than that of standing with bowed head to receive from God "the crown of life" (1:12).

On the foundation of so victorious a statement of faith, James erects a set of guidelines for practical conduct. It is not easy to decide which of his rules apply in a given situation and which should be modified. Perhaps that is one of the reasons why so God-intoxicated a seeker as Martin Luther considered this epistle as having little value.

Ponder the challenges of James with a receptive heart, however, and you are likely to agree with me that he quickly brings you under conviction. Practical-minded as he is, the apostle makes demands that require every hearer to confess himself impotent to "keep the law" and therefore in need of grace. Compared, say, with Romans, this tract certainly is thin in its theological content. But the same man who insists that "faith without deeds is useless" (2:20) has already trumpeted the warning that failure at any point brings guilt everywhere (2:10).

Perhaps, therefore, the church of the first century and of the twenty-first needs the corrective emphasis of James as desperately as the clarion call of Paul. We are indeed made just only by faith—but "faith without deeds is dead" (2:26).

Tenth Day *Read James 3–5*

Every aspect of life and conduct involves challenge and struggle. The tongue, for example, is one of God's richest gifts to us. Yet it throws us into an arena in which there is no quarter. Because the tongue illustrates the way we can use our gifts for good or for evil (3:9–10), it furnishes God with an opportunity to test us in order that, through fortitude under stress, we may grow more like him (1:2–3, 12–15).

As with the tongue, so it is with every hope and wish. Ambition, without which we will do nothing, can easily defeat us.

Our total inability to master ourselves should serve to make us aware of our limitations and hence cause us to depend only upon God. Such a mood is hard to enter and even harder to maintain. By concentrating our attention upon the coming day of the Lord, we will gain power to be steadfast in the struggle now.

Another powerful source of help is the fellowship of other pilgrims. Although each of us is frail, we who could never stand alone may succeed in remaining vertical when we help hold up our companions and in turn are bolstered by them.

Peter

Eleventh Day *Read I Peter 1–2*

Modern Americans live in a nation that has always been considered Christian. Most of us find it hard to imagine ourselves in the role of "strangers in the world" in remote outposts of a pagan culture (1:1). However, it is not typical for churchmembers to have their daily life dominated by consciousness of being "chosen," "destined," and "sanctified" (1:2).

For us to understand Peter's meanings here, we must try to be the kind of readers he addresses. We must be aware of the gulf between the church and the world, conscious of our alienation from a culture that includes us. Only to the degree that we succeed in becoming a little island whose shores are perpetually assaulted by tides that threaten our existence, will we achieve a transforming encounter with Peter's Lord.

Fearful though it is, the apostle asserts that exile in the flesh is not to be taken seriously. It is transient and passing. It will be swallowed up in the new creation whose existence is guaranteed and revealed by the resurrection of Jesus Christ. In the light of so great a victory—not limited to the future, but being bestowed in the present—a sober but joyous life of endurance in hope can overcome all adversaries. Not only those foes on the outside but also those on the inside that include "sinful desires" (2:11) must be overcome!

Twelfth Day *Read 1 Peter 3–5*

How clearly these chapters reflect the paradoxical nature of the gospel from which they spring!

Peter's words are maps indicating highways that lead in opposite directions simultaneously. Here are sources of comfort and solace, but they also prick and goad. Singing sentences that offer power are also sources of condemnation. It is only in glimpsing the glories of spiritual mountain peaks, which we know we can climb with God's help, that we are impelled to look at the ground under our feet and discover how short a distance we have yet come.

This brief letter exemplifies the fact that *salvation history* unfolds to engulf you and me in creative tension, where we must perpetually choose between spirit and flesh, where failure runs like a red thread through the whole mortal coil, and where response to God's ceaseless overture brings victory in past, present, and future tenses simultaneously.

Thirteenth Day *Read 2 Peter 1–3*

Those who take fragments of the message conveyed by God through Christ and elevate those bits of it into a "gospel of their own making" are living with futility compounded. Nevertheless, such persons often attract weak and silly followers in substantial numbers (2:17–22).

Instead of chasing after myths and emphasizing some one phase of the gospel to the exclusion of all others, we wait as well as act. Not everything depends upon you or me. God will usher in "a new heaven and a new earth, the home of righteousness" (3:13) regardless of how much or how little we do. In a sense, he demands passive submission as fully as active striving.

Once more, we are confronted by a demand for a coherent and systematic pattern of belief, thought, and action. Fortunately for us, the interconnectedness of all aspects of salvation presents us with an advantage as well as challenging us with its immensity. Provided we will be in a state of mingled striving and surrendering, God will set chain reactions in process. Faith will comingle with virtue, and virtue in turn will produce side effects upon knowledge. Increase in knowledge, whether oriented toward self-control or not, will affect the pilgrim's balance and steadfastness—and so on (1:5–6). All of God's stupendous promises, therefore, have capacity to transform not just one aspect of our belief and conduct, but our entire selves. This mysterious work of Providence, mediated by Jesus Christ and so magnified in him that we can see it even with our dim eyesight, operates to offer salvation to all who will continue in the process of dedicating mind, heart, and soul. It is the whole person, and not a mere portion of ourselves that God offers to redeem!

John

Fourteenth Day *Read 1 John 1–3*

Gloriously and incredibly, mere mortals really can come into meaningful encounter with God! That is the message of the entire Bible. If everything else had to be omitted, this central proclamation would have to stand. Earthbound creatures really can hear the Creator's voice with their ears, and with their they hands can touch the evidences of his presence (1:1–2).

Second only to this great central affirmation is the assurance that our coming into transforming encounter with God is best effected through the God-man, Jesus Christ.

All else is subsidiary and derived. Here is the core of the gospel.

To have personal experience with God, we must think and hope, struggle and dream with stalwarts of the mind and spirit. Then, and only then, we seekers gain capacity to see the light in which we have been bathed all the while. In the glory of this vision, we must strive harder than ever to see more light—to "live in him" (3:24).

To try to achieve this state of victory under tension, the result of accepting rescue through striving, we have read the entire Bible. Here, in John's so-brief epistle, we see that in nearing the end of our course, we have just begun. Instead of ceasing to run, we must pump harder than ever with muscles made firmer by our striving!

Fifteenth Day *Read 1 John 4–5*

Divine love is beyond our experiencing or describing in its entirety, yet it is ours for the acceptance. God's ceaseless outpouring for us and to us partakes of the both/and nature of his supreme self-disclosure in Jesus the Christ.

This love may be claimed here and now, but it does not reach its absolute in this life. Nevertheless, it is the tasting of it now that enables mortals to lay hold of eternal life then.

Any attempt to explain such exalted ideas as the experiencing of divine love is inadequate. To talk of God's love is, inescapably, to overlook some aspects of it and to distort others.

God, therefore, sent his Son to exhibit that love which defies description. By laying hold of love through faith in Jesus Christ, surrendered and rescued believers experience love in a fashion so sublime that they transcend the limitations of thought and language. Such entering into the revelation of personal religious experience is the highest state mere mortals can attain. By making such encounter with God our aim, we overthrow the Evil One and enter into eternal life—here and now!

Jude

Sixteenth Day *Read 2 John, 3 John, Jude*

These documents are but snippets and fragments, but they point to a way of salvation. Uniquely, though momentarily, they serve as heralds for the church. Notice, for example, that one of the most powerful of all benedictions appears in the final verses of Jude's little-read letter.

Alone, no letter in this trio offers the whole gospel.

Still these little "books" are Scripture! We are here dealing with the inspired Word of God. We are not permitted to judge it, for it sits in judgment upon us!

In the dilemma we here encounter—one which we cannot in honesty sidestep—the Bible itself offers a potent illustration of a perennial danger. We are human, caught up in our mortality. Hence we can distort and pervert and twist even Scripture!

Because we are frail and human, even the most devout reader of the Bible may mangle its message. Those who select a few fragments and proceed to make them the measure of the measureless gospel, have consciously or unconsciously edited the Bible. Through such a process, one can "prove" almost any doctrinal position whatever and find support for almost any rite or practice.

Once more, we are persuaded that for balance and perspective, we need the panoramic view that comes from surveying, over and over, the whole Bible as well as all of its parts.

Revelation

It would be possible, I think, to make some changes in the sequence of its individual books without substantially altering the nature of the Bible. For example, Paul's letters are arranged in the approximate order of their length. If they were grouped according to time of writing, the sequence would be quite different, but their total impact might not be greatly altered.

That is clearly not the case with the first and the last books of the Bible. Revelation is just as essential to the closing as Genesis is to the beginning of *salvation history*. Like Genesis, Revelation points both backward and forward. Like the matchless account of the beginning of things, this scintillating summary of meanings that converge at the end of things is great literature and an eloquent witness of things divine.

No book of the Bible has been more greatly abused than this one. Because of its obscurity, many readers have opened its pages only long enough to whiff the aroma of sanctity that lingers here, in somewhat the same fashion that ozone remains after lightning has struck. Conversely, seekers for light have been dazzled by gazing at John's masterpiece painted in blood and fire. As a result, many have become so enamored of Revelation that they have, in effect, elevated it to the place of a bible within the Bible. Using it as the key to unlock all doors leading into places of holy mystery, such readers have wantonly and violently committed the precise errors condemned in the brief letters that form stepping stones leading to Revelation.

The distortion of title by which many a pious pilgrim has spoken of this book as "Revelations" is not to be dismissed lightly. For John's witness is as clearly plural as it is singular. It really does deal with hidden things as well as with that one sublime secret in which the meaning and fate of the world are engulfed.

In its title, therefore, we are again confronted by the paradox of the one and the many. Here is the both/and factor that has emerged so many times in our striving to burst the outer kernel of confining words and enter into the heart of the Good News that deals with Jesus Christ: altogether divine and utterly human.

Guard against too great an absorption with one word, or a few phrases, or some potent visual image, or a mind-dominating number such as 666 or 144,000. These symbols are fluid rather than static. They issue great invitations and pose grave threats; a reader can become so fascinated with the antics of a squirrel on the limb of an oak that he no longer sees the tree—to say nothing of the enveloping forest.

We would be far poorer not to make our way through the turbulent waters of Revelation, but we must not spend our lives here. We need the balance that comes from living with the whole Bible—but when we next approach Psalms or Romans, our eyes will be sharper for having peered at the heavens through the unduplicated telescope fashioned by John in response to God's prodding of the apostle's soul, heart, and mind.

Seventeenth Day *Read Revelation 1*

Belief in the meaningful encounter between God and his people is basic to the Jewish-Christian point of view. Without such belief, there could be no covenant and no unfolding of *salvation history*. Revelation, or the self-disclosure of the Creator to the creature made in the divine image, is the door (and the only one) through which we can walk into an atmosphere in which we and the universe have more than finite meaning.

Revelation is the basic work of all Scripture; again it is the central role of Jesus Christ in whom "the Word was made flesh" in order that flesh-bound humans might hear the things of God. Revelation can and does proceed through every work of the Creator; the world of nature sings the praises of our Maker (Ps. 19). And Revelation flows through God-centered people who serve as megaphones through whom our Creator shouts, in order to be heard and understood by those too dull to catch the voice of their Lord except when mediated through personality.

Because John of Patmos stands at the very peak of disciplined listeners, his proximity to God makes it difficult for us ordinary mortals to grasp the full import of the secrets and warnings and promises he would transmit from heaven to earth. It is dreadfully easy to become so absorbed with, or puzzled by, the figures and symbols of this witness that his God-given message is obscured instead of clarified.

In this opening chapter, we are likely to be repelled by shadowy metaphors, if we are not wooed into that fierce spiritual pride which centers in claiming mastery over the occult.

Speaking for God and not for himself, John clearly has a message for those who seek to apply Calvary's poultices to wounds of their souls. The historical churches he is addressing do not matter. His audience here is the human heart for all centuries. John has a message so potent that he can hardly make it articulate. He has seen a vision so stunning that he was thrown into a trance. He would speak to the sons of men about the things of God, and, in order to do so, he uses images and symbols, metaphors and double meanings. He is trying to utter unspeakable things. Even in this comparatively sedate first chapter, we recognize ourselves to be in a strange and almost alien atmosphere.

Eighteenth Day *Read Revelation 2–3*

John's brief letters, or proclamations, address not simply a group of seven first-century churches but all Christian congregations everywhere. Since the imagery of these two chapters is less obscure than some later ones, they are easier to read. We do not have great difficulty in seizing upon the promises and warnings that seem directed especially to those who read.

Notice that using seven, "the perfect number," John has shaped a seven-sided delineation of qualities that cluster about Jesus Christ. For a breathtaking glimpse of the apostle's intoxicating view of his Savior, meditate upon descriptions included in: 2:1; 2:8; 2:12; 2:18; 3:1; 3:7; and 3:14. Jesus Christ, whose fullness is so far beyond us that we can only absorb snatches of it, is all that John says and infinitely more. To take these descriptions in a literal sense and try to define the physical or spiritual nature of the Savior by combining them is worse than useless, it is heresy. For each individual set of clusters, and all of them together, will illuminate the mind and spirit if treated as a "pointer to divinity," rather than a box holding some portion of it.

It is superb how John the listener becomes John the speaker With unmatched grandeur these seven little "letters" exhibit the both/and character of the gospel in their organic combination of warnings with promises, condemnations with commendations.

Nineteenth Day *Read Revelation 4–5*

Every attempt to know God, and to communicate what is known, requires the seeker to recognize two sets of limitations. On the one hand, human thought is not big enough to explore divinity. Likewise, human language is so geared to the realm of created things that it cannot speak of the Creator without being deficient. That is why worship at its highest has always leaned heavily upon symbols, figures of speech, rituals, music, and other media that liberate us from the constraints of words. But the more exalted a passage, the harder it is for nonbelievers to understand its sublime meanings.

Because John was granted a vision so exalted he was near the top of the Mount Everest of religious experience, his report of that vision sounds almost incoherent to persons who have only glimpsed the mountain from a distance. Even those who have climbed its lower slopes are dazed and bewildered.

We must not let ourselves be blinded by sunlight reflected from snow fields at the crest of the mountain. We must put on our dark glasses and admit only enough light to see some prominent landmarks.

In these chapters we find: (1) that mere men (John, for example) actually can press through the door into God's realm of glory; (2) confronted by God, the presence of his grandeur is so overwhelming that it can be hinted at only by means of mystical symbols and figures of speech; (3) the supreme work of the God-man, Jesus Christ (Lion of the tribe of Judah, Lamb of God slain from the beginning of the world), is to transmit the things of God to the sons of men. The Incarnation is indeed the axis of existence—the central point of the whole unfolding creation in general and of *salvation history* in particular. Incredibly, illogically, unbelievably, in and through the God who was man, all men may know God. This is the gospel. This is salvation. This (and this alone) gives meaning to a creature made in the image of God and placed within a context of time and space-bound to the earth by his body, and potentially one with God through his soul.

Twentieth Day *Read Revelation 6–7*

Jesus Christ, who reveals the things of God to the sons of men, pours out a message that is "both one and many." He opens many seals, disclosing a multitude of truths—all of which come from God and point to God. Like the Creator of whom they witness, these messages "give light darkly." They reveal—but not to the naked eye of the first-time viewer.

God is majesty, power, justice, death, and life. His outpouring of himself is not "all sunshine and joy"; in his self-revealing there are elements that strike dread into the hearts of all who behold.

In the midst of the "falling of the mountains" which occurs over and over to civilizations as well as to every individual, there is stability. Face to face with death, a great multitude will enter life. (The number 144,000 is figurative and symbolic, not literal.) Many who are rescued by God will come from the chosen people of the Old Covenant, but hosts of others from "every nation, tribe, people and language" (7:9) will join them. Salvation, though mediated through Israel, is universal. All who believe in Jesus Christ thereby enter through him into the company of God to know their Creator in a state of surrender that includes unspeakable joy.

Twenty-first Day *Read Revelation 8–9*

Revelation proceeds from God to man; communication proceeds from man to man. In our capacity to receive divine things through revelation and our God-given power to transmit intangible ideas to others, we are unique among creatures. But because communication as well as revelation is so sublime a process that it "smells of divinity," there are a hundred ways for every message to run aground. In these chapters (and perhaps the bulk of this book), John offers such scintillating metaphors and such brilliant flashes of thought that for most of us he dazzles rather than illuminates.

Clearly, these chapters "say" that terrible woes will come to mankind in the day of the Lord. Even more clearly, they underscore the conviction that though we know judgment is inescapable, only a minority of us will order our lives in keeping with that certainty (9:20–21). These two fundamental proclamations are at the heart of today's reading. If we try to decipher details, I fear that we will be in danger of losing our way in the subtleties of John's thought and the exuberance of his imagery. We must not, we dare not, become absorbed with tracing brush strokes of this master painter and thereby take our eyes off his masterpiece as a unified whole.

Twenty-second Day *Read Revelation 10–11*

Clouds of glory, like vapor above the surface of a mountain lake, hover here and make vision difficult. Yet if these chapters, and their companions, had to be summarized in one exclamation, I think you and I would agree on the message if not the language: "How great is our God!"

Allegorical allusions (clearly stipulated by John in 11:8) which must have had obvious meaning to first-century readers puzzle us, when we do not overlook them altogether. We cannot, by any amount of striving, read these pages through the eyes of early Christians expecting martyrdom by Rome. But if we have lost something, we have gained much.

Precisely because Revelation does not have for us the immediacy it surely possessed for those who first read it, we are the better equipped to penetrate beneath the surface of this book and find its rich veins of ore. Because we do not vibrate to the tread of Roman legions, we can center our attention on every clue that will help us reach that pinnacle on which, with our own ears, we can hear the seventh angel blow his trumpet as a prelude to joining our voices to the heavenly chorus that proclaims: "The kingdom of the world has become the kingdom of our Lord and of his Christ, and he will reign for ever and ever" (11:15).

Twenty-third Day *Read Revelation 12–13*

It is futility compounded to attempt to discover precisely what details may be signified by each of the ten horns and the seven heads of the beast that rose from the sea (13:1). Such allusions give power and grandeur to the imagery of this mind-absorbing vision, but they are not to be regarded as doorways into secret realms.

Whatever else he may be telling us here, John is using every resource of the poet-prophet to warn us that we cannot extricate ourselves from involvement in cosmic forces. There is a more-than-human struggle between the powers of good and evil, between the ongoing work of creation and the forces of degeneration.

You and I are caught up in combat that, for us, is mortal. We are tested and assaulted by one "beast" after another. There is no peace in this life. Yet, paradoxically, we can have absolute peace through participation in the conquest effected by "the blood of the Lamb" (12:11). Thus, the battle is won before it begins; absolute victory by God is assured, in spite of the fact that, for you and me, the struggle for life is personal, ceaseless, and to the death!

Twenty-fourth Day *Read Revelation 14*

As with poetic metaphors, so with symbolic numbers. To treat figurative language literally is to drive out the spirit and leave an empty shell. Far more than 144,000 readers of John's book have wandered off the path to life by trying to determine precisely what twelve groups of twelve thousand persons have God's signature upon their foreheads!

John is saying that we are divided into two categories. Some tune their ears to God's melody ("the music of the spheres" as well as formal systems of verbal witness, such as the Bible). Others prostrate themselves before created things and thereby witness their unwillingness to attempt to hear the divine harmony.

Members of both groups are marked by their goals. Some bear the mark of God, while others exhibit the mark of the beast. This inevitable and perennial dichotomy, or state of division, is itself cause enough for ceaseless strife and woe. Even if there were no divine agents of judgment, wielding their sickles in the harvest day of the Lord, people in this world would be perpetually in turmoil and strife because seekers after God cannot be at peace with adherents of the beast.

Here the whole problem of evil and the doctrine of Providence is brought to focus. God is wholly and altogether good, and he has nothing except bounty for the creatures made in his image. Yet it may be that God could not give his richest gifts to us without placing us in a growth-inducing context of struggle. So viewed, evil becomes a tool of Providence, an instrument of a larger good in which it is included. God's work of creation continues in and through us, spurred to creative striving by being forced to work out our destiny in an environment in which there is no peace except through ceaseless struggle.

Twenty-fifth Day *Read Revelation 15–16*

In the chorus that constitutes the Good News, the songs of Moses and of the Lamb become one. Separately and together, they help us heighten our capacity to listen and understand hidden things.

One of the heavenly mysteries, revealed since the beginning of divine-human dialogue but perpetually requiring individual and cultural rediscovery, centers in "the wrath of God." Altogether good and so prone to forgiveness that he sent his own Son to pour out his life for your sake and mine, God is yet a God of justice. His tenderness is that of a mother who in agony must punish her child in order to implement the flow of her love.

Always, it is easy for us to stand and cheer as God takes the offensive against beasts, dragons, and foul spirits. Always, it is infernally hard for me to see myself as a patriotic citizen of Babylon, my allegiance to that great city making me—even me—a rebel against God. Part of the work of John in his gloriously obscure and radiantly dark book is to give me new perspectives whereby I can see that the warning/promise of the Gospel is written especially and particularly...for me.

Twenty-sixth Day *Read Revelation 17*

Who is this great harlot who lures men away from God? Ah! John is too sensitive a listener to God, and too skilled a singer to men, to be trapped by the specific, the concrete, the created. Deliberately he has framed harmonies that lend themselves to a great variety of stanzas.

Instead of being merely a specific time- and space-linked power of evil, the harlot is evil itself.

She is Rome, sprawled over her seven hills, of course. She is also Caesar lying awake at night to map new conquests by his legions. She is imperial tyranny and official corruption in the first century. She is idolatry flourishing in temples scattered about the shores of the Mediterranean. But the harlot and the beast are also evil in high places within twenty-first-century democracies. This professionally soiled woman is official corruption within Christian institutions. She is lust for power and for sensual experience, bidding for the allegiance of all men everywhere. Most fearfully of all, she is the jeweled one who will occupy the throne of my own heart if I do not remain in the act of surrender to Jesus Christ in order that he may unseat her and rule in her place.

Twenty-seventh Day *Read Revelation 18*

God's call to "come out" is both specific and general. Through John of Patmos, he does indeed challenge his own to separate themselves from the Babylon of empire that surrounds and includes them. But the imperative is not limited to a demand that Christ's own must refuse to sell themselves to the Roman Empire in return for her favors.

God's act of entering into covenant with a *chosen* people implied and involved their separation from other peoples. God called on Abraham's descendants to separate themselves from the death-conferring security of Egyptian slavery. Perpetually and perennially he calls to the church, the bride of Christ, to separate herself from all her lovers. With a yearning that never takes no as final, he calls upon you and me to go apart—deliberately to renounce "the world, the flesh and the devil" in order more perfectly to love and serve our God.

Perpetually and perennially, people—all people—enter into commerce with Babylon. "The great city," wherever it may be and whatever forms of power are concentrated there, must and will fall. But we find it woefully hard to order our lives in the light of this certainty. It is to fortify us, convict us, and encourage us in fear and trembling to be continually in the act of separating ourselves from her—now—that John pens these lines.

Twenty-eighth Day *Read Revelation 19*

Throughout this book visions take place in sequence. Every time we think we have reached the final pinnacle, another and higher peak looms in the distance. When it seems that, with John, we have been wrung dry, spiritually and emotionally, we are urged to lift our eyes and glimpse new cataclysms and fresh glories.

That the time sequence of Revelation is not to be taken too literary is indicated by the fact that 19:11–21 echoes the earlier report of chapter 18. Still, there is a special quality in the ringing "After this…" with which the present chapter begins. Babylon is fallen. Evil has been unhorsed. Almost, it would seem, the logical next step would be to write "The End."

Although the end is in sight, we are not yet upon it. There is more. Heaven and Earth must join in a glad chorus of praise to God, who in his triumph over evil has won the cosmic battle—not simply for himself, but also for John and his intimates, for you, me, and everyone. Now the marriage feast may be held. Now the true union of heaven and earth, divinity and humanity, God and me, may take place!

Twenty-ninth Day *Read Revelation 20*

Yesterday we noticed the vexatious problem of sequence in John's account. From one perspective, it almost seems that events of the day of the Lord are hopelessly scrambled.

Part of the dilemma is due to the nature of verbal communication. John cannot put everything before us at once, in the fashion that Raphael, at one fell swoop, confronts the viewer with each and every detail of his painting depicting *Saint George Slaying the Dragon*. In order to write at all, John must describe first one detail and then another. This factor becomes confusing if we permit the human limitations of the apostle to persuade us that the sequence of his visions declares God to be incapable of doing *simultaneously* all of the things described in the entire Revelation.

Again, time does not limit or confine God. It is a necessary structure for ordered human life—at once conferring great power and binding us in chains partly of our own forging. God is above and beyond time. With him, a thousand years are as a day—and a day as a thousand years.

With the troublesome time-factor transcended, these chapters (once more) echo with shouts of praise and victory. God has conquered, and in his victory those who believe in him through the Lamb find not simply rewards—but meaning for life. Here (and only here) is the way to personal significance not grounded upon transient created things, but is rooted in eternity and omnipotence.

Thirtieth Day *Read Revelation 21–22*

It is the nature of the Creator perpetually to be creating—making "everything new" (21:5). That is why every human attempt to know God absolutely is futile, if not actually heretical. Such efforts assume a static universe, so small that the whole of it can fit within the human skull.

God is all in all; we are creatures—limited, cribbed about, confined within our humanity. But this humanity is only a husk that surrounds and for a little while nurtures the inner self that is made in the divine image. This second and higher person—the soul, if you please—has capacity to shake off all the limitations of the flesh.

In order to do so, and thereby achieve the end for which God created the world and me, I must seize hold of—appropriate—divine gifts that I cannot win or earn. Jesus Christ, Son of God and Son of Man, will enable me—if I will enter creatively into his whole cycle of striving, surrendering, suffering, and dying—to be in the process of becoming God's own. Fully revealed through the words and deeds of the Word made flesh, the Good News of personal rescue that offers more-than-finite meaning to me is the secret shouted in every page of John's Revelation. Nowhere is it put more succinctly and more compellingly than in the final invitation (22:17): "The Spirit and the Bride say, 'Come.' And let him who hears say, 'Come!' Who is thirsty, let him come; and whoever wishes, let him take the free gift of the water of life."

Conclusion

We have reached the end of our odyssey. Starting with the primeval act of creation, we are now in sight of the New Jerusalem. Its spires and turrets are too distant to be viewed in detail, but we know that it is there, a present reality rather than a dream.

In coming to the end of our journey, I think we realize that we are just beginning! Instead of being surfeited, we are more eager to know the Bible—and through it, God the Father, God the Son, and God the Holy Spirit—than when we started.

I once watched a television documentary on the Nile River. Starting at its remote sources deep in the heart of Africa, the commentator took his viewers with him along the four-thousand-mile waterway. He showed tumultuous waterfalls, enormous lakes, and ancient Egyptian monuments that would soon be flooded by the backwaters of a dam being built.

Finally, each person who had "traveled" the length of the Nile emerged, with the river, at the Mediterranean Sea. There the joy of having traced the course to its end changed into fresh wonder at the scene of the setting sun drawing water from the sea to send it back to a new watershed, to begin another journey along whose course it would move turbines to produce power, support the vessels of voyagers, slack the thirst of parched lands, and once more move out to sea.

As with the flow of water down the Nile, so with a pilgrim's progress through the Old and New Testaments. Having reached the end, it is time to make a fresh start.

There are many ways to read the entire Bible. If this has been your first complete journey, you may decide to retrace your steps during another year. Should that be your decision, I promise that your second journey will be far more exciting than the first. If, on the other hand, you prefer to vary your quest by adopting a different pattern of reading, there are other plans available. Some of the best ones are offered by The American Bible Society. You can call them toll free (800-322-4253), look up their Web site (www.americanbible.org), or write them (1865 Broadway, New York, New York 10023) for information about study materials.

Consult denominational headquarters for guides and reading programs endorsed by leaders in your own church. Or investigate some of the many plans available from private groups such as The Bible Study Hour, ACE, 1716 Spruce Street, Philadelphia, Pennsylvania 19103. You can also call them (800-956-2644) or look up their Web site (www.icrn.com/The_Bible_Study_Hour/).

Whatever you do—do something!

Should you decide against a return visit in company with *A Guide to Reading the Entire Bible in One Year*, and find yourself not fully satisfied with any available published program, then you might like to draw up your own travel itinerary. For example, spend time searching out and meditating upon the prayers of the Bible in the many excellent modern translations.

Personally, I find the "chain reference" approach less than satisfying. Most or all of these systems tend to concentrate upon isolated verses, phrases, or even single words. To use such an approach consistently over a period of years is, I think, to slip gradually into concentrating upon only a tiny portion of Scripture and consequently, in effect, to "edit" the Bible by neglecting whole regions of it.

Provided that the chain reference type of reading appeals to you, I doubt if it will do you any harm to follow it part of the time—say, one year's reading in every five or ten.

Biography is still another doorway; you might set out to reread all the passages that deal with persons, as opposed to abstract ideas that predominate in the letters of Paul, for example. But after a season of tracing the footsteps of Moses and David, Simon Peter and Jesus Christ, you might—for balance—concentrate upon the great biblical themes: sin, salvation, judgment, grace, fear, joy, and the like, tracing the development of each through the Old Testament as well as the New.

There are as many ways to read the Bible as there are personal interests. Whatever way you do it, I beseech you to continue the practice of daily exposing yourself to the Word of God in Scripture, thereby bridging the gap between creature and Creator as you receive news bulletins from God.

INDEX